CW00704504

dumb angel

the life and music of
Dennis Wilson

CREATION

DUMB ANGEL
The Life And Music Of Dennis Wilson

Adam Webb
ISBN 1 84068 051 2
Copyright © 2000 Adam Webb
First published 2001 by
CREATION BOOKS
www.creationbooks.com
All world rights reserved

Author's acknowledgements
Thanks to the following people for their time and memories: David Dalton, John Hanlon, Stephen Kalinich, Carli Muñoz, Daryl Dragon, Fred Vail, Stephen Desper, Stanley Shapiro, Billy Hinsche, Hal Blaine, Van Dyke Parks, David Leaf, Kingsley Abbot, Marilyn Wilson, Roy Carr, Bobby Gillespie, Paul Lester, Sean O'Hagan, Rian Murphy, Peter Buck, Bob Whitaker, Bill Bentley, Bill Scanlan Murphy, Carol Kaye, Bengt Stenstrom, Paul Cairns, Fred Scerbo, Hans Arne Nahrem, Stefan at Marina Records, David Dalton, Jon Stebbins, Sebastian, and anyone I forgot.

To Richard Farrow, Tom & Lawrence Epps, Anne Stafford, Maria Comiskey, Michael Wolstenholme and Stephen Goddard for their support and comments over the past year. Thanks also to Miranda and James at Creation for giving me the chance to do this thing.

To the memory of Dennis Wilson: will just one record company have the guts to release what you wrote.

I dedicate this book to John William Webb.

CONTENTS

PREFACE

When Brian Wilson abdicated his leadership role in the Beach Boys post *Pet Sounds*, most fans assumed that the band was effectively over. How surprising then, that it should be Dennis Wilson who stepped forward as a composer and producer. After all, prior to the *Friends* album the only recorded composition by Dennis was "Denny's Drums", a drum solo on the *Shut Down Volume 2* album. And yet over the space of *Friends*, *20-20* and *Sunflower* it was Dennis' songs which most closely matched Brian's in quality.

Personally, I've always loved the production touch that Dennis had in this era. The effect of his world-weary voice and deft production on songs such as "Little Bird", "Be Still" and "Forever" were as moving as anything on *Pet Sounds*. There's no question that along with his other strengths, Dennis was the most soulful of the Beach Boys, as both a writer and a singer.

"Slip On Through", which opens *Sunflower*, would not have been out of place on a contemporaneous Stevie Wonder record. And I've always had a soft spot in my heart for "Got To Know The Woman". Who could resist the sound of Dennis breaking into laughter while exhorting his woman to "do the chicken"!.

I found it quite surprising that during the creative doldrums which the Beach Boys intermittently suffered in the seventies that Dennis wasn't pushed more to the fore creatively. I guess that we can be thankful in a way, because his relative lack of song writing credits on *Holland*, *Carl And The Passions* and *Fifteen Big Ones* forced Dennis into recording his solo album *Pacific Ocean Blue* – possibly the best Beach Boys-related album of the decade.

—*Peter Buck, REM*

INTRODUCTION

"They say I live a fast life. Maybe I just like a fast life. I wouldn't give it up for anything in the world. It won't last for ever, either. But the memories will."
 —Dennis Wilson, sleeve notes to *All Summer Long*, 1964

"What a person is, he brings with him when he comes to music."
 —Marvin Gaye

"What the hell's wrong with freedom man? That's what it's all about."
"Oh that's right. That's what it's about alright. But talkin' about it and bein' it, that's two different things. I mean it's real hard to be free when you're bought and sold in the market place."
 —Jack Nicholson's George Hanson replies to
 Dennis Hopper's Billy in *Easy Rider*

"I think that the crack in his voice was the crack in his life between beauty and pain. Between pain and liberation. At the same time as he had the pain he had the joy. Not knowing that the same thing that caused the joy could be applied to where the pain was. So it's blurred for him rather than integrated."
 —Stephen Kalinich to the author, 1999

"I love everything there is to do."
 —Dennis Wilson

I don't know what Rock'n'Roll *was*. I was born after 1969. It claims to have been a lot of things and those myths still linger.

What Rock'n'Roll is *now*, is the soundtrack to the mainstream. A corporate circus. Choreography. So safe and without danger that our leaders get elected to it.

Back in 1954 it was born under the sole untamed possession of teenagers, but Rock has grown old to become respectable and safe and adult and all those other adjectives that were supposed to be its antithesis. Three chords of energy and excitement has somehow mutated into another beast altogether; and it's been analysed to death and it's been flogged to death. All that dumb beauty: debased by those seeking to intellectualise the subject – those who have no business in the area. Come on down Hanif Kureshi and Salman Rushdie. Come on down MTV and vacant PR corporate culture. Thanks for squeezing the wide-eyed innocence from our hearts.

The recording industry resembles more than ever the fraudulent Behemoth that roamed the pre-Beatle '60s. Manufacturing music, it sells us a lifestyle and version of rebellion more suited to a drinks or hygiene product. Once again our pop stars have become the inventions of nameless be-suited professionals. One monumental and endlessly unreal

Coke advert. The spin-doctored no-risk representation of the lifestyle we *want* to hear about – a Prozac Nation, quite literally. "Neutered and Spayed." The real taboos – the taboos that are apparently non-existent – are held in check by Twentieth Century self-denial, while our true mavericks are so often ignored. So cautious and so bland you'd wonder if the true recklessness of a prime Jerry Lee or a Little Richard would be allowed today. The real freaks have found alternative channels of expression.

Conversely, in the monthly periodicals and their polls of "The Greatest 100 LPs", we read that the greatest albums have already been made. "All the great books have been written, the great sayings all said." The Top Ten will consist of The Beatles, The Stones, *Blonde On Blonde*, *Astral Weeks*, *Never Mind The Bollocks*, *What's Going On,* and *Pet Sounds*. In the 1990s you might add *Nevermind* or *O.K. Computer* to the list. Debate is over. Aside from the Sex Pistols' debut these all date from the glory years of 1965 to 1972. Marvin Gaye represents the pinnacle of black music and female contributions are denied, as if not intellectual enough to stand next to Dylan or Lennon. As a reflection of the magazines themselves, the charts are mere acts of self-congratulation for the domain of white-standard-blues-inspired-male-rock-music.

How on earth did we end up back here? A journey that began with such excitement – transported us to incredible places – only to finish further back from where we started. We view Rock music now as art; as museum pieces. So submersed and staid in our culture that it is both entertainment and some intangible "other". Some great cultural force of benevolent power. A force that simultaneously can Feed The World, while allegedly inspiring the teens of small-town America to slaughter their peers. As the cult of celebrity grows proportionately to tabloid circulation, so the claims bear less and less relation to the actual achievements.

We view Rock with contradiction and pretension, as if it can provide great meaning in dumb statements – as if musicians are prophets. Bob Dylan did not change the world and neither did The Beatles. They played music that reflected their times, and became unnecessary when they did not reflect their times. Period. And if they did stir things up, what was the result? Endless world tours, greedy coke habits, soft drink sponsorship and the soulful sound of MTV Unplugged. The "revolution" of the 1960s failed because it was based on self-delusion. "Blowin' In The Wind" meant and achieved nothing compared to "Dancing In The Street".

Rock music (pop music – whatever) is about feeling, not something to be analysed in the Sunday papers in a space next to Opera and Ballet. How can you legislate for your favourite moments, describe properly the perfection of sound? The power of pop music *is* that it is dumb and commercial and that it swallows itself in the race towards the new. Go to a gig now and stand in line and put out that cigarette and sit in Row C and wait to be entertained. The energy present in the 1960s, when little girls would pull out their hair, has now transferred itself to club culture.

It was not always this way of course.

From 1954 to 1958 pop music was the domain of the insane. All constrictions were lifted. To make it big was to go louder, faster, sicker, and more outrageous than what went before. America was spoilt rich in a world recovering from war and every one of its citizens could seemingly afford a washing machine or a television or a spacesuit. A new age of commercial equality – the fulfilment of the American Dream – seemed to be dawning.

No longer the exclusive domain of some Harvard minority, prosperity now affected the white trash masses and a teen culture was born. Elvis, UFOs, James Dean, Little Richard, Jerry Lee Lewis and The Creature from the Black Lagoon all existed and were born into the America of McCarthy. Meanwhile the UK and Europe faced grim austerity. From conception, the roots of Rock'n'Roll were/are based in consumer dollar prosperity. In 1958, in a conservative country, officially paranoid of communism and entrenched with racist laws, a cross-dressing black man was Number One in the music charts. AWOPBOPALOOPBOPALOPBAM-BOOM. This said everything that needed to be said. Rock'n'Roll was pure freedom and empowerment.

Or it was for a few years anyway: the Empire was soon to strike back. Coinciding with the deaths of Buddy Holly and Richie Valens and the imprisonment of Chuck Berry, the first wave was over by the end of the decade. Phil Spector became the peerless "Tycoon of Teen" while Goffin and King emanated a conveyer belt of classic hits from the Brill Building. Pop became mass production as the big record companies manufactured their own groups. Pat Boone covered all those distasteful Negro tunes in a clean white style and the initial rush of electric madness was replaced with romantic ballads. Those first Rock'n'Roll records raged deviancy but Spector's girl groups sang about settling down and small town domestic bliss. "Wait Till My Bobby Gets Home", "Baby I Love You" or "Not Too Young To Get Married". The weird went underground or their behaviour was censored behind company respectability. And in 1961, in Hawthorne California, a family dressed in identical Pendleton shirts and sunny smiles, cut a disc entitled "Surfin'".

The story of The Beach Boys has always been the story of Brian Wilson. The non-surfing creator of the Californian sound; the man who composed to God from his sandpit; the man who went to bed for a decade; the 250lb man who returned to life after therapy; and the genius behind *Pet Sounds* and (the greatest never-to-be-released LP) *Smile*. For every stage of his life an alternative myth or headline can be woven. A combination of musical brilliance and drug-induced mental illness that has proved irresistible formula for all those wanting to document the darker side of 1960s pop music or romanticise about beautiful losers. The endearing notion of a social misfit creating heavenly pop music against all odds – the "tears of a clown" – touches the pathos within all of us.

Much of this is justified. The compilations of Beach Boys' product that still sell in there millions consist of nothing but 100% Brian Wilson compositions. "California Girls", "Surfin' USA" and "Barbara Ann" are all now synonymous with a time of innocence: between Elvis shedding his quiff to join the army and the birth of Hippy. The songs and sounds he created between 1963 and 1967 stand testament to a natural talent that broadened musical horizons and set new standards for Pop Music. *Pet Sounds* in particular, as a chronicle of genuine teenage feeling was a staggering achievement for Pop, and a bridge between the throwaway world of the 7" single and the advent of Rock music. In its wake *Revolver* and *Sergeant Pepper* followed. The otherworldly arrangements of songs like "Don't Talk (Put Your Head On My Shoulder)" or "I Just Wasn't Made For These Times" articulated perfectly the stresses of turning from teen to adulthood. "I dreamt I had a halo over my head," wrote Brian in 1990. "This might have meant the angels were watching over *Pet Sounds*." When "Good Vibrations" was released in 1967, rewriting the rules of record production again, it seemed that Brian's dream of composing "a teenage symphony to God" was about to be realised. It was The Beach Boys, and not The Beatles, who would triumph in the race to become the transatlantic kings of the Pop charts.

But the new "Crown Prince of Hip" (formerly the "Crown Prince of Square") was to take one acid trip too many. The project known as *Dumb Angel* a.k.a. *Smile* would remain in fragments. Its bones would be picked over for the next ten years. The acknowledged Genius, who had made even Leonard Bernstein gush with the beauty of his music, would drop any grand pretensions to create art and gradually retire altogether from song writing, and then from life. The talent and the drugs prompted a two-year torrent of brilliance before becoming a trickle to nothing. After 1967 Brian Wilson was the leader of The Beach Boys only in spirit.

Dennis Wilson was just the drummer.

He lived and breathed the Surf Bum lifestyle that Brian was to encapsulate in three-minute harmonies. He even suggested they start singing about the craze that was sweeping the West Coast. But his group membership was initially tenuous – due only to his Mother's insistence that he not be excluded from his brothers' new passion. His ability behind the kit was limited to a thumping backbeat and his voice was sandpaper compared to the angelic sound of Brian or Carl. On wax, session man Hal Blaine often played Dennis' parts, and like Ringo his voice was used sparingly – upfront on only a few cuts per album. Effectively banished from the recording process, the black sheep of the Wilson family could freely and happily devote himself to touring and the excesses that went with it.

A hyperactive and rebellious child, unable to concentrate on anything that was non-gratifying, his main contribution to the group aesthetic was image. In a band of misfits, Dennis the blond muscular surfer stood out like Steve McQueen amongst the toothy Al Jardine, the portly Carl, and the receding comb-over of Mike Love. In a band of such differing personalities his sex appeal was all-important, lest they were seen as contrived, or a manufactured one-hit novelty[1].

---

[1] A spoof documentary for a 1971 tour of Europe highlighted this – while the other boys are merrily sight-seeing, Dennis parodies his playboy image: drunkenly arising in the back of a limousine. "Should've seen the blonde from last night," he smirks aloud upon waking to the camera.

And this being Pop, Dennis held another equally important role. He attracted girls. It was a vocation on equal par with his drumming. When he strolled from behind the kit to deliver "The Wanderer" or "Do You Wanna Dance?", his hand cocked over his left ear, the screaming began. On those early pre-*Pet Sounds* television appearances the clapometers surged into red every time the cameras sought him out. Flailing wildly in the background Dennis was the epitome of teenage daydreams – natural, charismatic and untameable. Four courses of Beatlemania directed onto one personality, and a sea of teenage fucking to swim in. The carefree life of surfing, cars and sex was one that big brother Brian, sporadically wracked by low self-esteem and obsessed with music, could only dream of. For Dennis it was all his macho fantasies come true, nothing more than a means to an end. To get paid and to get laid.

Or so the myth goes. For after 1967 more and more of Dennis' indefatigable energy was transferred into writing music. Already living a lifestyle beyond the further extremities of his peers and absurdly at odds with the group's image, the supposed playboy of the band had begun conjuring some remarkable songs. Dense and soulful, sometimes dark and sometimes joyous, his intensely personal music reflected a California where golden beach innocence was becoming but a distant memory. Always a champion and reverential towards Brian's more experimental music, Dennis had quietly begun twisting the Beach Boys sound to his own specifications. While the rest of the band ignored his lead and slipped off into a drawer marked self-parody, it was their drummer – the "dumb, no-talent and drug-addled womaniser" – who offered the creative vision that could and should have paralleled the achievements of *Pet Sounds*.

The reality was that Dennis was a complex individual who refused to be pigeonholed. He moved too fast to be pinned down. In his adult life he was both gigolo and family man, drug addict and athlete, man and child. From a sex symbol he became a virtual bum, alcoholic and homeless, albeit a member of America's most famous band. His generosity was legendary, in both his heart and his wallet. Dennis would think nothing of casually relieving himself of money or possessions – the number of "shirt-off-my-back stories" probably total into thousands. Cars and motorbikes were written off daily. Dollar bills were dropped in their thousands. Nothing stood before the pursuit of pleasure.

Living always for the moment, he would often hurt those close to him, yet Dennis ultimately disregarded his own health and well-being for the sake of others. Carl Wilson recalled his brother's "nervous energy" from an early age ("I've never witnessed energy like that!") and how he could throw himself entirely into any new project. In the process of recording his only solo album, the masterpiece that was *Pacific Ocean Blue*, he worked for days on end to the point of physical collapse.

Dennis was a pioneer. The first Beach Boy to surf, drag race, drink, take drugs, meet the Maharishi, star in a film, and release a solo album. Competitive desire became nervous obsession. And though his role in the band was often stunted for reasons of jealousy or whatever else, Dennis proved a great catalyst for both Carl and Brian, always supporting the more experimental course.

And it was no surprise that he was also the first to die. According to Dennis' close friend Fred Vail, his premature death, though shocking, was probably inevitable: "I knew that Denny wasn't the type of guy who would live to be an old man. It just wasn't in the general scheme of things. He was just constantly challenging the boundaries." The restlessness in his veins fuelled both creativity and self-destruction. While the raw soul of his music continued to reach new emotional peaks his marriages failed and drug dependency spiralled. The sexual desire that had already taken him by 1968 into the world of Charles Manson and his hippy-chick sex battalion remained unceasing. As a hedonist Dennis was total, his capacity for life too much.

Yet the myth remained, and still remains today, that Brian would be back. That he would somehow rise from his torpor and start making hits again. That somehow his God-given talent would shine through his neuroses and defeat mental illness. While this may have been quite understandable in the early 1970s, when nobody knew quite how far he had fallen or how serious his mental state, with hindsight The Beach Boys had become a totally different band by the turn of the decade. An uneasy combination between touring show band and champions of the new, desperate to win critical plaudits.

No-one expected Paul McCartney to produce music of Beatles' quality after the mediocre offerings from Wings, and the same John Lennon who co-wrote "A Day In The Life" was covering "Stand By Me" in 1975. (How cruelly short the shelf life of the Pop performer, in such a fickle teen-driven business.) But Brian Wilson was different. He was an acclaimed G-E-N-I-U-S – and possibly a mad man. Despite the fact that Dennis and Carl were writing brilliant songs that reflected their age and maturity it was still Brian that everyone looked to. Contradiction after contradiction led everybody (from the record labels, to the fans, to the group themselves) to same conclusion: Brian paved success in the past so therefore he was capable of bringing it in the future. Forget the fact that he was incapacitated and barely capable of feeding or dressing himself. Forget the fact that *Pet Sounds*, the one true reflection of his soul, was a deliberate move away from the clichés of surfing and car songs, a tilt at the celestial infinite. It was always back to Brian that the final hopes would rest.

No doubt there is a certain romanticism of "Victim Culture" in forming this evaluation. From Van Gogh to Syd Barret to Kurt Cobain, everybody loves a tortured artist – to equate pain with artistic fulfilment. While Dennis was beautiful and macho and seemingly self-confident, Brian was totally lost – describing himself, in an increasingly rare moment of song writing clarity as, "a cork on an ocean wave", barely able to keep from drowning. Despite the myths and the kooky stories Brian was actually scarily and seriously ill. There was nothing glamorous about his mental decline, whether it was induced by drugs or by the pressures on his notoriously fragile psyche. Tony Asher's comments that Brian was "a genius musician but an amateur human being" have been celebrated by Rock'n'Roll ghouls for far too long. We demand lives of excess from our

Rock legends, but in Brian's case there was nothing to aspire to, little to romanticise about. His existence from 1969 through to the 1980s became a living hell while he remained at the mercy of forces beyond his control. Eugene Landy, The Beach Boys, the Record Companies, and even his own legend were constantly pulling him apart at the seams.

The basic attraction of The Beach Boys is that they were the most simultaneously conservative, outrageous, apple pie, avant-garde and fucked-up of American groups. A family of harmonic perfection that mutated into a bickering soap opera played out on concert stages and court rooms. As a microcosm of California they appealed to both Charlie Manson and Ronald Reagan; to the pure pop fan, *and* to those who like their harmonies a little more experimental – to literally touch the sun. Far beyond the high-profile pretentiousness of The Doors, their legacy is a lasting slice of Americana and a perfect mirror of the slide from optimism into the 1980s. And that's not forgetting the creation of the "Greatest Pop Album of All Time". There can be no denying the genius of *Pet Sounds* or the longevity of its influence, but the fact remains that it was the pinnacle of Brian's achievements and always will be.

By contrast, Dennis' lifestyle was a chosen road. He too faced tragedy and saw his work under-appreciated and under-promoted, yet remained a victim only to himself. While Brian's life was stalled in some nightmare adolescent Never Never Land, Dennis expressed his emotions as an adult. There was nothing plastic about him and his music remained painfully honest; sung in a soulful croon that was at once weary and innocent, gradually stripped hoarse through the years. His melancholy was not only the product of a dark soul, it came from an inner compassion and a quest for the impossible love he continually sought. His good looks exuded confidence and flamboyance but inside he remained a romantic, hopelessly in love with being in love. In his own words, "The greatest success in life is to feel I'm something for someone; the feeling of falling in love, the newness of love." As a true Rock'n'Roll star and free-spirited nature boy, Dennis Wilson lived as he wanted. We need not feel sorry for him.

Despite being a US institution, the Beach Boys have always been held in the highest regard in the UK and Europe[2]. This was especially true in the years between 1967 and 1973 when American audiences turned their back on a group considered the epitome of washed up. Ironically this coincided with perhaps their most interesting body of work, when Brian Wilson relaxed his reign and the other members began writing and arranging, their records continued to chart regularly over here and their concerts sold out. And it was in Europe that Dennis cautiously attempted to launch a solo career with the release of a lone single in late 1970. The band's renaissance in 1974, marked by the success of the million-selling *Endless Summer* compilation, consigned the majority of this unbelievable

---

[2] As early as 1971 the *NME* was lamenting this fact: "Britain and Europe has always recognised the Beach Boys' genius. For every record sold in North America, the Beach Boys sell three in Europe. The band traditionally occupies a top-five position in Britain's annual fan rankings of all groups."

music – a large percentage written by Dennis – to the dustbin of history. While other members wrested control and took the money, his place was gradually airbrushed from the picture and his songs dropped and forgotten. Prejudiced and put-down, the genius of Dennis Wilson was restricted to those ears that stuck by the Beach Boys through their supposedly lean times.

The time has come to re-evaluate that talent, and the music that was so widely ignored during his lifetime. Aside from his stand-out contributions to Beach Boys LPs from 1968 to 1979, his work is scarce. A couple of solo singles and his masterpiece *Pacific Ocean Blue* are now all but impossible to find, while his Beach Boys material has proved too individualistic for most *Best Of* compilations. The classic road movie *Two Lane Blacktop*, in which he starred as the Mechanic, was unavailable for over twenty-five years and has only now crawled out onto video. The bulk of material that would have formed his second album, provisionally entitled *Bamboo*, remains available only on bootlegs. A few years back the discovery and release of several sub-par Beatles songs made the headline news, and yet this priceless treasure of recordings by Dennis remains in dusty vaults. The failure to release these extraordinary songs, which could well have saved the creative reputation of the Beach Boys or even made Dennis a star in his own right, was/is a debacle of *Smile* proportions.

Dennis belongs up there with Nick Drake, Tim Buckley, and Gram Parsons – all neglected talents in the '70s, and canonised now. More than that, he should have Smokey Robinson, Curtis Mayfield and Marvin Gaye alongside him too. In a sea of mediocre MOR rock, Dennis was one of the great white soul singers of the 1970s. Like them he sang his own mind in his own voice. Like those other mavericks Lou Reed, Neil Young and Iggy Pop did with *Berlin*, *Tonight's The Night* and *The Idiot*, he reported from an emotional place that crossed beyond the mainstream. Music that was literally *released* – the frailties and complexities of the individual laid bare for all to see. Soul music totally and utterly. It was in Dennis' songs, every passionate, fragile and beautiful second of them, that we saw the true individual.

To these ends it is not my intention to write a biography, or to disassociate Dennis from the Beach Boys. He was a Beach Boy, after all (*the* Beach Boy), and a whole lot else besides – the roles were indistinguishable. I just want this book to stand testament to a wayward and forgotten genius, and to relate a truly extraordinary story. Dennis Wilson remains the embodiment of a true rock'n'roller, someone who cared and who dared to try. That's more than enough in these plastic times, when we need just about all the soul we can get.

It's About Time.

WHITE PUNK

"I don't know why everybody doesn't live at the beach, on the ocean. It makes no sense to me, hanging around the dirty, ugly-as-shit city. That's why I always loved and was proud to be a Beach Boy; I always loved the image. On the beach you can live in bliss."
—Dennis Wilson, 1976

Since a teenager, the wayward life of Dennis Carl Wilson had been possessed by the tides of his beloved Pacific Ocean. That omnipresent horizon of water; stretching from Santa Barbara along the coastal highway, past Long Beach towards San Diego. The salt-water pull of the North Central Gyre.

Riding the rolling breakers on his 9ft blue board had offered release, away from a suffocating home life and an overbearing father. Dennis was lucky enough to be born in 1944: the good fortune of fate ensured he and his peers could take advantage of that whole glorious post-war Nirvana. A ticket to teenage heaven in a fashionable New World of music, woodies and girls on the beach – his passion for the surf turning on the musical instincts of elder brother Brian. The inspiration behind The Beach Boys, the ultimate musical encapsulation of huge unbridled teenage fun.

And so began the life of America's most successful pop group of the 1960s. The soundtrack to the Californian dream. Endless Harmony.

To Dennis, the ocean and the beach were freedom. A doorstep Paradise for a nature boy: a place to swim and to fish. A place to pick up girls and a natural haven for a troubled man. Just to lose yourself in that perfect swell of immunity and feel the energy wash over you. The sheer never-ending untouchable vastness of it all offered inspiration and possibilities – equal only to his own considerable love. The peaceful inevitability of each incoming tide a soothing contrast to his unpredictable nature. In adulthood his sailboat *Harmony* serenely cruised the Californian waters and became a temporary home when harboured at the Marina Del Ray. He would later despair about the destruction of its natural beauty.

Throughout his 39 years Dennis never strayed far from the beach. His blue music was laced with references to water and the hope it would bring redemption. Whatever his ills it seemed the Pacific Ocean would always provide a cure.

The last few years though had not been good. The promise of 1977's *Pacific Ocean Blue* – a truly magnificent "lost album" – had never been realised. The follow up was aborted and Dennis returned to his original role as drummer, a role he had struggled away from for almost ten years. He loved being a Beach Boy but the band had not produced a great record for some time. Their leader Brian Wilson was locked in a suicidal depression. Only enduring popularity on the concert circuit combined with the bonds of family ensured Dennis would return in times of crisis. As the decade closed he was marooned: the success of his past was nullifying his future – his independence and lifeblood gradually sucked back into the Love-dominated organisation that was parodying his teenage dreams.

Dennis responded the only way he knew. His foot hit the floor. He drank and fought in a ceaseless fury against a world past caring. 1983 had been particularly bad: in and out of clinics and kicked out of the band whose existence he could lay claim to. Spiralling downwards, consuming powder and alcohol, he had grown old through pain and confusion. The true King of California was barely recognised on the beaches of his youth. His once muscled body was now bloated and his voice, inflicted by polyps, was barely a voice at all. The anger and bravado that once propelled his life were now about to swallow it. Dennis could never reform what he was, and in the end he was a broken man.

That his final resting-place would be the ocean floor was somehow fitting. On January 4th 1984, at 5:11 p.m., his body bag was dropped at USCGC POINT JUDITH, 33-53.9°N by 118-38.8°W. This was three nautical miles from shore; the water depth in excess of 100 fathoms. An elegy he had composed for the late Otto Hinsche, *Farewell My Friend*, played on a stereo.

It was over twenty years before, on September 15th 1961, that a nervous group of teenagers entered Dorinda and Hite Morgan's studio on Melrose Avenue to lay down a track called "Surfin'". The familial nucleus of the band, then called *The Pendletones*, was based around the Wilson brothers Brian, Dennis and Carl and they were very, very young – 19, 16 and 14 respectively. The other members being Mike Love, the Wilson's 20-year-old cousin (who was already married), and a school acquaintance of Brian's, Al Jardine. As individuals they were already amateur veterans of the school prom and church circuit, but this was their first venture into a recording studio. To raise cash for their hired instruments the boys had broken into an emergency $200 left behind by the Wilson parents, Murry and Audree, who were spending their Labor Day vacation in Mexico City.

The chosen song was a simple ode to the craze that was sweeping the coast. The rhythm went "bop-bop-dip-di-dip-di-dip" against a 12-bar blues structure, while their nasally teen voices (soon to become a trademark) melted together in four-part harmonies. There was no masterplan behind the recording other than to cut a disc, but the sound was fresh with a professionalism that belied the years of the performers. "It started, we went into a room and sang and it got into the air. It was wonderful," Carl later reminisced with awe. As the by-product of a musical upbringing, harmony came naturally. Together they could create something magical.

For three straight days the boys had practised furiously the self-penned number, written hastily by Brian and Mike in response to Dennis' suggestion. (An earlier meeting with the Morgans prompted Dennis to brag how the band already *had* a surfing repertoire when a lack of originality in their material failed to impress.) On the day of recording however, Dennis was absent – recently suspended from school for hurling a screwdriver at the head of a fellow student. Brian decided to replace his brother's services with a local hillbilly drummer, who himself was dropped in favour of simple percussive finger clicks. The rhythm was finally added by Brian himself, tapping a snare drum. This was not the last time that the errant middle brother would find himself sidelined from the performances of The Beach Boys. It was in these early years of the group's existence that many of his future troubles stemmed and could be identified.

For from top to bottom the Wilson's were a family held together by music. When the other traditional bonds of clan were cracked and their inter-relationships unstable it was the music – and sometimes *only* the music – that kept everything together. As I've already stated, I'm not in the business of writing a biography (the facts about the Wilson boy's home life are well documented elsewhere, read anything by David Leaf or Timothy White), but for an understanding of everything that was to happen later a brief description is pretty much essential here. At their inception The Beach Boys were child stars, the original boy band, and in so many ways never outgrew their adolescent roles. The family was the group and the group was the music.

Outspoken and hardworking, Murry Wilson was the undoubted head of the household. For better or for worse his considerable presence straddled both personal and professional spheres, marking the entire band for the duration of their career. This was significantly so in the early years when acting as the band's manager. As a living embodiment of the American work ethic with his never-say-die desire to succeed, he was the most complex character of the whole family – admired and loathed in equal measure, but never particularly liked. Married to the easy-going Audree Korthof in 1938, the couple had settled in the inland lower-middle class satellite town of Hawthorne in 1944. Not quite the archetypal Californian world of sun-kissed beaches and orange groves (it was Ordinary Joe suburbia), but a sense of optimism prevailed nonetheless as the war dragged to its conclusion. By working at the local Goodyear plant he avoided any action himself but still emerged from the war years minus his left eye – the victim of an industrial accident.

After the war Murry had set up the A.B.L.E Machinery Company (Always Better Lasting Equipment), but harboured aspirations to be a songwriter. A stocky domineering figure (now with a glass eye), an ever-present pipe between his lips, Murry Wilson considered himself a talented tunesmith, and was opinionated about it too. A number of his quirky romantic numbers (influenced by the big band sound of Tin Pan Alley), were issued on the tiny Palace record label and he continually hawked his songs to an ever-growing list of showbiz contacts. His greatest success thus far was a cha-cha dance number "Two-Step, Two-Step" recorded by the improbably named Lawrence Welk Orchestra. From an early age he both encouraged and berated his sons' superior talents. Initially enraged by them wasting his hard-earned dollars at Wallich's Music City it was his "suggestion" that the boys record the first fruit of their labours. Murry knew Hite and Dorinda personally – they had published several of his masterworks and even met a 13-year old Brian, who auditioned at their studio when they were seeking a youthful voice.

Without Murry it is debatable that the band would have met success so quickly, or even at all. By common consensus the old man was dictatorial and outspoken (Beach Boys engineer Steve Desper's description of a "freight train in a library" summed up most people's opinion of Murry) but it was through his contacts and business acumen that the band signed to Capitol Records in 1962. Brian had a God-given talent for harmony but there were 100 other garage bands exploiting the surfing idiom in the early 1960s. Murry pushed that talent onto 7" wax and beyond. In the harsh craze-driven scene that was the Californian recording industry the band needed someone to play hardball for them, and so Murry put his own plans on hold and decided to live out his dreams via his offspring – the early pictures of five beaming white cherubs in identical clothing bore his stamp totally. His notion of what a group should look like and how they should act was grounded in the 1950s, and was an image that the Beach Boys would find almost impossible to break away from. His love of melody – of the standard classics – remained a subliminal influence on Brian, but that innocent striped-shirted image was theirs for life. By enforcing professionalism on stage and in the studio (the band were fined for swearing or not smiling "properly" for their fans) Murry instilled a work ethic that ensured his boys would be more than one-hit wonders. Their first LP *Surfin' Safari* was the result of one mammoth 13-hour session. Through sheer guts they would become *the* No. 1 band, with this ogre at the helm.

Murry's defiant protection of his vested interests, as his family had now become, would eventually enable his son the freedom to create separately from the rigours of business. Progressing even beyond Spector, Brian was the first to win some semblance of control over where his records were recorded, who played on them, and the track list of the finished product. His move to Studio 3 at Western Recorders in 1963 to achieve a desired state of excellence, a breakthrough that would benefit later artists, was testament to Wilson bullishness when it came to getting things right. When his considerable tenacity was directed away from his boys then Murry had an amazing propensity to get things done. But it also had a downside. The roles he played between manager and father were indistinguishable, and the latter role was weighted with far too much emotional baggage for the combination to remain successful. The myriad ways that Murry mistreated Brian, Dennis and Carl as children would continue into their adulthood and his position within the group structure would eventually become untenable. Murry's chauvinism was such that he had to be fighting someone, and if it was not some company executive trying to chisel money off the Beach Boys (*his* band) then he would be fighting the band himself. Like Brian he sought perfection from all those around him. Unlike Brian, his talent did not match his ego.

Frustrated in just about every venture in which he participated, the head of the Wilson household was a notorious bully to his kids. The exponent of a twisted "tough love" philosophy he expressed himself physically, thrashing them for the tiniest misdemeanour. The intention of rearing three God-fearing self-reliant citizens became secondary to promoting his own dictatorial image – an image that belied an acute inferiority complex. The recurring crux of a family argument would be, "Audree, if you love me, you will see my point and don't give in." If he could not control the world at large then he could at least control his household.

It is alleged that Brian's deafness in the right ear was caused by one of these childhood beatings, but it was the troublesome Dennis who always came off the worst. Most famously when he stole that glass eye for a school show-and-tell, but any far lesser acts of insolence caused Murry to react. There were no discussions or reasoning, only the back of his hand or a broomstick. On other occasions Dennis had his hands burnt with matches or was scalded with boiling water. He was forced to eat tomatoes until he was sick for daring to leave them raw on his plate. The floggings when they occurred were as public as possible in order to cause maximum humiliation. "He used to physically beat the crap out of us," spoke the victim as an adult.

Murry's bellicosity and cruelty had one exception, and that was the soothing sound of music, as Brian quickly discovered. "My dad was an asshole and he treated us like shit, and his punishments were sick. But you played a tune for him and he was a marshmallow."

"This mean motherfucker would cry with bliss, like the lion in the *Wizard Of Oz*, when he heard the music," added Dennis. (This family trait to literally break down and cry on reaction to a beautiful song was inherited by both brothers). Little wonder that the Wilson boys sung like birds at such an early age.

Any paternal affection emanating from Murry came through music. Though he was pulling in $15,000 a year with the machinery business, a typical evening's entertainment would revolve around the Hammond organ, singing duets with Audree. "We were all so poor we'd just sit around singing and on occasion drink a glass of brew. All they ever heard was music in the house – and on occasion family arguments," he later commented through rose-tinted memories. Brian had fallen in love with Gershwin's *Rhapsody In Blue* at an early age and was treated to a toy accordion, which he mastered soon after. As a teenager he was presented with a tape recorder which formed the basis of early experiments into Four Freshman-type vocal harmonies. Carl received guitar lessons and all three boys were taken to Sunday School where their singing voices developed. Save for brief drumming lessons with Carl's guitar tutor, Fred Morgan, Dennis was never given any formal tuition, but in-between performing menial chores at A.B.L.E. learnt to play piano himself. His father instead treated him to a surfboard and trips to the go-cart track – in their own way as important for the development of the band as Brian receiving a Four Freshman LP. Dennis' principal task musically was to stack the record player at home with 78s while Murry lapsed on the couch and barked orders.

Early recordings such as "Hawaii" and "Catch A Wave" highlighted Dennis' lack of technical ability next to Brian or Mike. On the latter surfing anthem, when taking the lead in the verses, his voice was flat and nervous, without the immediacy of Mike's R'n'B inflected vowels.

Brian's outrageous falsetto simply ran rings around it. As he confirmed in a 1976 TV interview, Dennis' musical training was confined to the back seat of Murry's car on a Friday night, singing numbers that had been concocted earlier by Brian. These would be some of the few times that he would be at harmony with his brothers as an adolescent. The voice that was to mature into such an expressive instrument in later years just was not suited to the Beach Boy recordings of 1962 to 1964. (Some irony this when Dennis was the only band member to have experienced the subjects being sung about). In any case the failure to emanate his brother's talents can hardly have aided his cause when faced with his father's wrath. Though, in truth, none of them would escape the long term scars resultant of growing up under Murry Wilson.

Brian, despite popularity amongst his peers through playing the clown, was prone to introverted moods and confidence-sapping attacks of fear. Being the eldest he was pushed the hardest, towards unattainable ideals which he was eager to live up to. His punishments were mainly psychological. "I used to catch it from him all the time," he later remembered. "It bothered me because it made me feel like I was goofing up, that I was inferior, it made me feel worthless and a number of emotions like that." Murry's considerable and aggressive work ethic, ("I try harder, drive harder") rubbed off in his son's search for musical perfection. Long adolescent days and nights spent divining the formula to the latest pop hit indicate how strong Brian's competitive urge was. The internal self-pressure to be "the best" would later spiral out of control when the band became established – praise and respect and acknowledgement of the music were to mean more to Brian than anything. Unfortunately Murry, partly out of resentment and partly out of his paternal "wisdom", could never fully praise his eldest son – as if it were a weakness or failing on his part. In the family that was the group Brian was doomed to fail even when he was succeeding. "He was critical of the first thing we ever did," he bemoaned on Murry's first reaction to "Surfin".

Solace was found in addiction to candy and soda, which he consumed with gusto, and in the daydream freedom of music. Brian's awkwardness was ever present in those early Beach Boy songs. The reverence towards surfing, cars and girls (none of which he had much experience of) becoming some sort of fantasy world – an outsider's perception of teenage ideals. For every "Surfin' USA" or "409" there was a soulful ballad from the heart such as "In My Room" or "Surfer Girl", which seemed to pin point the *real* Brian Wilson; an escapism via the melodies that ran around his head. His "regular guy" exterior concealing an acute sensitivity. Carl on the other hand tried to avoid his father altogether, and as a consequence was spared much of his wrath. He instead grew close to Audree and relied on her for protection. Of the three boys he was by far the most balanced individual.

And the most unbalanced was Dennis. While the rest of the family found a common thread in music, something to paper over the cracks in their relationships, he grew up virtually alone. For Dennis, who took no part in the communal Wilson singing sessions, was repelled by any activity based around the family unit. On reaching walking age he was out the door and inquisitively away from West 119th Street into a fantasy world of his own.

According to author Timothy White, Dennis was a childhood sufferer of acute nervous tension, a hyperactive condition filling him with a dread of time and huge doses of pent-up energy. Every second of the day bore down and seemed to oppress him. Every moment had to be seized. Unable to abide Murry's controlling presence and unreasonable punishments he stalked the neighbourhood as a teenage punk. While Brian and Carl could immerse themselves internally and find some release through music, Dennis rebelled. The regular beatings seemingly had no effect beyond the barriers he raised. A lack of attention and sympathy among such a musically attuned household created a tough-necked independent personality. Though not an overly malicious child he reacted to the stresses of his homelife by fighting, cutting school and running wild – in Al Jardine's own inimitable expression Dennis was always off somewhere "raising heck". Known locally as Dennis The Menace he was arrested several times for minor offences – starting brush fires or petty theft – his demeanour tense and shiftless. A typically revealing *NME* interview from late 1966 (entitled "Danger Spice of Dennis' Life") had Dennis describing his formative years as a Hawthorne alley cat:

"If my dad hadn't given me a BB [pellet] gun when I was 9 years old my life would've been completely different. With that gun I had something I could take my anger out on. Hunting, fishing, racing have been my preoccupations ever since. After I got that gun, I built a fort in a tree in our backyard. Whenever my parents got me upset, I'd go sit in the fort and start shooting – at birds, windows, trees, fences, anything. I was in a completely different world out their – my own. I was like that in school too – in my own world. And I always made trouble – or it made me. If anything wrong happened within a 20-mile radius, some would say Dennis Wilson did it. Lots of time I did."

The same interview confirmed Dennis' love for speed and his destructive nonchalance. He boasted of his involvement in numerous car crashes, even while at High School – "I must be the only guy in Hawthorne ever to knock down two trees and a lamp post on the front lawn of the police station." The external brashness in actuality concealed personal confusion with the world of Hawthorne – its rules and strictures suffocated the spirit. Included in White's book is an entire High School essay – all 50 words of it – from 1961, revealing much about his character:

"Sports car racing is very dangerous. Just think, you are going about 120 miles per hour down a curved mountain road, then you have to make a hard right or left. The main thing is you have to keep your eyes on the road, not in the deep blue sky."

Behind the loud-mouthed punk persona beat the heart of a romantic.

The one place that Dennis could find contentment and

comradeship was 5 miles away at Manhattan Beach. Since the turn of the decade the Californian coastline had become a Mecca for the surfers. The fad was fast becoming a lifestyle choice, and Dennis was a willing participant[1]. Weekend excursions to avoid Murry's menial chores, occasionally fishing with Mike on Redondo Beach, soon turned into regular truancy as Dennis spent more of his life on the sands than at Hawthorne High. The intriguing combination of an exciting new sport gift-wrapped in a scene of girls, cars, alcohol and weed and all served up with its own language and codes was attraction enough for Dennis' insatiable curiosity and his love of the new. Among the surfing beatniks, with their laid-back communal lifestyle, Dennis at last found a kinship that was lacking at home. The calming influence of the ocean was evident enough for Brian to notice his middle brother's new habit of trawling through trash cans, in the hope of finding something of use for his new beach buddies. "I guess he's gone from being a sports guy to a nature boy."

Many have commented that Dennis had much in common with the characteristics of Murry, and that his quick and impulsive temper made him his father's son. To some extent this is true. When Murry died in 1973 it was his middle son, whom he had battled so physically throughout his life, who grew closest and was most affected by his passing. Dennis certainly inherited the confidence and rough exterior that belied a sentimental heart full of romance. He also retained his father's disarming honesty – in both his personal and public life. But he was not beneath learning from Murry's failings. Outspoken and rebellious he might have been, but any cruelty on his part was confined to childhood and the merciless tormenting of his overweight younger brother. (He was certainly never less than loving to his own children, despite long periods of absence, and as an adult often found it easier to relate to their total honesty). Most people who encountered him during the Beach Boys 1960s zenith, like the publicist Derek Taylor, found the twenty-something Dennis to be a mixture of the childlike and the childish. David Leaf, in a posthumous tribute, stated that the Dennis he knew was a "perpetual bad child" whose intense curiosity with life and to "know everything through experience" was fuelled by "a combination of blind faith and innocence." According to Leaf, Dennis was a total natural who had "never been taught how to deceive people" – aside from himself.

Another significant difference between father and son was his protective stance towards Brian and his music, which remained reverentially so in his time as a Beach Boy. Dennis recognised early on that his place in the dream was solely down to the talents of his eldest brother and he never forgot that. During later recording sessions he would become humbled by Brian's mere presence, and considered his own

---

[1] Some debated whether Dennis even stood on a board before the birth of the band – Nick Venet, who signed the band at Capitol before falling out with Murry, claimed that all three brothers gained their knowledge from the movies. This seems more a case of sour grapes: at the very least Dennis had experienced the surf lifestyle that Brian and Mike would so eloquently put into song.

Dumb Angel

talent a mere diversion before the master. Even in 1977 when his solo career seemed to be taking off and Brian was all but wasted, Dennis would recall the time around 1964, gazing at him and thinking, "'This guy's my brother?' I was famous because some guy was 'beautiful', and I got a chance to play drums and sing with him and take part in this great ride – God, what a fuckin' honour." While others later used the Boy/Man genius for their own ends Dennis' concerns remained genuine, if occasionally misplaced.[2]

This respect for Brain's talents coupled with his own lack of formal tuition would only fuel Dennis' inherent sense of isolation and insecurity. When the band recorded their follow up to "Surfin", which by early 1962 had risen to number 75 in *Billboard*'s Hot 100, Dennis purportedly broke down in front of the Morgans, claiming his life to be phoney, that he would rather be a writer than a pop musician. "I'm a duck who was born with two chickens," he allegedly cried. On that second recording session at Western Studios, making the demos that would see the band sign to Capitol, Dennis actually played the drums, but consistently behind the beat. His inclusion in the group was down to his mother's sense of familial democracy rather than his ability – it was only fair that Denny should be in the band, since the idea to sing surfing songs was his. Within the group (within the family) he was the perennial outsider, destined to be misunderstood. This tenuous position, coupled with his own frailties, would haunt Dennis with recurring feelings of inadequacy and guilt. A *Rolling Stone* article from October 1977, that witnessed one of the band's frequent splits, had Dennis confessing to writer John Swenson, "Mike Love never wanted me in the band. For that matter Brian didn't either, or at least not at first. My mother took my part and told Brian I had to be in the group. I never even knew this myself until two years ago."

Yet even without any greatly recognised talent, Dennis embraced the joy of early success. His life was heading particularly nowhere and there is no doubt that rock'n'roll life suited his extrovert tendencies. For five shit-kickers from the suburbs it was the realisation of fantasy – a passport to travel, adulation and excess, when middle class anonymity was the only viable alternative. The defining moment was in Brian's car: switching the radio dial to KFWB and hearing "Surfin" played for the first time. The joy on Brian's face, his teenage dreams accomplished in those two-minutes and twenty-eight seconds, was for Dennis the "all time moment". He might not have played on the actual record but he could celebrate its success, tearing down the street and screaming at the neighbours. At last he was part of *something*. The music gave Dennis

---

[2] Brian's ghost-written biography' *Wouldn't It Be Nice*, which gave free reign for his psychologist Eugene Landy to distort the band's history while offering occasional insights from its supposed author, contained two sentences in the acknowledgements that stand as a wonderful testament to his brother's importance: "I often think of the one family member who would've stood on my side and helped me fight my current battles. Dennis I miss you." In a book filled with Stalinist re-writes, I like to think that this is the true voice of Brian Wilson.

direction and some small connection with his family. "If there wasn't The Beach Boys and there wasn't music, I would not even talk to them. But through the music I fell in love with my brothers."

In the words of Hal Blaine, the beat behind Phil Spector's Wall Of Sound and a session man for over 350 Top Ten hits – including the majority of the Beach Boys' – "Drummers are all show-offs. We always seek attention." Considering the stereotypes of Keith Moon and John Bonham, this seems a fair assessment. The physical demands of the drum kit have attracted more than their fair share of lunatics. And certainly for Dennis, lacking the proficiency to do much else musically, the drum kit was the perfect instrument for his high-octane temper. Lacking the subtlety demanded to realise Brian's sophisticated pocket symphonies Dennis was more of a "beater" who came into his own in the live arena. Early concert footage shows his swaggering frame hammering away with primitive delight – mouth wide open, his eyes manic stars while attempting to over-ride the volume of adolescent screams. That hour on stage provided another chance to prove himself to his father and his brothers. Thumping out the crude rhythms demanded by the majority of material (surf covers such as "Let's Go Trippin'" and "Miserlou" or Beach Boy originals "Fun, Fun, Fun" to "I Get Around") he found his true home on the drum riser, sitting behind the static formation of Al and Carl on guitar, Brian on bass and Mike on lead vocals. Attempting nothing more than a driving 4/4 on his four-piece kit, Dennis propelled the show onwards into teen frenzy.

In the studio Dennis was more than happy to allow Hal Blaine to take his part. As Brian sought to emulate and overtake the gargantuan productions of Phil Spector he came to rely increasingly on the talents of The Wrecking Crew, his hero's own backing band. The Beach Boys may have been the greatest white vocal group but they were far from the greatest musicians. Consequently the likes of Blaine and musical gun-slingers such as Glen Campbell, Carole Kaye, Larry Knechtel, Jerry Cole, and Leon Russell, amongst others, etched into vinyl the multi-layered sounds that ran through Brian's head. The ever-turning, ever-demanding Capitol Records conveyor belt, that sought hit after hit from Brian Wilson, in addition to the promotional tours and appearances from his band, also demanded this situation.

Since the release of "Surfer Girl" in 1963 and up until after 1967 Dennis played on few of the Beach Boys records. As Brian's compositions outstripped his rivals in complexity and sophistication his brother was shifted to the shadows. These were the songs that made them famous, that have appeared on endless compilations since, and his contribution was limited mainly to background vocals. According to Gary Usher, the first of Brian's successful songwriting partners, this was another unwanted secular weight on the prodigy's shoulders – that he must hurt his brother's feelings (and risk a family quarrel) by omitting, and admitting, his second-rate talent. In truth though, Dennis could hardly have cared less. The discipline of recording hardly suited his lifestyle or his temperament – according to Brian he was, "The most messed-up person I know. He has to keep moving all the time. If you want him to sit still for one second, he's yelling and screaming and ranting and raving." Dennis' hyper-activity was just not conducive to those legendary mammoth sessions, as Brian procured take after take to achieve pop perfection. If Brian wanted to use someone else that was fine by him, it just meant more freedom to live out the Beach Boy fantasy out on the road or on the beach. And in any case the practice of using session musicians was hardly unusual for the times – Blaine played on the Byrds' groundbreaking version of "Mr Tambourine Man", "California Dreaming" by the Mamas and Papas, and numerous other West Coast classics, along with his Wrecking Crew stalwarts.

No, Dennis' importance lay elsewhere, in other means. Successful pop music is usually a combination of style and substance – Elvis was living proof that a great haircut can be the equal of a great tune. Dennis was the catalyst – the one who actually went off to the beach or to the car track and reported back what he saw. He knew the importance of looking cool. While Brian had the Midas touch and the other boys had the angelic voices, it was Dennis who provided the whole package with some sort of identity. In every sense he was the archetypal Californian male – beautiful, bronzed and carefree, the total opposite of his other band members, particularly the overweight and introspective Brian. It was his lifestyle (even unwittingly) that provided much of Brian's inspiration. Similarly to Brian Jones' role within the early Rolling Stones, Dennis provided a talismanic presence that teenagers could connect with. If the Stones were sold by Andrew Loog-Oldham's maxim "they're not a band, they're a way of life" through Jones' sheer dandified decadence, then Dennis with his love of the beach and his love of girls was the essence and soul of the Beach Boys. What the former embodied in "Swinging London", the latter reflected in mid-'60s California.

The Manhattan Beach lingo that Dennis introduced to Brian and Mike, enabling them to write "Surfin", was just the first instance of this inspirational flow. Since Brian was scared of water ("I hated the ocean; its murky darkness and power frightened me") and only Mike offered slight competition in outdoor pursuits, Dennis was relied upon to provide a first-hand account of what was currently hip. The Beach Boys were not a surfing band per se but merely a band who sang about the sport. Their name, which is now synonymous with a board cruising on golden waves, was the momentary idea of record agent Russ Regan and they had scant connection with the local scene concentrated around the staccato Fender attack of Dick Dale. Through Dennis they had stumbled upon fame and simply built upon the mirage. After "Surfin" came "Surfer Girl", "Surfin' Safari", "The Surfer Moon", "Surfin' USA", "Catch A Wave", et al. The image was aeons away from the real imaginations of Brian Wilson, but Capitol Records (whose tunnel-vision saw only short-term returns in such a craze-driven teen market) milked it for all it was worth. The Beach Boys had little control over this matter, and hardly cared in those halcyon days before 1966, but in many ways the band aesthetic was less about the songs of Brian than the lifestyle of his younger brother.

The recorded conversations between Paul Williams (founder of *Crawdaddy* magazine) and David Anderle (Head of Brother Records

1966–67) after the death of the *Smile* project are very revealing on these points. Both men were among the inner circle of onlookers when Brian was at his creative heights, witnessing firsthand the craziness that was going down at Laurel Way in 1967. Williams described the band's drummer as completely on the edge ("You never know with Dennis at any second whether he's gonna explode or not") and as someone who lived as "a free animal who is almost always controlled by his emotions, and very seldom by his head". This was evidently a prime source of enjoyment for Brian, who would "spend a great deal of time talking about Dennis, just going into raps about Dennis". Anderle in turn recalled the close brotherly bond and the creative spark that was achieved: "All the fantasies Brian would get, Dennis would take even farther. Brian would say it would be really groovy if everyone got into the ocean, Dennis would buy a boat. If Brian said, 'God, it would be great to have motorcycles,' Dennis would have a motorcycle outfit, a motorcycle, and would be doing the most incredible mountain-climbing numbers you've ever seen. That's Dennis."

In this vein Dennis was his brother's predominant source of material. When Brian decided the band could not live off surf songs alone and began collaborating with the likes of Gary Usher and Roger Christian on "car songs" such as "409", "Little Deuce Coupe" and "Shut Down" he again looked to Dennis' ability to lock onto the "next big thing". The car itself was a potent symbol of the new teenage America – an automatic representation of freedom, speed, affluence and success. That whole James Dean/Marlon Brando rebellion package was bound up by wheels of one sort or another. The kids who lived away from the coast might only dream of surfing but they could identify 100% with songs about automobiles and aspirations of cruising the town to shut down inferior opponents.

The emerging dragster scene was correctly recognised by Tom Wolfe as the true face of Americana in his 1964 essay for *Esquire* magazine, "The Kandy Kolored Tangerine-Flake Streamline Baby". By worshipping a union of pure aesthetic and dollars, US teenagers had broken off from the Old World of the '40s to create something culturally all their own. "Here was this incredible combination of form plus money in a place nobody ever thought about finding it, namely, among teenagers... In fifteen years stock car racing has replaced baseball as the number one sport in the South." Wolfe perfectly summarised the power of these post-war trends – the potency of pop culture over an irrelevant and conservative establishment: "Stock car racing, custom cars – and, for that matter, the jerk, the monkey, rock music – still seem beneath serious consideration, still the preserve of ratty people with ratty hair and dermatitis and corroded thoracic boxes and so forth. Yet all these rancid people are creating new styles all the time and changing the life of the whole country in ways that nobody even seems to bother to record, much less analyze."

Christian and Usher as a partnership were to become responsible for a significant number of the one-hit wonders that made up the Californian pop scene between 1962 and 1964. The Beach Boys may have crossed over to nationwide prominence with the release of "Surfin' USA" in 1963 (their first national top ten hit) but their backyard was still home to numerous garage groups hoping to follow the Wilson's leap from local station KFWB to stardom. The two songwriters promoted and created bands at an astonishing rate in those years for the record company sharks who, scenting a quick buck, were snapping up and releasing anything surf and/or car related in a frenzy. While Brian preferred to perfect his craft and mastery of the studio Capitol, BMG, Columbia and MCA were releasing 45's with a machine gun logic. Roll the tape, cut the record and ship it out – if this one fails don't worry, another ten are out this week. That one-hit Usher/Christian wonders like The Astronaughts ("Competition Coupe"), The Super Stocks ("Surf Route 101"), The Knights ("Hotrod High") or The Sunsets ("Chug-a-Lug") lacked the sophistication of Brian's arrangements was immaterial to the money makers. One only has to listen to the beauty and depth of a song like "Don't Worry Baby" from 1964, where the car race is presented as love story, to realise the Beach Boys were in a different league to the majority of these one-dimensional garage punks. They did not represent competition in the same way as Spector or the Beatles or Motown. And yet to Capitol, Brian was perceived as no different to the bandwagon. He wrote pop songs that sold for the time being, and his name on the credits was a decent assurance of cash in the bank. The subjects of his success were girls, cars and the beach. That precept was to remain a constant throughout his career, even after the years of 1966 and 1967 when he was first recognised as some sort of genius. In the four-year journey to *Pet Sounds* eighteen Top 40 hits were squeezed out of that increasingly frazzled mind.

The first collaboration between Gary Usher and Brian was "409", a homage to the power of the Chevy, and released in 1962 on the flip of "Surfin' Safari", in addition to being covered by Terry Melcher and Bruce Johnston as The Rip Chords. Gary's expertise on all matters car-related was used by Brian in much the same way that he relied on Dennis' love of the surf. He provided the inspiration and language to create commercially viable pop songs that connected with a ready audience. Usher was an avid hot rod racer at the San Fernando Airport Dragstrip and his pop career had taken off when performing with Carol Conners and Ginger Blake (later of the Honeys) at the Orange Show Fairgrounds in San Bernardino. It was there that he bonded with KFWB DJ Roger Christian over the latter's 1955 Corvette. The two roared back to Usher's house at an average speed of 90 miles per hour and the partnership was cemented.

Despite co-writing several of the Beach Boys earliest and most enduring songs, the bond between Brian and Gary was resented by Murry – always quick to dampen any loss of his paternal control. (In the summer of 1963 Brian had enraged his father and Capitol executives by gifting Jan and Dean a Number One hit in the shape of "Surf City"). Brian was keen to emulate Spector's svengali-like operations, bestowing his songs liberally wherever and with whoever he pleased, which was anathema to his father's perception of the Beach Boys, as an extension of the family. Murry became instrumental in promoting the talents of Roger Christian after he criticised "409" on his radio show as a "good song about a bad car". He subsequently stepped seamlessly, and with apparently remarkably little friction, into his partner's still-warm shoes. While Christian took on the mantle of Brian's chief songwriting buddy the ousted Usher sought companionship with the band member who he perhaps had most in common with: Dennis.

Dennis had been a regular visitor to the drag strip throughout the early-to-middle '60s. Racing his yellow cobra against Usher's 426 Plymouth Hemi Superstock the two quickly became friends. When Murry ousted Gary from writing with Brian they became allies, united in their mutual resentment of old man Wilson and their absence from Beach Boys operations. For a short time in 1963 they actually lived together, forming the studio-based Four Speeds[3] after a benzedrine-fuelled road trip to Tijuana. Under this pseudonym three 45's were released on the Challenge label: "Cheater Slicks", "R.P.M.", and "My Stingray". Existing around a mercenary pool of session players and co-written with Mike Borchetta, Dennis brought his primitive drumming skills to the latter two tracks. At odds with the Beach Boys' slick production standards the songs were pure garage nuggets – two minutes of car worship and speed culture[4] built around dirty three-chord structures and interlaced with the sound of screeching tyres. Lost in the ether, The Four Speeds were never more than a diversion from the day job. But their existence was proof that Dennis could strike out on his own musically, as well as personally.

His swaggering confidence was most noticeable though when transferred to the third subject matter that concerned the Beach Boys 1962–67: GIRLS. If Californians could identify with surf boards and Americans with cars, then the whole world could identify with girls. And if the others had little knowledge of the two former subjects at least Dennis was not needed to give pre-packaged instructions on the third. He and Mike certainly dived straight into the pool of excess. The early tours of school hops and youth events became exercises in teen bacchanalia as the two competed for the female population of California and beyond. The two 15-year-olds, Carl and David Marks, would reportedly lose their virginity to prostitutes on the band's first official tour of the mid-west (the latter coming down with a case of VD), encouraged all the way by the behaviour of their elder bandmates[5]. *Teen Scene* editor Earl Leaf, who had unlimited access to the band at the start of their career,

---

[3] The Four Speeds would make their only public appearances in the autumn of 1963 as third-support to the Beach Boys and the Honeys. Dennis drummed for both groups on those nights.

[4] Sample lyric: "A brand new injection makes it really move along."

[5] According to Brian, both Dennis and Mike spent over $1,000 in brothels on this jaunt alone. Mike would also find himself visiting a Munich cell – the result of an altercation with a German hooker's pimp.

witnessed similar scenes of revelry on a subsequent tour of Europe: "Mike Love was awful, girl-wise he'd fuck anybody... But Dennis was the worst. Dennis was an animal."

How must Brian have looked upon this? By the age of 22 he was married to Marilyn Rovell – though unsure in his voyeuristic fantasies whether he actually wanted her kid sister Diane – and physically loyal. Chained to the studio and resentful of touring Brian weaved his own fantasies, putting the opposite sex upon a pedestal and concocting his dreams around them. In a case of the song mirroring life, Brian's subject matter would always remain unobtainable and in the realms of his daydreams – a "Pom Pom Playgirl" or the "Girls On The Beach" (just out of reach). Introverted and awkward he would never be able to play around like the other guys. Akin to his fear of water Brian had a fear of girls that made him consider his younger brother with awe; "I'm not like Dennis, I'm not a real cocksman. I'm a subtler kind of guy. I do it all on a conversation level," he rued at one point.

This alienation was even more pronounced on the tour dates that Brian was beginning to hate in equal measure to his brother's delight. "I remember the first time we heard girls scream," he recalled. "We thought there was a fire." Dennis was the only animated presence on stage – seeking attention with every flail of his arms and hair and every opened mouth grin. While the others looked conservative and professional running through the same goofy routine, Dennis brought an element of danger that the audience was quick to comprehend. When he left the kit to sing "The Wanderer" the decibel level surged through the roof, aggravating Brian's one good ear and causing Mike to burn with jealousy. "In Sacramento they knocked us out of the way to get to Dennis. What an embarrassing trip!"

This of course gave Dennis some power. The Beach Boys might be living off songs based upon his own punk existence – and for which he was receiving no real credit – but on stage he received payback in kind. Relegated on record, for those 45 minutes on stage he was bathed in lust and loved every second of it. His role as sex symbol thus cemented – a role that would soon enough hinder his attempts to be treated seriously as a composer – he became the recognised face of the Beach Boys for all the teen magazines and pull-outs, understandably less interested in Brian's latest studio techniques. As the NME noted in 1967, while Brian was being proclaimed a genius Dennis had become the King of California for those a thousand miles away from its sun-kissed beaches ("what the men don't know, the little girls understand", indeed):

"When they're on the stage at Ashbury Park, Finsbury Park or the Paris Olympia, the girls gaze longingly at Dennis Wilson, the mad impetuous drummer and imagine the sandy beaches of Malibu filled with Dennises – tall, strapping, athletic youths grabbing their surfboards with a cry of joy, paddling out over the whitecapped waves silhouetted against the brilliant sunset."

Articles in the fledgling US pop press went even beyond that. Earl Leaf's

Teen Scene portrayed Dennis as nothing less than California's own love-god – half Cupid, half Adonis:

"A complete out-going extrovert, blue-eyed blondish Dennis is the group's glad-hander, good-timer, mad-mixer and sex-pot. He loves to mill around the theater, flirts with the chickies and often brings them backstage to meet the other lads. Once he was nearly caught in the tender trap but now he plays the field. He loves to run barefoot through the fields of flower-eating starlets. He intends to remain single as long as matrimony is not compulsory."

So while the rest of the band remained anonymous, Dennis provided the requisite press angle needed to sum up what the Beach Boys stood for. The mindless fun, fun, fun that Brian wrote about came signed, sealed and delivered in the shape of his middle brother. For outsiders he exemplified the myth of free and easy California – the post-war glamour, light years away from Steinbeck's struggling Joad family. Lacking decent pin-ups in the US to rival McCartney, Jagger or Jones, the centre-spreads came thick and fast. "Danger Spice of Dennis' Life" ran one, or "The Beach Boys' No. 1" or "He's a Peach of a Boy", or "Always Dennis' personality demands ACTION!" Described as everything from surfer, to drag racer, to hunter, to animal lover, this was all grist to Dennis' ego and a bitter pill to the four other Beach Boys. While he swaggered they smouldered. Tragically, they would never see through the image, and sometimes neither did he. When Dennis did emerge from Brian's shadow in 1967 then Mike and Al would remember these times well – and his talent was spurned.

Yet, while Dennis' star was in the ascendant, the combination of inherent personal popularity and family democracy demanded he be given higher-profile roles than drumming. He may have been considered an untalented waster but there could be no denying his importance to the Beach Boys. Facing new craze after craze on top of fierce competition from their new Capitol label-mates The Beatles, Dennis kept the band perennially hip. As they were to find after 1967, without that intangible factor it would be curtains for number one hits, adulation and all the trappings. (That was the problem with hipness: either you had it or not – if you had to work for it you never would, and once lost it was so, so hard to win back). His rebellious spirit caused consternation but without him there would have been no link to the outside world – no-one to report back what was happening out there on the beach. Minus Dennis, the Beach Boys would have been revealed as fakes: four squares who'd never set foot on the sands, more relevant to the Johnny B Goode America of the '50s than the teen-driven '60s.

And so Dennis was given the opportunity to sing lead on at least one song per LP. His voice hardly in evidence on the other tracks below the perfection of Brian, Carl and Mike, this concession at least gave the little girls a chance to sigh and Dennis the excuse to stop the show and take centre stage. This unwritten détente kept a lid on the pressure. With

Brian rolling out the hits everything somehow stayed together: Murry continued to "manage", Mike continued to dominate the live shows for which Carl and Al provided the motor, and Dennis sealed the whole package with a veil of authenticity. Brian of course pulled the strings by writing and producing, but every member of the family basked in the ego of their own little roles.[6]

As 1964 closed however, he pulled the lid off and nothing would be the same again. In Brian's words, "The rubber band had stretched as far as it would go."

What happened on and after *that* December 23rd flight from Los Angeles to Houston when Brian suffered his first public breakdown has been well documented[7]. The stresses of being leader and lynchpin had already been evident during gruelling tours throughout Europe and Australia. Wrenched away from his recently married wife and pumped to the brim with paranoia, the snowball of doubt was already rolling. Brian's hero was Spector – he wanted to produce not perform, to find his own path of perfection rather than follow in the wake of dictation. Weighed down by his father's barking inanities, Capitol's timetable of demand for hits, the rival success of the Beatles and the expectations of his band, he was crushed by responsibility. Brian's domain was the studio or the bedroom, not the beach or the concert hall. The volume of the crowd and the amplifiers was agony to his good left ear while Mike and Dennis' off-stage puerility was the antithesis of his monogamous heart. At 22 he could no longer be an adolescent *and* a man.

Pre-dating the Fab Four, Brian made the decision to remain full-time in the studio writing music. The band were to act as apostles, returning to record vocals between the tour dates that were spreading the gospel according to Brian. The fundamental structure of the Beach Boys was thus re-moulded and collectively, being a conservative beast, they hated it. The roles everyone lived so comfortably were being threatened. Why change when five Beach Boy LPs had recently dominated the charts simultaneously and they remained second only in popularity to the Beatles? Why worry about art when the royalties were pouring in and the guys were getting laid worldwide? Damaged egos resulted in shortsighted conflicts. The world would soon see the cracks that flourished beneath the harmony: "Mike lost his cool and felt like there was no reason to go on. Dennis picked up a big ashtray and told some people to get out of there or he'd hit them on the head with it... Al Jardine broke out in tears and had stomach cramps. He was all goofed up,

---

[6] The songs on which Dennis sang lead from the Beach Boys' first albums were: October 1962, "Little Girl (You're My Miss America)" from *Surfin' Safari*; September 1963, "Surfer's Rule" from *Surfer Girl*; March 1964, "This Car Of Mine" from *Shut Down Vol. 2*; and October 1964, "The Wanderer" from *Beach Boys Concert*.

[7] Brian lapsed into catatonia only five minutes into the flight screaming, "I can't take it," and was sedated for days afterwards. Glen Campbell immediately replaced him for the Beach Boys' contracted live dates and stayed with the touring band for six months.

---

and my mother who was there, had to take care of him." Only the sedate presence of Carl managed to allay the fears of the others.

Throughout that fateful year Brian had begun working on the *Today* album that was to redefine what the Beach Boys represented. The songs that came to dominate side two of that record – "She Knows Me Too Well", "Please Let Me Wonder" and "Kiss Me Baby" – were all recorded between June and December 1964 at Western studios. Revelling in a sophistication and sadness hitherto unheard of on a Beach Boys' record, they brought new words and feelings to the sunny Californian lexicon. Juvenile notions of finding the love-you're-going-to-marry beside the soda stand were replaced by doubt, pain and an unbearable longing. Rather than imaginations of what life was like on the beach these characterisations sounded frightfully real. The delicate blue textures of the music, augmented by a subtle use of horns and strings, reflected perfectly the introverted mind of their maker. Propelled inwards by the effects of grass, Brian seemed to bathe in the tears of his soul.

In fact, *Today* was a record of two distinct halves – side one, stacked with current pop hits like "Dance, Dance, Dance" and "Help Me Rhonda", suggested it was business as normal. The former reached Number 8 on *Billboard* while a re-mixed version of "Rhonda" hit the top spot, appeasing Mike and the Record Company. Brian's new music was left to slip by almost unnoticed on the reverse – having not yet attained a sufficient position of strength, he had to act tentatively. Only years later when *Pet Sounds* was so revered would listeners check back to these songs and trace the beginnings of that journey. Indeed, "She Knows Me Too Well" and "Please Let Me Wonder" could have slipped pretty seamlessly onto that LP – a fact true of a number of Brian Wilson compositions from this time. Songs like "Guess I'm Dumb" (a 45 Brian composed for Glen Campbell), "Let Him Run Wild", "The Little Girl I Once Knew" and – most famously – the breathtaking intro to "California Girls" were all lyrical or sonic precursors of the record that would later define Brian as a genius.

However, the biggest leap forward on *Today* was side two, track five. Recorded in January 1965, "In The Back Of My Mind" stands as one of the strangest and compelling pre-1966 Beach Boys songs – and Brian gifted it to Dennis. Following the shockwaves of his decision to retire from touring the two brothers had grown surprisingly closer – Dennis was genuinely intrigued with Brian's new direction, respecting the desire to follow personal emotions rather than interpret second-hand tales. Sensing a kindred spirit in such maverick behaviour Dennis would from now on stand behind Brian whenever the issue of "the new direction" arose. Brian would still accommodate Dennis' lifestyle as a template for songwriting, but the decision to use his unbalanced voice on "In The Back Of My Mind" was deliberate and inspired.

The song itself dealt with topics that would only be fully realised a year later via "I Just Wasn't Made For These Times": a fear of the future and that a relationship would be shattered by the pursuance of a dream. The notion that even with apparent wealth and contentment the fears at the back of your mind never cease – "happy times when I break down in tears" – was very *Pet Sounds*. Very Brian Wilson. To have Dennis sing these words alone without the usual Beach Boy choir and in his imperfect voice – its cracks and nuances accentuated through double-tracking – was a master-stroke. The very fragility and nervousness of the execution only heightened the foreboding sense of dread. A fact particularly evident in the final few bars as Dennis strains to reach notes beyond his range and succeeds only in pro-ducing a strangulated howl. (Carl may have had perfect pitch, but he could not do this). And this from the playboy of the group too, whose previous performances had rarely elevated above average – the cover of "Do You Wanna Dance?" that kicked off the LP was dull and throwaway by comparison. "In The Back Of My Mind" was the first indication of Dennis Wilson's soulful potential. Brian had dis-covered the strength of his style from the supposed roots of its weakness. The decision to use Dennis to make his point had been deliberate.

On tracks like "I Get Around" or "Dance, Dance, Dance" no single sound had been super-fluous. The layers upon layers of perfect vocals and chugging beats were *the* winning formula for Beach Boys' singles. Confident and exuberant, aside from the Beatles no other band could compete with such a mastery of the studio. The sound of a Beach Boys' single was the definition of positive. But this was no longer true for the instru-mentation on "In The Back Of My Mind" – it hardly seemed to exist at all. While Dennis attempted to follow the lead offered by a simple guitar picking and oboe, huge

swells of strings and muted strums and echoed offbeat percussion were dropped into the mix. They seemed to wander over from a different song than the one Dennis was singing and threatened to overbalance him.[8] The whole giddy exercise appeared in constant danger of collapse and ended in some relief, the vocals reaching their state of desperation in a rushed attempt to conclude matters. In short, it was a pivotal moment for the band.

With the move towards matters of the heart and psyche and with the band beginning to loosen their image with a collegiate look, Dennis too moved on. Rising to Brian's challenge, some distance occurred between himself and the rest of the band. While they moved only grudgingly away from the "old look", Dennis combined his sports jock persona with full support for a more experimental future. On *Pet Sounds* he would not take a single lead vocal – in fact he would not do so on a Beach Boys album until 1967[9] – but his allegiance to Brian was as important as any musical contribution. Somehow the two true geniuses of the Wilson family were coming together.

Then, in 1966 Brian Wilson, with minimal help from the rest of the band, produced *Pet Sounds*. It is/was the greatest pop album ever made.

In 1967 he nearly made a better one.

---

[8] The foundations of "Let's Go Away For A While", the strange and ethereal instrumental on *Pet Sounds* that seemed to literally waft away ("Try to hum it!" commented Brian of his musical conundrum) were all here.

[9] On the follow-up to *Today*, *Summer Days (And Summer Nights!!)*, Brian's sleeve notes claim that Dennis was supposed to sing lead on a track but he had fallen asleep outside the studio in his camper van.

TEENAGE
SYMPHONIES
TO GOD

Unsurprisingly, this era is where the whole Beach Boys legend rests today. Forever they will remain at the summit of that ephemeral flicker when pop music peaked; before the derivative volume of the 12-bar blues boys usurped beauty and subtlety for what could have been forever. This was a mantle born not of the candy floss surf music that popularised the group (and that certain members would have had them remain playing) but the soul and inspiration of their leader. From the sublime depths of *Pet Sounds*, to the unfinished glories of *Smile*, in this brief 18-month period Brian Wilson actually challenged the Beatles and George Martin head-on in the creation of beatific astral pop music. *Smile* was to be the point where his talents as composer, singer and producer transcended one another to be promoted in a single sparkling word: GENIUS.

And yet – and this is an essential piece of the legend – the world was not ready for Brian Wilson. Too many ideas, too many harmonies, too few kindred souls... whatever. The masses didn't get it, or weren't given the chance to get it. And like the forlorn and desperate characters he now sang about, Brian too was destined to be misunderstood. The original Lonely Planet Boy, or, in the words of his incredible song, where even the drums began to sing: "I Just Wasn't Made For These Times".

The pursuit of the Holy Grail – the Teenage Symphony to God – would leave Brian's powers shattered. Like some Cold War scientist granted total freedom to master the studio, he fought and lost an unofficial battle versus The Beatles to push forward the boundaries of pop music. To explore the outer limits of songwriting in a kaleidoscope of sonic possibilities. Standing on the threshold of artistic breakthrough, the Wilson-Parks vision of Gothic Americana was never welded together and the follow up to "Good Vibrations" was crippled by delays. Thousands of sleeves and an elaborate 12-page art book had been printed, while a specially recorded promotional radio ad ("we're sure to sell a million units!"), claimed *Smile* was coming out in January 1967. By May, still nothing. The multi-part "Heroes And Villains" took an age to nail down and Brian's struggle to keep his project coherent was becoming apparent. In its stead, Capitol Records impatiently issued a two-year old recording of "Then He Kissed Me" – proper Beach Boys music in their view. Dejected and depressed the thread was slipping away, and the greatest what-might-have-been story in '60s pop had begun.

The band's fortunes suffered accordingly. In late 1966 the Beach Boys returned to Anglophile LA from London as the world's premier band. The End Of Year *NME* Reader's Poll had them voted as the Number One

Vocal Group, beneath the headline "Beach Boys Beat Beatles".

By 1968 their time as a potent commercial force was over. They would only see mass popularity again as a touring show band when Nixon had left the White House. It was a rise and fall unprecedented in pop music before or since.

1966 was perhaps the last great year for pop music. A watershed year, before the implications of Dylan's conversion to rock'n'roll were debased by the burgeoning San Francisco scene, and before the mass spawning of UK revivalists who would soon proclaim Eric Clapton as their God. The year of "The Sun Ain't Gonna Shine Anymore", *Revolver*, "Eight Miles High", The Who, Dusty Springfield, Smokey Robinson, "Paint It Black", "River Deep Mountain High". Groundbreaking and sophisticated pop, without embarrassment decades later. Pop that kicked the doors open for *Forever Changes, The Velvet Underground & Nico, Sergeant Pepper* and – unwittingly – a sea of long-haired no-talents trying to catch up and make polemic. That way lurked the pretentious dinosaurs of the next decade. Concept albums, eight-minute singles, double-live albums, performance art and other highbrow nonsense, in the name of "progression".

But '66 was paradise – the mythical Kennedy-dreamt Sixties, before the intellectualisation of music at the expense of its soul.

The context of the era makes *Pet Sounds*, undoubtedly a fantastic album, seem even more incredible today. Though it might stand accused of being too innocent or too romantic for the cynicism of some Twenty-First Century tastes, Brian's masterwork was a massive step forward for '60s culture. At a time when pop music was not considered worthy of analysis or deconstruction, *Pet Sounds* was a quiet revolution. Cycle bells, theremins, woodwind, coke cans and orchestras were all somehow incorporated to creating this vision of love. Everything was turned inwards on the self as the sound became of equal importance to the lyrics. What Coltrane and Davis were doing with jazz, Brian Wilson did with pop music: initiating a real Year Zero, redefining what sort of instruments and arrangements could be used, what could be sung about. It was the next stage in the lineage from "Heartbreak Hotel" to "Be My Baby" to *Rubber Soul* – a real artistic whole in an arena where art was not supposed to exist. Completely out of step, not only with the surfing albatross of The Beach Boys, but also with the efforts of their contemporaries. Considering the recent successes of the throwaway *Party* LP and the "Barbara Ann" 7" you can almost imagine the collective jaw dropping at Capitol Records when this introverted, ethereal holy music was presented to them. And with not a babe or pearly sunshine smile on the sleeve but rather the band feeding goats at the zoo. The Beach Boys lacked the fanfare and hipness of a Beatles or a Hendrix (the clean-cut image marketed for them would see to that) but it was they who opened up the possibilities for others to be taken (too) seriously.

In many ways Brian was the fall guy for the entire music industry on both sides of the Atlantic. Ahead of his time, setting the standards, but unfortunately never reaping the full extent of the rewards. Furthering the achievements of Spector's Wall of Sound, his studio methods had already transformed the way that records were made in California. Emphasising the importance of the producer, Brian made music at will where he wanted and for who he wanted: taking up an unheard of residency at Gold Star studios, providing hit singles for outsiders, giving up touring in late 1964 and henceforth pouring his creative energy into the pursuit of perfection – recording as many takes as it took to strike gold. If there was a true Rennaisance composer of the time then it was Brian Wilson. As Nick Venet, the man who originally signed the band, said, "Brian was the first guy to do it until it was right. A lot of us would get chicken after four hours and say, 'We better get off that tune'. Brian would hang in there for nine hours no matter what the cost. I used to think he was crazy, but he was right." In the best Hollywood traditions commercial success bred artistic freedom. The result being the pursuit of musical perfection as opposed to the mere practice of making records.

But *Pet Sounds* was the start of the beginning of the end – sowing the seeds of Brian's reputation and his destruction. Recognition and praise for its groundbreaking techniques from peers like Paul McCartney and Pete Townsend, and the support of a few key writers such as Paul Williams at *Crawdaddy* and Jules Siegel at the *Saturday Morning Post* momentarily shifted the focus for invention and style California-bound. Though he had been homing in on the sound and beauty of *Pet Sounds* for at least two years, for many the finished article was a revelation – a real bolt from the blue. In the sea change provoked by its possibilities Brian was keen to seize the moment and bask in the glory his talents deserved. Ex-Beatles publicist Derek Taylor was employed to promote gospel of "Brian Wilson as Genius" and the Californian movers and shakers descended on Chez Wilson to witness the daily miracles being performed there, most especially a song firstly earmarked for *Pet Sounds* called "Good, Good, Good Vibrations".

As part of *Smile*, that single was just a fragment of the album that was going to cement Brian's reputation in the stratosphere. The project was to be a psychedelic masterpiece – an all-encompassing surrealistic American opus to everything: including an "Elements Suite" between the humour of "Vege-Tables" (humour, and its healing powers, was Brian's big scene at the time) and the truly heartbreaking "Surf's Up". Fuelled by Brian's increasing consumption of acid and Afghani hash it would satisfy all bases: a million-selling single for the record company alongside freakier numbers like "Mrs O'Leary's Cow" a.k.a. "Fire" and other excursions into the avant-garde.

But, while *Pet Sounds* was a true original, the rules had changed and were changing fast as 1967 progressed. In 1966 such a personal cry from the heart, in a business centred so purely on cold entertainment, was unprecedented. No white pop band had bared its soul quite so nakedly or so eloquently. The Beatles had obviously taken massive steps on from their slavish impersonations of Buddy Holly but they were hardly experimenting to the levels they would in the coming years. Dylan had replaced his canvas of folk with electric Chicago blues, while the Stones were still looking for an exit from the R'n'B cul-de-sac of their own making. When "Good Vibrations" hit Number One on both sides of the Atlantic it was confirmation that Brian was the current leader of the pack – nobody had straddled the highbrow and lowbrow so effectively. It would not take long for the others to catch up though.

The Summer Of Love was the event that changed everything. If, as planned, Brian's new music had been unleashed in early 1967 then maybe things could have been different, but six months later the market was saturated with psychedelic music. Everybody shed their skin to groove with the Love Generation and sell more records. The Stones posed as five awkward wizards on the cover of *Their Satanic Majesties Request* (and even allowed Bill Wyman to sing a song), Jimi Hendrix became the black musician it was OK to worship, and even The Monkees went freaky with the release of *Head*. More risqué ventures like The Doors, Jefferson Airplane and the Grateful Dead thrived. And then there was *Sergeant Pepper*, the LP that broke the California-Liverpool quid pro quo firmly in the Beatles' favour. The Beach Boys, the band who started it all and should have claimed their crown, were forgotten like they'd never existed. The cruel short-term memory of the music business ensured that the image of young conservatives was retained. Their non-appearance at Monterey only confirmed that the band had missed the love boat – a fact that undoubtedly pleased several of its members.

Certainly for Mike Love, Brian was moving too quickly into unexplored territory. Writing off the new direction as Brian's "ego music", he voiced similar concerns to the Capitol Records executives who had taken the wind out of *Pet Sounds*' prospects by launching a parallel *Greatest Hits* compilation release to coincide. His own pride damaged by the fact that Brian had chosen to collaborate with Tony Asher and Van Dyke Parks, Mike had nothing but contempt for a counter culture he did not understand and that threatened his apple pie view of America. As the band's live emcee, the move to more esoteric musical shores only compounded this loss of influence. The introspective and complicated new material was hardly suited to your typical Beach Boys show and songs like "I Know There's An Answer" or "Don't Talk (Put Your Head On My Shoulder)" sounded like they should be performed in a church rather than a concert hall. Unlike The Beatles who disengaged from playing live as an entire unit, The Beach Boys were two separate entities living polarised existences: Brian on his way to uber-hipness in California and the touring band members promoting the word in their uniform striped shirts. Had the situation been reversed maybe the world would have debated the meanings of "Wonderful" or "Cabinessence" rather than "Lucy In The Sky With Diamonds". Maybe.

In fact only one member of the band supported Brian's experiments totally and wholeheartedly throughout this period: Dennis. The period 1966 through 1967 would prove to be his inspiration and musical education.

That's not to say Dennis was exactly all over Brian's masterworks. He wasn't. Since "In The Back Of My Mind" he had not sung lead on a single Beach Boys composition save for a reverential reading of "You've Got To Hide Your Love Away" on the *Party* LP that was both earnest and distinctive for the fragility of his voice. His importance (and given the opposition to Brian from the staid triumvirate of band, father and record company this cannot be underestimated), was his total support for the "new music".

After the relative commercial failure of *Pet Sounds* in the US it was Dennis who stood up for Brian's new direction when the rest of the group were worried that, to paraphrase Bruce Johnston, "we were gonna have the biggest hit in the world or the career was over". Interviewed by the *NME* in early 1967 it he who made the grandiose claim that *Smile* was so good it made its predecessor "stink", and in another article that it was "100% better" than that "honest album". The notion of playing "feels" and incorporating strange instruments and jazz styles was obviously intriguing and he went on to name check Hal Blaine's percussion on "Let's Go Away For Awhile". Mike would only bestow faint praise on either project with tactical hindsight (as if to say, "Good Vibrations" was only a hit because *I* helped write the lyrics, and tempered them for mass consumption) but Dennis was a believer from the start. Obviously excited at this bizarre way of making records – stoned, wilful and beautiful – his allegiance was recognised by Brian when reflecting upon the album's opener: "'Wouldn't It Be Nice' has a very special and subtle background. One of the features of this record is that Dennis sings a special way, cupping his hands. I had thought for hours of the best way to achieve the sound, and Dennis dug it because he knew it would work."

The ultimate tribute however was the working title for the ambitious LP in progress, which went under the nom de plume of *Dumb Angel*. This, apparently, was Brian's pet name for Dennis.

And despite being lost in the Brian-Carl-Mike dominated vocal stack of *Pet Sounds*, Dennis was finally making his own tentative experiments with the recording of the ill-fated follow-up. Claims that he played keyboards at the apex of "Good Vibrations" might have been wishful thinking but his talents were in evidence elsewhere. For one was the fragment entitled "The Old Master Painter" on one of those 466,000 soon-to-be destroyed record jackets – a slow-motion orchestral snapshot that segued into a minor key version of "You Are My Sunshine", for which Dennis overdubbed a suitably mournful vocal in November 1966. (Brian deliberately changed the context to "you *were* my sunshine" to exacerbate this). Two months later he was conducting his own solo sessions without Brian's guidance, on the piano rather than the drums, the end result being an unreleased instrumental filed under the title "I Don't Know". (Dennis recorded a song with the same title a decade later, though such non-descriptive tags were commonplace for works-in-progress – "California Girls" was originally entitled "Yeah, I Dig The Girls", for instance.)

It was "Cabinessence" though – the most densely complicated of the *Smile* tracks – that Dennis loved the most. Featuring a Van Dyke Parks' lyric that somehow interwove the three Frontier myths of "Home On The Range", "Who Ran The Iron Horse" and "The Grand Coulee Dam" the song was a lunatic arrangement of banjo, "Doing-Doing" backing vocals and a huge slab of fuzz bass. Concurrently it was Mike Love's nightmare

and the fulfilment of Brian's psychedelic dreams. Searching for comprehension, the former attacked Van Dyke Parks' stream-of-consciousness wordplay ("Over and over the crow flies uncover the corn field"), unable to appreciate its free-form beauty. Dennis just rode with it. Throughout the swirling "Iron Horse" chorus he could be heard half-singing, half-talking in a manner that sounded almost subliminal. "On 'Cabinessence', there's a line in there – 'truck-driving man' – which I sang. I got off so much doing that. It's mixed way down in the track and it's syncopated all the way through. Right there is my biggest turn-on."

The incredible music that Dennis himself made from 1968 onwards was a direct result of these sessions. Unlike some of the pastiches that the band as a whole were liable to produce (music in a Brian Wilson style) he learnt directly from the master that feeling and emotion were the keystone to making good records. "As life goes on, you learn a lot. It's the same here with the boys and Brian. He writes about his experiences in life. That's all you can write about. You can't write about things you don't know. That's what we're doing with *Smile*." Even during the cocaine-session-player-rock-hell of the mid-to-late '70s his voice and music remained wrought with soul. The dense textures and arrangements to songs like "Be With Me" or "Celebrate The News", or even "Holy Evening", recorded some ten years later, were all evidence of his artistic flowering in this period. Brian, by comparison, would never visit these places again, save for in his shaking memories.

The reasons for Dennis' allegiance to his brother in the face of so much opposition were several.

Number one fact was that the terminally fashionable Dennis was in tune with his surroundings. While Mike Love was busy buying deerstalkers in London, Dennis was investing in beads and growing his hair. (It was becoming pretty obvious that the likes of "Be True To Your School" were not going to be cutting the grade in a technicolour future). Recently married with an adopted son, the incoming Flower Generation seemed to have an effect on Dennis, appealing to his romantic side. According to Derek Taylor, Dennis was going through a "thing rather like George Harrison did" and aside from Brian he was the only band member who was turning on – when he wasn't talking about music or drag racing then conversation was punctuated with a hazy "I love people" or "The kids are wonderful". Brian's sudden interest in astrology and spiritualism sparked off similar pseudo-hippy impulses in Dennis, who was by now well on the road to fulfilment that would lead him into the sphere of both the Maharishi and Charlie Manson. As a *Teen Beat* article would have it: "He hurls the word 'beautiful' about like someone invented it for him – uses the word 'love' in a spiritual sense – talks about men's clothes being 'pretty' and declared sincerely that the fans' welcome gave him 'a nice feeling inside'."

Secondly, Dennis' security within the band was not a result of talent or, equally ironic, surfing. He may have planted the seed back in 1961 but nobody had artistic expectations of Dennis so he had nothing to lose; no reason not to follow the lead of Brian's pied piper. He wrote no songs and had secured his tenure on looks alone; to everyone else Dennis had merely rode to success on the coat-tails of his more talented brothers and cousin. Why shouldn't he have faith in Brian, his genius brother who had created his whole fantasy lifestyle? Equally, why would he not want to move on from the whole surfing scene that was threatening his credibility? Derek Taylor recalled one astonishing conversation with Brian and Dennis where both claimed "never having written surf music or songs about cars: that the Beach Boys had never been involved in any way with the surf and drag fads." Clearly both were as desperate as each other to leave the past behind.

On the opposite hand were Mike and Al, who owed everything to the old music, had both composed with Brian, and were stuck in a 45 rpm groove that was perennially 1964. As the live face of the group, with a reputation to match, they had every reason to fear these new studio-based wonders that seemed to spell the end of their influence and a reduction of their bank balances. Mike had always known the value of money since The Beach Boys offered an escape route from the "oil and gas business" – working the pumps at a gas station. The two true artists of the group carried on spending the funds as if it were Monopoly bills – Dennis would soon give most of his away while Brian was forking out on tents and sandpits. If they could not produce the new songs live, the new songs that were not doing so well on the charts compared to the *Greatest Hits Vol 1*, then they would cease to exist. So there was a real schizophrenic battle going on here as to who were the "real" Beach Boys – Brian or the band; God music or surf music. This almost exact same scenario would be repeated in the mid-70s with the absurd conclusion of perfectly brilliant Dennis and Carl tracks being sacrificed to Mike's crowd-pleasing good old rockin' favourites.

The exception to this was obviously the immense success of "Good Vibrations", which resulted in the purchase of four spanking new Rolls Royce Phantoms from a London showroom for the Wilson brothers and their cousin. Bruce and Al, not being members of the PLC, received a hefty clothes allowance.

A third reason was drugs. Hash, acid and speed were all vital ingredients in the journey to *Pet Sounds* and beyond. Unleashing a fearsome swell of creativity in Brian from the stoned and introspective side-two of the *Today* album in 1965 to the full lysergic blast of *Smile*, they cemented the divisions in the group still further. Already prodigiously talented, the chemicals offered Brian an opportunity to reach out further, to drop his ego and reveal true thoughts. Enough of that surf music already! Let's play for God.

"About a year ago I had what I consider to be a very religious experience. I took LSD, a full dose of LSD, and later, another time, I took a smaller dose. And I learnt a lot of things like patience, understanding. I can't teach you or tell you what I learned from taking it. But I consider it a very religious experience."

Dennis, who had undoubtedly smoked reefer with his older surfing buddies at the start of the decade, was only too happy to join his brother on this particular journey. Providing a level of sympathy and understanding for Brian's projects that was both unexpected and singular among his band mates, he alone stood up for the new direction. Quite simply, *Smile*, like its nemesis *Sergeant Pepper*, would not have happened without LSD. The practice of erecting tents and sandpits in your living room, of conducting business meetings in your swimming pool, and writing paeans to vegetables and wind chimes were all a by-product of Augustus Owsley's finest products. Songwriting born of an expanded consciousness, and taken into the realms of higher leanings like FAITH, BELIEF and ART. Dennis knew the place Brian was coming from and vice versa – Brian's fried lifestyle brought him closer to Dennis' high-octane spirit. The crude demarcation of Brian-Dennis on the left, Carl as the peaceful mediator, and the clean living of the Mike-Al-Bruce axis was thus carved into stone for the future.

For Mike Love, over twenty-five years later, this was the point where Dennis split irrevocably from the Beach Boys' image. "Around the *Pet Sounds* era, he started getting involved in the same type of medicaments that my cousin Brian did, but Dennis' nature is different to Brian's, he's more of a rebel, more physically aggressive and stuff. Nobody could tell him what to do. If you told him, 'Hey Dennis, maybe it wouldn't be a good idea to drink two bottles of whatever it was, or take all those drugs' he would not listen to you on purpose."

This was still mostly recreational use, distanced from the arduous and professional duties of making records, and far from the full-scale pursuit of powders that afflicted the '70s. However, bootlegs for one session in October 1966 for "Our Prayer", the beautiful and wordless acapella hymn that resurfaced on *20/20*, do reveal Brian questioning whether his band "can feel the acid yet" as well as pressing Dennis for stimulation – "Denny, do you have any hash joints left? I know you do..." Recalling his time with the band up on Bellagio Drive in 1967, *Rolling Stone* scribe David Dalton, remembered Dennis' narcissism firsthand. Belying the normality of appearance, when offered a joint he sniffed it "in the way a dog might do" before commenting, "When I smoke grass with someone, I don't know whether to kiss them or run screaming out of the room."

But what a fantastic time to be making music, as the '60s turned from innocent to jaded. When every decision seemed to hold infinite possibilities in an era of wide-eyed wonder; before corporatism fully infiltrated the new underground, signalling the return of the pop record as mere unit shifter. For a very short twelve months the likes of Brian Wilson, buoyed by the freedom of success, moved beyond the forces of commerciality that traditionally harnessed the artist to short term commodity. The record companies did not understand, and it would take a year or so for them to tap into the linguistics and sales potential of the counter culture – bringing to mind Peter Fonda's "they stopped shaking their heads in incomprehension and began nodding their heads in incomprehension" analysis of Columbia executives' reaction to the success of *Easy Rider*. As Dennis commented in the midst of the delays for "Heroes And Villains", "We've got afraid to put anything out unless it comes up to a certain standard. We're not just putting out singles to sell thousands and earn money. We're not that sort of group. Money's a deadly thing when you're dealing with anything artistic. And we believe that the music we offer to the public must come first. It has to be something we believe in – so we won't be rushed."

Signalling the arrival of new-found freedoms for music makers, the steady drip of thinly-veiled allusions to the perfect trip had already begun. They would soon become a flood: "Younger Than Yesterday", "Rainy Day Women #12 & 35", "Tomorrow Never Knows", "I Had Too Much To Dream (Last Night)". The reality of an Age of Aquarius was wrought largely by liberation through mass psychedelic experimentation – a nation of musicians innocently coming up as one, seeing the world with new eyes before the collective come down of the next few years. Forever re-treading old ground, we'll seemingly never escape the heights of '66/67.

And so many troughs too. Though it might have made the Great momentarily greater, the psychedelic revolution also propelled the bandwagon jumpers and the hangers-on to the front of the queue. Expanding the minds of the mindless, bad ideas became worse and pop started to resemble a vacuum of ideas with long hair. Major labels assimilated the language of the Haight to score hits. Pills down the throats of the talentless only increased the volume of voices until everyone was lost in Tower of Babel. For the rest of the decade it was pretty much downhill without anyone sufficiently advanced musically to pick up the baton. Somehow from the eggs of expectation emerged ugly hatchlings like Canned Heat, The Grateful Dead and, eventually, The Eagles. The horror, the horror. As it happened, "A Day In The Life" and "Good Vibrations" marked career pinnacles for the joint-leaders of the pack of '66 – never again would they attempt such a surge for the stratosphere. The Beatles marked a return to basic songwriting with the sprawling mixed-bag that was the *White Album*, the cracks in their relationships beginning to show; while the Beach Boys followed *Smiley Smile* (the very distant cousin of Brian's opus, that was rush-released in September 1967) with the simplistic and soulful *Wild Honey* – "music for Brian to cool out by", according to Carl.

Would things have been different had *Smile* been released in January 1967 as originally planned? After all, according to Van Dyke Parks, in 1966 the pre-*Pepper* Beatles "had gone to LA to listen to the eight-track *Smile* sessions, and what they were looking for is revealed on that album." In such a rapidly changing musical climate, timing was all-important. Had the Beach Boys sustained the credibility of *Pet Sounds* and delivered the quick one-two sucker punch then history could have been altered. *Sergeant Pepper* would have passed its sell-by-date on release and who knows where Brian's talents would have led him next.

But Brian was a born competitor. As a composer one of his major strengths was staying one step ahead of the game – tapping into the currents surrounding him through the likes of Dennis, Gary Usher and Van Dyke, and divining the sea changes in LA. The ascent from surf songs to car songs to love songs to acid songs had sustained The Beach Boys while their rivals became debris. That moment you stopped to look over your shoulder, as Mike would have had the band do, was the moment you died. Through sheer determination and workflow The Beach Boys had been spared.

By delaying the release of *Smile* the moment of its potential passed and the band became irrelevant. Pop might have made room for art, but it was still the cruel business founded on hype and transience that it always had been. Only now the sceptical likes of Jann Wenner at *Rolling Stone* were questioning the validity of Brian's hype, and writing off Derek Taylor's claim of "genius" as so much "promotional shuck". When *Smiley Smile* was allowed to limp out, the movement was already towards a rootsier sound – that of *John Wesley Harding* and *Sweetheart Of The Rodeo*, and – ironically – the sound that Brian produced with *Wild Honey*. *Smiley Smile* has the reputation of an anti-climactic failure – that it died in the charts because it was cobbled together and was not the real deal. Dennis himself wrote it off with the underwhelming comment that it was "just something we were going through at the time, connected with drugs, love and everything". But it was still a strong record – how could it not be containing both "Good Vibrations" and "Heroes And Villains", as well as versions of "Wind Chimes", "Vege-tables" and

"Wonderful". The real problem was in the all-important timing, a factor that would have dogged the release of *Smile* proper had it too appeared nine months behind schedule. It might as well have been nine years.

The masses did not fail to buy *Smiley Smile* because of the production or because it was not the "legendary" *Smile*. They did not buy it because, as Brian has stated, among other reasons, "We got a little arty about it, and it got to the point where we were too selfishly artistic and we weren't thinking about the public enough." Distracted by drugs and attention, and his new group of friends, Brian had committed the mortal sin. He stopped to look over his shoulder.

He was still sufficiently attuned to pre-date the sound of country rock with *Wild Honey*, but by then it was too late – the public perceived The Beach Boys – unsurprisingly given their name and the wishes of Capitol Records/Mike Love – as a good-time surfing band. The release of several pivotal 1967 tracks in the years ahead – "Cabinessence", "Our Prayer", and finally "Surf's Up" – did little to reverse this opinion. Similarly to Scott Walker, who went from number one solo success to commercial obscurity in the space of four albums, The Beach Boys lost their core audience and failed to gain a new one. Contrary to popular belief, Brian did not go into hibernation directly after the debacles of 1967 (he faded gradually through 1968, and not completely until Murry – unbelievably – sold the publishing rights to his songs in 1969) and the band continued to make some brilliant music, albeit out of step with the rest of America.

This was the beginning of the "lost period" that lasted until 1974. The period that saw the hits dry up, the band unable to draw 200 people to shows in New York, and albums that failed to breach the Top 100. The period that saw The Beach Boys in the headlines more because of Brian's drug intake or Dennis' involvement with Charlie Manson than because of their records. Ironically these same records, ignored *en masse* at the time, have now become the aural blueprint for numerous contemporary artists.

Brian was now no longer at the helm, and the Beach Boys themselves were forced into the process of writing and producing. What followed were a series of unbelievably disparate records where each member attempted to stake claims on the band and determine their collective future. This marked the first flowering of Dennis' talent, as it was he more than any other member who came closest to touching the glories of 1966.

The real question therefore is not what would *Smile* have achieved had it emerged in September 1967, but rather what would have happened if there had been two functioning geniuses in the band instead of one? For after the release of the next LP, *Friends*, the working genius of the Beach Boys was Dennis Wilson.

LITTLE BIRD VS. THE LOCUST EATERS

"But two cuts by Dennis Wilson and Steve Kalinich, 'Little Bird' and 'Be Still', are tight, emotional and beautifully done, with fine lyrics that don't exploit the California-nature-youth idiom that is, as vision, as artistic as the music itself."
—Excerpt from Arthur Schmidt's review of *Friends*
– *Rolling Stone*, August 24th 1968

"And then I got my mantra, and as the Maharishi was giving them to us he said, 'What do you want?' I said, 'I Want Everything. Everything.' And he laughed and we meditated together. It was so wild."
—Dennis on meeting the Maharishi in 1967

"Holy Men eat locusts. Holy Men don't have press agents. They certainly don't stay at the Plaza. A lot of people who were ready for the Maharishi's 'technique' of meditation were put off by exposure to the prophet in person, especially the liberal New York press establishment. How could he be a genuine holy man if he wasn't indignant about Vietnam and gave the poverty problem a qualified ho-hum."
—*Rolling Stone*, March 9th 1968, in reference to Maharishi's
press conference set up by PR firm Solters and Sabinson

The Beach Boys were now making music in a void. "Good Vibrations" had shipped in the dollars but credibility did not follow. The band were effectively dry docked in LA, their faces pressed against glass looking in. According to Jules Seigal in his infamous essay of October 1967 "Goodbye Surfing, Hello God", the pertinent question for LA taste-makers, still wary of "Little Deuce Coupe" or "Surfin' USA", had been "whether or not Brian Wilson was hip, semi-hip or square". From a nearly making the grade status, they were now firmly entrenched in the latter camp.

Drawing parallels with the failures of *Smiley Smile* and *Smile*, context here was again the everything. Listening to the *Friends* LP now, with its combination of middle-of-the road spaciness and pretty never-trying-too-hard laid-back harmonies, it seems like the epitome of a too hot Californian afternoon. Lazy, beautiful and healing to equal parts mawkish, tepid, saccharine and uninspiring. Literally effortless. Like so many of the band's post-*Pet Sounds* efforts it was an uneven affair; the handful of genius moments hidden amongst some worrying lapses. In truth it was the perfect reflection of a rudderless group going nowhere – fumbling for a sound and direction and fighting a losing battle the only way they knew how. While music changed – while America changed – The Beach Boys kept singing in harmony, treading water and waiting for a change in fortune.

Following the Carl-dominated *Wild Honey*, (itself released only three months after *Smiley Smile* and spawning minor hits with the Motown-like title track and "Darlin'"), *Friends* was the first true commercial failure of their career. It fared no higher than #126 on *Billboard*. An infinity in pop terms. And while Brian was actively involved in ten of its twelve cuts there was not a suitable single on the thing. Capitol Records began gearing up to dropping what they saw as a lame duck, and for the third consecutive year the release of new Beach Boys material was smartly followed by the next volume of the obligatory *Best Of* package.

Certainly there would be no return to the pre-'67 days, when the unveiling of a Beach Boys 45's was an "event". (Less than twelve months earlier, like a gift from the gods, an exclusive "Heroes And Villains" acetate had been delivered late night for its premier spin on KHJ-Radio by a procession of limousines). Now that all six members were writing, the band collectively was being forced into a state of prolificity previously unknown to them, only they were operating in alien territory and their proven hitmaker was becoming anything but concerned with furnishing hits. Setting up camp in his bedroom that would soon reach a state of semi-permanence, Brian was content to drift through the business of making records. Happy to sustain a constant high through weed and coke he would appear intermittently from his domain, providing a little tweaking here and the odd fragment of an idea there. Brian still had talent to burn but his personal songs on the album, "Busy Doing Nothing" and "Passing By", spoke volumes through their titles alone.

Yet ironically, the Beach Boys' struggle to exact reasoning for their leader's new found ambivalence to commercial success and to come to terms with the Love Generation make the album all the more interesting to today's ears. Listening to their hit-and-miss experimentalism, as six very different individuals seek to divine the secret formula of their previous success, you can almost hear the desperation to be loved – to make The Beach Boys viable again. That they get it so wrong so consistently only makes the record more endearing. Perhaps unsurprisingly, given the blood and sanity he expended making *Pet Sounds* and *Smile*, *Friends* stands today as Brian Wilson's favourite Beach Boys LP. Created so organically it just lay there, as easy as ice cream or sunshine, "It seems to fit the way I live better – it's simple and I can hear it without having to get into some mood... *Pet Sounds* is by far my very best album. Still, though, my favourite is *Friends*."

If only they had caught that one last wave to the Summer of Love and Monterey and beyond. But 1968 meant the Siege of Chicago, My Lai, and the deaths of Martin Luther King and Robert Kennedy. Not only that, but the coming to power of Richard Nixon – confirming the true whereabouts of power in late-60s America and the inherent conservatism of a nation. Against such venality their one collective act of a social conscience was Carl's refusal to take the draft, backed up in interviews by

Dennis. And *Friends*? It must have just seemed so *inappropriate*: brimming with concepts of TM and childbirth, wrapped up in a cover of pastel impressions and clouds. The abiding impression was one of contentment with your lot – a true depiction of the idle lifestyle of your average over-the-hill Californian pop star combined with all the narcissism overload of a strongly sugared candy bar.

With hindsight you could view this as heroic or principled, but at the time of course it was a suicidal release. Twelve songs with an overall theme of domesticity, a majority under two-minutes long when the average was creeping past four. All phasers set to flop. The two tracks that attempted a response to the zeitgeist of "issues" – "Anna Lee, The Healer" and "Transcendental Meditation" – sounded forced and ridiculous, jumping the woolliest concepts of the underground. Unsurprisingly they were written by the Mike-Al axis that had resisted Brian's wooing of the counter culture so vehemently. As America burned and its heroes were murdered in that blistering summer of hate, *Friends* took all the wrong options. While others protested at the crimes committed for their benefit in Vietnam, The Beach Boys sounded ambivalent. They carried on playing pop while The Beatles and The Byrds now played rock – living up to the adolescence of their name while the rest of the world grew up.

But behind the backs of the journalists and the great American public who ignored them, The Beach Boys were still keeping on. Some desire was keeping the heart still beating. No longer feeding on the manna of popularity that had been their lifeblood, they were metamorphosing into something else, something different. The greatest white singing group who had ever existed – America's Number One Surfing Band – the eternal teenagers, who had not even played on most of their greatest hits, were learning to write songs. Holed up in Brian's home studio with engineer Stephen Desper at the controls, the process of rebuilding would become a public exercise that would be committed to vinyl for the next few records. Where once their fortunes were nailed solely to Brian's genius, they now emerged shakily to embrace a potential future without him. Plummeting sales did not necessarily equate with plummeting talent, and *Friends* was the first of at least six truly experimental records. These were the sound of a band battling with itself, with each other, and with the remnants of its audience. Boxing in the dark and sending out hopeful messages to a world ceased caring.

That's not to say much of the cold shoulder was without justification. There are some pretty lame moments on *Friends*, that even the passing of time cannot conceal. Exhibit A were the two TM songs already mentioned. Plain embarrassing, they were hokey, twee, and an advertisement for every journalistic criticism of hype levelled at The Beach Boys. An obvious example of the squares making out to be hip – and missing the point entirely. The preppy ra-ra-ra of yesteryear just did not transfer to songs about yogic brotherhood. Yet Mike and Al were not the only guilty parties in quality control, for some of the Harmony King's own material was little more than half-baked. The instrumental "Passing By", though a pretty enough, was little more than 2 minutes 24 seconds of divertory tactics to hide a dearth of new material. Too spaced to sing, Brian hummed instead, like his mind was far far away. (A style that would have improved "When A Man Needs A Woman", with its own brand of trite lyricism, considerably). By comparison the Hawaiian-style instrumental, "Diamond Head", was far more evocative being drenched in watery sound effects against a lapping slide guitar.

Other great songs on the album included the title track, which reached number 47 when released as a single, where waltzing harmonies were perfectly pitched to the theme of brotherly love. When the group could so easily have fallen apart at the seams it sounded no less than therapy. Equally as good were "Be Here In The Morning" and "Busy Doin' Nothin'". The former was a catchy but complex singalong featuring Brian's voice tweaked to a pitch it had no rights to reach combined with the contrast of Dennis' croon during the breakdowns. Melding together about ten different melodic fragments, with a witty lyric and imaginative instrumentation, it was the most successful "group" effort of the era. The line "No calls from Korthorf, Parks or Grillo", in reference respectively to the band's personal assistant, road manager and business manager was classic, and indicative of the post-*Smile* mood within the camp. A kind of spaced-out "what do we do now?" – "where have we been?". The latter song was all Brian. Showing ample evidence of a sense of humour, there was also the dread realisation of inertia setting in. Seemingly recorded ad lib to a bossa nova backing, the lyrical flow provided directions through Bel Air to Brian's house, where you could eventually find him inside occupied by nothing. Both sad and amusing in its whimsy, the world could now witness the changes that had befallen yesterday's genius – having reached the end of the line there was nothing left to prove but this playful reaction.

But the truly great songs belonged to Dennis. Against the prevailing languidness it was his two stark and simple cuts, "Little Bird" and "Be Still", that really stood out on *Friends* – because of who sung them as much for what they sounded like. The innate spiritualness of Dennis' voice might have been highlighted on 1965's "In The Back Of My Mind", and his tendencies towards the left-field evident during the making of *Smile*, but until now there had been little reason to suspect he might become the saviour of the band. In 1968 he was still looked upon as "Crazy Dennis", unpredictable and foolish, and the rest of the band refused to work on his compositions. These first faltering steps though, so compact and heartfelt, were revelatory. And so fully realised too. From rudimentary dabbling in the studio he had struck gold almost immediately and without precursor. Months of watching Brian bare his soul had obviously rubbed off, and from the beginning Dennis' music was wrought with the same emotion and pain that made his elder brother's creations so great.

Dennis also learnt the necessity of collaboration to achieve a variation on the Beach Boys sound. Only by reaching outside of the family unit towards different lyricists and musicians could the slumber of conservatism be broken. For three numbers on the album he worked with the rest of the group, but for the first of his own material he wrote with Stephen Kalinich, a little-known Californian poet [see Appendix]. Kalinich had been working as an in-house writer at Brother Records since 1966, when Arnie Geller, Brian's personal assistant, had picked up on the folk song, "Leaves Of Grass", he had written with Mark Buckingham. Despite drawing inspiration from the figure of Walt Whitman, the alleged marijuana connotations of the lyrics meant the song was not released, despite being cut and produced by Carl. But the Wilson brothers thought highly enough of Kalinich's poetry to bring him on board – indeed he would be the only "outsider" to work extensively with all three of them, and aside from Gregg Jakobson, was the only person to collaborate with Dennis over the span of a decade – providing the song "Rainbows" to *Pacific Ocean Blue* nearly ten years later.

On both numbers Dennis essentially provided musical backing for Kalinich's holistic words. Together they trawled the Venice Beach District either by foot or in Dennis' chauffeur-driven Rolls ruminating on ideas of world peace and spiritualism, and churning out ideas that would provide the basis for songs, most of which remain unreleased. "Despite all the things you read about Dennis, there was a side of him that wanted to give," stated his co-writer. "Little Bird" was inspired, according to Kalinich, by the view from Dennis' window and "the little bird up in a tree who looked down and sang the song to me of how it began". From this concept a finished poem was left on Dennis' piano, and by the next day was transformed into a song.

With its plucked bass, "Cabinessence" banjo, "Child Is The Father" horns and drowsy strings, layered atop of a minor key piano riff, "Little Bird" was greatly reminiscent of *Smile*. The sense of adventure and sheer wonder, present in all the best Beach Boys records, was evident in bundles. Yet being shot through with requisite personality and style ensured this was no pale imitation or mimicry. The subject matter was light, but the vocal – all gravel toned and serious – pushed all the right melancholic buttons. Carl's pitch-perfect lines threatened to elate the emotions ("What a day, what a beautiful day") but Dennis wrestled back a sense of the sombre with his world-weary tone. The hookline, written by an un-credited Brian, was executed with all the sense of grandeur and tragedy that would exemplify his later recordings – "Where's my pretty bird, he must have flown away; if I keep singing he'll come back some day."

Dennis was not a "natural" musician, and was not taken seriously as a creative force within the band, but this only served to make his compositions all the more singular. Despite some support from Carl and Brian, he was not encouraged to enter the studio – the majority of his songs were executed during all-night sessions with Stephen Desper after the band had packed up and left for the day. This did little to quell the creative flow however and Dennis' work rate started to reach Stakhanovite proportions, according to the beleaguered engineer: "I worked 17 or 18 hours a day and sometimes slept under the console because Dennis wanted to record in the morning. The Beach Boys would finish at 3 in the morning and then Dennis would be there until 10.

Finally Brian gave me a bedroom in his house and I'd go home at the weekend." This was a far cry from the days when, according to Carol Kaye, Dennis would "come in and said hello, listen to a take or two and then leave".

The whole recording process was treated with a reverence that bordered on religious – being a self-taught player, the mechanics of writing were drawn out through exploratory sessions of playing "feels" to find a correct backing for the words. Dennis had to work hard at his art and this would be the primary reason for the individuality in his music – without tutoring there were no boundaries, no well-trodden path of reason. As with all great rock'n'roll, textbook talent can never compensate for soul and feeling. The music flowed sub-consciously through Dennis' fingers and imagination as opposed to some pre-conceived action. The Wilson ear for melody had been there all along, but Dennis would never be constrained by notions of the commercial. His voice and work would remain timeless. The same angels that Brian felt looking over the making of *Pet Sounds* were here too.

Back-to-back with "Little Bird" was another gem of prettiness sung in that weary moan, pitched between the fragility of tears and the

emotion of a smile. "Be Still", which came from the Biblical "Be Still and know that I am God", was simplicity itself, just vocals and a pump organ. The adjective "hymn-like" was invented for it: "You know, you know you are / Be still and know you are / Your life is meant for joy / It's all so deep within."[1]

The tender reading of these words was pretty hard to reconcile with the tough-guy persona promoted by magazines only three years earlier. Unbuffeted by the Beach Boys harmony swell, Dennis sounded not a little lost and not a little alone. His naked emotions reflecting a growing personal interest in the TM phenomenon that was attracting so many in the rock world, not least Mike Love and Al Jardine. Yet while Mike's "Transcendental Meditation" and Al's "Anna Lee, The Healer" held all the subtlety and allure of a Billy Graham rally (though in fairness both would

---

[1] Stephen Kalinich recorded an extended spoken-word version of the song in the mid-1970s. It appeared as part of an unreleased poetry album recorded with the assistance of Brian. The version played to this author was well over the 1 minute 22 seconds that the *Friends* version clocks in at. Brian is clearly audible playing the organ and sings back up on one further track.

---

write far worse on side one of *Carl And The Passions: So Tough* and on 1978's *MIU* LP, the real nadirs in The Beach Boys canon), Dennis sounded truly holy. Not for him the amateur dramatics of Jim Morrison or the slight quirkiness of his fellow Beach Boys – Dennis might have been labelled a fool by his bandmates, interested in nothing but frivolity, but here, in total seriousness, he sounded like a true believer.

In fact it was Dennis who first turned the band onto the joys of meditation. Mike played the role of holy Bahaadvista throughout the '70s and used his position as the Beach Boys MC to spread the word of Maharishi Mahesh Yogi, but he met his guru through Dennis in late 1967. It was then at a UNICEF concert in Paris that the inquisitive drummer first encountered the long-haired Indian holy man, talking with John Lennon and George Harrison. Echoing opinions he would soon share about Charlie Manson, Dennis was immediately impressed with the sage's wise counsel – "All of a sudden I felt this weirdness, this presence this guy had. Like out of left field" – and called the boys over from London to check him out. And so began the Beach Boys close and long term affiliation with transcendentalism – fashionable for all of six months in 1968.

Since this was a counter cultural fad without dependence on drugs, it was seemingly the perfect vehicle for the band to hitch a ride back to pop's summit. Every member could participate with TM and it was certainly the primary influence on the concept of *Friends* – the whole group drawn back together through peaceful vibrations and religion-lite. At one swoop a lot of headaches would be solved: Mike and Al would have some affinity at last with their contemporaries, Dennis would be preoccupied with a new obsession, somnolent Carl just seemed well-suited anyway, and there was always the hope that Brian might find a crutch to aid creativity. It would also put The Beach Boys back in step with The Beatles, who had found space for one of George Harrison's sitar numbers on each of their last three LPs. The East gave the Haight a spiritual kick and Ravi Shankar was the future of music.

While other bands turned their back on TM, through boredom or, in the case of the Fab Four, because of the secular failings of their instructor, it was becoming an obsession for Mike. John and George had finally upped sticks in disgust from Rishikesh after two months – Lennon writing the sarcastic "Sexy Sadie" ("You made a fool of everyone") about his experiences – and the Maharishi was seen as a fallen and discredited idol. Yet the Beach Boys were convinced to pump their own money into his proverbial basket and go on tour with him. In June 1968, Paul McCartney, as part of a PR drive to end The Beatles' association with his holiness, made direct reference to this "immensely tasteless" event – "On top of everything else it was a flop." *Rolling Stone* commented that "This sort of left the Beach Boys holding the bag, and Donovan holding his hand". Mike was more than happy with his role of mouthpiece, spreading the yogic gospel, but The Beach Boys were fast becoming synonymous with a dead duck.

"When a new fad comes along we'll be the first to ride it," claimed Brian in 1965. He was not wrong, and the band treated TM in much the same way they had with cars and surf boards in the years preceding. Their seemingly oblivious promotion of its merits only confirmed the loss of a magic touch that had sustained them for five years.

The tour of state capitals that was to have taken place in mid-1968 was an unmitigated disaster. Billed as half-concert, half-lecture the crowds stayed away in their thousands. Unsurprisingly, the thought of an hour's "teaching" combined with an all-the-hits-and-more roadshow was not a huge draw. Over $500,000 from the group's finances was wiped out almost overnight – a more than considerable sum in 1968 – leading to Al Jardine's infamous comments, in reference to the ornate stage sets, that the only benefactors from the whole debacle were the florists. The Beach Boys would need all the meditation they could muster to get over this. Following an aborted tour of the southeast that coincided with the shooting of Martin Luther King and the Chicago riots, the non-allure of the Maharishi succeeded only in widening the financial black hole for a band used to frittering thousands. Both events were, according to business manager Nick Grillo, "a fucking nightmare".

(The Beach Boys' perilous financial circumstances continued spiralling out of control until they signed with Warner Brothers in 1970. The previous year saw them embroiled in the courts with Capitol Records before Brian scuppered a potential deal with Deutsche Grammophon with a highly public admission of penury: "If we don't pick ourselves off our backsides and have a hit record soon we will be in worse trouble. We all know that if we don't watch it and do something drastic, in a few months we won't have a penny in the bank.")

In attempting to court The Beatles' audience, the Maharishi succeeded only in ostracising himself. Remarking that poverty was caused by a lack of intelligence or laziness (perhaps reflecting the conservatism of a certain band that sang "Let the bees make honey, let the poor find money") and surrounding himself in western luxuries, he hardly endeared himself to the Class of '68. Appearing insincere and slick ("Smile, meditate, profile, sniff flowers, smile", wrote one commentator of his spin-doctored roadshow) his charm offensive ended in acrimony and protests for his mere being in America. Run out of town, it looked as if the Beach Boys were soon to be joining him.

Rolling Stone was particularly scathing, commenting that the Maharishi was now the fifth Beach Boy and ridiculing Carl's naivete in regards to a proposed tour of South Africa when he commented "as far as segregation is concerned we're apolitical"[2]. Even Brian was not spared and in a spoof column predicting the stories of 1969 his masterworks were openly mocked: "The Beach Boys will cut an album of Christian hymns entitled *Prayer Sounds*. Side One will be composed entirely of traditional hymns... while Side Two will consist of Brian Wilson originals, among which will be 'Outtasight Saviour', 'The Surfer's Prayer', 'A Teenage Confession', 'The Big Shut Down' and a remake, with new lyrics,

---

[2] To be fair to Carl it was his idea to sign The Flame to Brother Records, while Jann Wenner's favourites The Byrds toured South Africa – minus Gram Parsons – only a year later.

of 'God Only Knows'." They were seemingly everybody's favourite whipping boys.

Yet while the Beach Boys had gambled everything on TM, Dennis was moving in his own distinct circles. Socialising with the likes of Neil Young his time was being spent on the Strip, immersed in the whole psychedelic experience, consuming acid and allowing his hair and beard grow to the standards of the Californian hip elite. This was something far more interesting than the Maharishi, and though he continued to meditate with the band Dennis was never stationary long enough to commit to anything or to anyone. His marriage to Carol Freedman was already starting to go awry and by the middle of 1968 he was ready find a new guru; someone more exciting than his Holiness – someone more attuned with the spiritual *and* the physical. While Mike Love was disparaging and phased about the whole East Coast scene ("Those psychedelic groups make it in about five cities in America and in the rest they wouldn't draw flies"), Dennis recognised the need to get involved. Throwing himself into the aftermath of the Summer of Love, knowing that the Beach Boys had to respond to their surroundings, he began the pursuit of a new direction.

It was a decision that was to herald some life-changing consequences and, as it turned out, *Rolling Stone* could not have predicted a future so wrong. 1969 was no laughing matter and it would see the Beach Boys become more synonymous with the Devil than with God.

COMING DOWN FAST

"Fear is nothing but awareness. I was only frightened as a child because I did not understand fear – the dark, being lost, what was under the bed! It came from within. Sometimes the Wizard frightens me. The Wizard is Charlie Manson, who is another friend of mine who says he is God and the Devil! He sings, plays and writes poetry, and may be another artist for Brother Records."
—Dennis Wilson to *Rave* Magazine, 1969

"Dennis Wilson is writing songs and producing two tracks. Someone crashed his Ferrari, they completely ruined it. Then someone came along with a tow truck and stole it"
—Bruce Johnston to the *NME*, March 22nd 1969

"Dennis Wilson's brotherhood took my songs and changed the words. His own devils grabbed his legs and pulled and held him under water."
—Charles Manson

The fateful nights of August 9th and 10th 1969 – nights that concluded with the brutal and perverse slaying of the occupants of 10050 Cielo Drive and 3301 Waverly Drive – have achieved a macabre significance in rock'n'roll folklore. The blood of Sharon Tate and Rosemary LaBianca, scrawled grotesquely across the crime scenes, have stained forever the '60s notions of Peace'n'Love. An enveloping darkness was coming down. To an entertainment industry that had mutated so waywardly in eight years – from the solid conservatism of coiffured pop stars wearing ties to the same pop stars embracing mysticism, politics and weed – Charles Manson and his philosophy came on like the Angel of Death. A wake-up call to realities outside of the sunshine bubble.

All in all it was some package to end the schizophrenic decade: a predatory satanic cult, The Beatles, acid, sex, murder and a leader who considered himself an embodiment of both Jesus Christ and the Devil. The ex-convict and aspiring musician, who had mixed with Hollywood's great and good, was to become wholly synonymous with the Dark Side of California. Combined with the separate tragedy at Altamont, the murders committed by his "Family" have become epochal. As clear a sign of innocence lost and idealism wasted as the press and historians could hope for, and a chain of events beyond the most nightmarish trip. So strange and complex in fact that we'll probably never know the true story behind what really happened.

The cold details tell of seven senseless deaths. Stephen Parent, Jay Sebring, Sharon Tate, Abigail Folger, Voytek Frykowski, Leno LaBianca and Rosemary LaBianca, all slaughtered over those two nights. Save for Parent, every one suffered an incredulous number of stab wounds. Frykowski alone had been stabbed 51 times. The murderers were predominantly female. Sharon Tate was heavily and evidently eight and a half months pregnant. The man who reputedly ordered the bloodbath killed nobody (on those two nights anyway). And, in a final twist of perversity there was evidence of darker, perhaps Satanic forces at play: sloganeering on walls in the victim's blood, a fork protruding from Leno's belly and "WAR" was carved into his flesh. No robbery, no rape – just merciless killing with a reasoning unknown.

The motive, according to D.A. Victor Bugliosi at least, was "Helter Skelter" – Charles Manson's theory of evolution, decoded from the grooves of The Beatles' *White Album*. The ignition of a quasi-religious black-white war, allowing the Family leader to fulfil the destiny of his acid fantasies and become Jesus Christ on Earth. In other words the murders, in a script straight out of Hollywood or Marvel Comics, were all part of a grand scheme to shock the world and change the course of civilisation.

Given the conflicting evidence, whether this was even warm to the whole truth is debatable. Bugliosi's day by day diary of the trial, that was published in 1974 as the best-selling *Helter Skelter*, was an almost equal mixture of chilling insight and vigorous bravado in his own legal prowess. Passages that tantalisingly hinted at Manson's almost supernatural powers only fuelled the notion of the man as folk devil or at least some dastardly aberration in American society. But beneath the hallucinatory testaments of Family gospel was a current of common criminality, the significance of which was underplayed in the D.A.'s summing up. By his own admission Manson was/is a gangster, immersed, like several of his victims, in the Los Angeles underworld. Was it really coincidence that Frykowski and Sebring, the latter known as "Hollywood's Candyman", were high on prototype MDMA tablets on August 9th? Or that a rival drug dealer, Billy Doyle, had been humiliated and flogged by Frykowski at Cielo Drive only a week earlier? Or that Rosemary LaBianca, a seemingly random victim, had connections running amphetamines for biker gangs? There were a thousand pieces to the jigsaw and many lay untouched when the sentences were read out.

Central precepts of "Helter Skelter", like the interpretation of messages in Beatles lyrics, have since been derided by Manson's co-defendants. There were other reasons to have unleashed fantasy into murderous reality – sometime Family member Bobby Beausoleil spoke later of the desperate conditions out in the desert; of living in a barren pressure cooker environment and eating bugs for survival. Life on Spahn Ranch was so strange and isolated that who knows whether the killers even knew why they acted or even what *truth* is. If Charlie famously had a face for every occasion then the murders he inspired can be interpreted to any of them.

To garner some sort of understanding as to why Dennis Wilson wrote with a man soon to be considered evil incarnate, and even allowed him to share his plush Pacific Palisades home, we must press the rewind button back to 1968 and forget momentarily the hideousness of early

August. Forget HELTER SKELTER and lay aside the murderous implications of words like PIG or RISE – to a point when such weirdness could surely not have been imagined.

We must also consider some wider questions of where rock music was heading in the late '60s as well as events in the war zone that was America. History, written by the winners, so often creates monsters or illusions of individual evil in order to protect the guilty – as if the West was blameless in the rise of Sadaam or Hitler, or if these fiends appeared as freaks from nowhere. Debate and reasons as to *why* are censored from the agenda: let's not make things too complicated, or, God Forbid, blame ourselves... And it's much the same with Manson. Twisting the man's already twisted words: "Mr & Mrs America... I am what you have made me and the mad dog devil killer fiend leper is a reflection of your society." The crimes were shocking and bizarre but The Family were a true product of their era. Their death culture mirrored the other death culture that surrounded them: Vietnam, Chicago, Watts, Hollywood. Their actions must be judged against the prissy demonic flirtations of seemingly every two-bit pop star.

Ironically, compared to many others in the rock fraternity Dennis, the man who apparently acted as a catalyst in introducing Charlie to the high life, was a relative innocent. An extreme and forceful individual certainly, a sometimes maniac and reckless individual, but hardly a candidate for the deep-seated fascism with which Manson would soon be associated. Indeed, in most characteristics they seemed almost polar opposites. Yet, as unsavoury as the fact might be, the few songs Dennis wrote under his influence would be among the best and most powerful in the Beach Boys canon. At the very least there can be little doubt that the "Wizard" had a profound effect on Dennis Wilson's second wave of songwriting.

Dennis would first meet Manson in mid-1968. According to his good friend, and later lyricist, Stanley Shapiro, their paths crossed after Charlie trailed Dennis' chauffeur off Benedict Canyon and up to the house he shared with his first wife Carol. The driver had been to drop off a purse to a pregnant hitchhiker they had picked up earlier. When Charlie traipsed up the drive, his guitar a permanent fixture on his back, Carol freaked. She was already paranoid about Dennis' affairs on the road and here was one of the strangest men she had ever met seeking out her husband. The resulting fight saw Dennis move out, temporarily to a powerboat in Marina Del Rey, and then to an opulent pad in Beverly Glen.

Other sources had them meet either buying drugs at the house of Gary Hinman or, tying in with Stan Shapiro's account, when Dennis picked up hitch-hiking Family members Ella Jo Bailey and Patricia (a.k.a. Katie) Krenwinkel. Hinman was later slain by sometime Manson associate and ex-Zappa guitarist Bobby "Cupid" Beausoleil on July 31st 1969, while Krenwinkel was to be convicted on seven counts of first-degree murder. Either way, the foundations of mutual attraction were there from the start, and they were narcotic or sexual.

At the time Manson had been out of jail but a short while. Set free from prison on March 21st 1967 at the age of 32 he had been incarcerated for over half his life – a shining testament to US penal rehabilitation. Graduating through a cyclic and spiralling process of capture-offence-release-capture, a petty string of misdemeanours clung to his name. As a terminal and habitual criminal he knew no alternative to the jailhouse and ultimately resisted his freedom – as far back as 1961 an official evaluation noted that "institutions have become his way of life and he receives security in institutions which is not available to him in the outside world". Like so many of our "monsters", the self-consciousness and realisation of his position in the grand scheme of life (to play the part of a zero) lay crucial to his future actions. Charlie was born with nothing, had inherited nothing and had nothing to lose. The cold amorality that guided the killings of 1969 was ultimately the product of a life behind bars.

Charlie's reality was a void of alienation. A white trash fate beneath even the "niggers" and women he so despised. What had the Great Society done for him? Where was his place in the Dream? Isolated since birth, his every waking minute he had felt condemned, scraping existence at the sharp end of those cruel contradictions inherent in Twentieth Century America. Denied love and a childhood he viewed his country with the hatred and vitriol of a fundamentalist. God Bless Amerika.

By 1968 he was not alone. Great swathes of the good public were consumed with identikit thoughts. Spurred by the ridiculous war in Asia and increasingly draconian measures used to suppress the subsequent protests, particularly in Reagan's California, the question as to quite where the country was heading had reached new levels of mass consciousness. The Anti-War Movement, the Black Panthers and the Yippies were merely the most prominent examples of widespread proto-revolutionary fervour – a fervour in evidence around the globe from Paris to Budapest to London.

Like anyone with an inherent animosity toward straight society Manson gravitated towards the Haight, the heart of a burgeoning youth culture, where he was accepted, like every other bedraggled newcomer, with open arms. As Charlie's innocent hippy face put it to a writer in *Tuesday's Child*, "We slept in the park and we lived on the streets and my hair got a little longer and I started playing music and people liked my music and people smiled at me and put their arms around me and hugged me... It just took me away. It just grabbed me up, man, that there were people that are real."

Yet while the Panthers were fighting literally for basic human rights, the exertions involved in flying the Freak Flag were diminutive by comparison. In the "struggle" against the Establishment, the ownership of long hair was enough to ensure hero status in the Underground; a quick two-fingered salute could win the trust of your Brothers. Protests against the War and a society represented by Spiro Agnew and J Edgar Hoover succeeded in motivating and politicising a generation for answers. Momentarily the doctrine of Timothy Leary seemed the perfect solution for those who did not want to come home in a body bag. Dropping out would ultimately prove easy; the problem was: *what next*? Once you had rejected the pigs and the straights and the Man, then solutions would have to be sought elsewhere. And it was amidst this void that Charlie's answers seemed so persuasive and correct.

The search for the esoteric seemed to permeate every level of pop culture.

Take, for example, the *Rave* magazine from 1969, where Dennis gave the infamous interview that name-checked "The Wizard", for a period low-down of the pop culture concerns of the day. I'll deal with Dennis' piece later, but turn to pages 44 through 46 of that issue and you come to an article entitled "If God didn't make the little green apples – Who did?". There follows the intimate and pretentious thoughts of Robert Plant, Keith Emerson, Blodwyn Pig and Chicken Shack on the meaning of life. While these now seem so laughable in their seriousness (Exhibit A Plant: "The Scottish, Welsh and Irish Nationalists, the black nationalists, should take note of what John Donne said many years ago – 'No man is an island unto himself'."; and Exhibit B Emerson, on the polarities of "great music": "blues from the tormented Negro and at another extreme the *St. Matthew Passion* (from Bach)". The remarkable thing was that these pearls of wisdom were printed in a teen girls' pop magazine between a romantic short story and Valderma spot cream adverts. To ask pop stars deep and spiritual questions was normality. The opening gambit of the *International Times* to Paul McCartney in 1967 was: "In the last few thousand years only the materialistic side of man has developed and been built upon." Eighteen months earlier he would probably have been asked: "What's your favourite coloured milkshake?"

And what of the big boys? The bright lights of the American counter culture, who laid the foundations for this type of banter. What was their agenda? What sort of vibrations were they sending out? Pretty confused ones if truth be told. The shape of the New Society was becoming a hole of ideas into which metaphysical notions of revolution, togetherness and love were poured. The conclusion to these most often involved the call for some kind of Agrarian Year Zero and a re-programming of the consciousness through LSD. A 1967 "summit conference of hip" between Allen Ginsberg, Timothy Leary, Gary Snyder and Alan Watts for the San Francisco *Oracle*, presented a typical mish-mash of ideas. The four celebrity head honchos of the subculture appeared like the People's Judaean Front – psyching-out one another's ego with self-centred stoned humour. The following are random quotes:

Snyder: "...the people of the ants are all going to be tribal people. That's why it's going to work [dropping-out to live in communes]. We're going to get the kids and it's going to take about three generations."

Leary: "Drop out of school."

Ginsberg: "Where are you gonna learn engineering, or astronomy, or anything like that?"

Leary: "The way men have always learned the important things in life. Face to face with a teacher, with a guru."

Watts: "Each one of us is what is real and has been real for always and always and always and ever will be... That's what you and I are, and we lose our anxieties and we lose our terror of death, and our own unimportance."

Snyder: "A group marriage is where, a number of people – as a group – ...announce a marriage is a social announcement of commitment... announce that we will be responsible for the children we produce and for each other."

Leary: "I suggest that the next issue of the *Oracle* carry a half page, or a full page manual on how to form your own religion."

Leary: "I'm going to take LSD once a week and I'm going to take hashish once a day at sunset and I'm going to have babies and I'm going to learn from our babies."

All succinctly put and utopian and beautiful. But you really had to fear for existential daydreams given the viciousness of America A.D.1967 going into '68. Did these "leaders" really believe their own hype, that there was a valid movement happening here? Many commentators were proclaiming the death of a media-defined subculture before the summer was even over. While such romanticism thrived so could Mayor Daley, Richard Nixon – and Charles Manson.

Given the extent of Hippy submissiveness it was little wonder that the Peace'n'Love bandwagon was eventually so completely hijacked by the denizens of commercial culture. Unlike the Jefferson Airplane, Eldridge Cleaver was never going to be advertising Levis. Beyond a hardcore of believers spewing forth impossible idealism, any mass movement was confined to submission in the face of government strength. Dropping out meant apathy and apathy meant a susceptible weakness to suggestion. The Achilles Heel of Hippy would be the propensity to blindly follow wrong answers in the pursuit of truth, whether that was the Maharishi, Zen Buddhism or The Process Church of the Final Judgement. Witness even now the witless proclamations of Ken Kesey (that acid would stop bombs falling on Sarejevo) to realise that 1969 was ripe for Manson's brand of cult terror. Granted that Uncle Sam was training its own hired killers bound for the jungles of Vietnam and Cambodia, but even after the Family's involvement in seven grisly murders was apparent he was still proclaimed "Man of the Year" on the cover of *Tuesday's Child*. *The Liberation News Service* meanwhile (paper of the Weathermen) praised the killing of some "rich honky pigs" under the headline MANSON POWER – THE YEAR OF THE FORK.

Things seemed to have got a little out of hand within the counter culture. A little confused and directionless when psychopathic killers were given free advertising space for their records and treated with such reverence. A little too far beyond rationality. Falling for a scruffy shaman with a busload of free girls and drugs was one thing but to so openly praise this death culture was quite another. Dennis Hopper might have allegedly wanted membership of the Tex Watson Fan Club (on the premise that the Tates and Polanskis had "fallen into bestiality and sadomasochism") but the murdered themselves were hardly establishment figures. As Joan Didion wrote so poignantly on hearing of Sharon Tate's death in her essay "The White Album": "I remember this, and I wish that

I did not: I remember that no-one was surprised." This was when the '60s truly ended: the common enemy was no longer identifiable.

In prison Manson picked up two obsessions that would define his destiny. The first of these was Scientology and the second was music. The former provided a methodology of mind control while the latter acted as a vehicle for his message.

By 1968/9 Charlie was already one step ahead of the current obsession with Eastern philosophy and the Maharishi. Faith in Karma and Reincarnation must have seemed like so much old hat to someone well briefed in the concepts of Scientology, as Charlie had been from the early 1960s. Both words had strong undercurrents in his spiel and, since his tutorage in jail from fellow prisoner Lanier Rayner, he had become interested in using Scientological practices as a means of autosuggestion or "auditing the personality". By no means a total convert (though he once claimed to have achieved the ultimate level of *Theta Clear*) he did bastardise many of its teachings as a means of deceiving others. To impose your will upon another's mind was a powerful trick in the con man's armoury and Scientology was evidently popular with more than several McNeil Island inmates. Additionally, this new "religion" provided the means of improving the self without submitting to any hang-ups over morality – perhaps a reason for its enduring popularity in Hollywood today. Through Scientology Manson came to the half-baked conclusion that would both dominate Family thinking and attract the many pleasure seekers who rode with them, including the 24-year old Dennis Wilson: that All Action is Positive. Everything is Right – Nothing is Wrong.

When exhausted of L Ron Hubbard's teachings Manson progressed to a fascination with the Occult. He became an admirer of The Process Church of the Final Judgement – a UK-based quasi-Satanic organisation whose founder Robert DeGrimston (*nee* Moore) also twisted the concepts of Dianetics before preaching *Armageddon*, *Fear* and an omnifarious worship of both Jesus and the Devil. These were all ideas thrown into the mix of Charlie's millenarian gospel. *Fear* in particular served day-to-day needs very well. Though preached as the ultimate key to unlocking feelings of awareness, its saturation allowed for mass group domination. In an animalistic pecking order the Family hierarchy was sustained through fear of the leader that was sold to them as love. "Paranoia is the other side of love," Manson quipped to *Rolling Stone* writers David Felton and David Dalton. "Once you give in to paranoia it ceases to exist. That's why I say submission is a gift, just give into it, don't resist." As Brooks Poston, who hooked up with the Family at Dennis' house, was to comment to the D.A.: "Fear turns Charlie on."

If prison was the place to learn these tricks then gullible San Francisco was the perfect environment for the Wizard to practice his magic. His favourite mind games included the "Imagine-I'm-your-father-when-we-make-love" Freudian chat-up line, or the "I-understand-your-parental-hang-ups" routine, or just simple flattery to those seldom flattered. Men were lured into the flame with promises of servile women and drugs. On meeting Dennis, Charlie apparently fell to the floor and kissed his feet.

Uncovering and exploiting feelings of alienation among the unwanted drop-outs of the Haight was hardly a low percentage tactic of enrolment. The Summer of Love peaked in 1967 but the impending winter saw kids homeless, freezing and starving. Put down your acid and shoot up some speed. To an experienced con like Manson it was easy pickings. Preying on isolation of the weak and offering a surrogate family unit is the lifeblood of all cults from The Moonies to the Jesus Army. To the psychedelically altered heads of America's deserted sons and daughters a few choice ideas from the Scientologist lexicon could seem like the ultimate wisdom. A desire to escape the confines of "straight society" left many without a compass. Submission of the ego, a belief in the Now, and the universal importance (or unimportance) of all living things were beliefs well in step with transcendentalism, mantras, astral projection and spiritualism. Everything was inter-linked until the message became impenetrable and made perfect sense to those wanted to believe it. Throw in a liberal diet of LSD and it's quite possible that a man could become God.

A fixation with the power of music was the other key component of Mansonism. In jail Charlie had become a prolific writer of songs, tutored on guitar by an ex-gangster, Alvin "Old Creepy" Karpis. By the time of his release in 1967 he had probably composed hundreds. He might have been a '50s child and incarcerated away from the cultural metamorphosis in San Francisco, but the con man within must have realised the changes in audience perception of rock music. In a world that was turning on, singers had become poets – their standing elevated beyond entertainment to embrace social commentary and whatever else. Music had always been central to black culture, traditionally denied avenues of political expression, but as white youth became disaffected with Presidents then Dylan, The Beatles, The Stones and even (God help us) Jim Morrison filled the void. The medium was afforded a respect and authority it would never reach the peaks of again. Quite simply, if you sang then people listened.

So music became a vehicle for Charlie's ideas and his lyrics were littered with pseudo-Scientological concepts, summed up by the song he would soon sell to Dennis, "Cease To Exist". Other masterpieces that came on like evangelical rants sung in a Johnny Cash croon included "Old Ego Is A Too Much Thing", "You're Home Is Where You're Happy", and "Always Is Always Forever". Humans as data-filled computers, the prisons of the mind, revelation, an ever-encompassing love and paeans to the Garbage Dump were Charlie's concerns. Sinister meanings can be read into them, but at the time they must have appeared merely far-out cosmic folk songs. Typical hippy fare plugged into the spiritual zeitgeist. But in the context of the Family home (the whole group around the camp fire, singing in unison), the scene was impressive enough for Gregg Jakobson, Dennis' close friend and co-writer, to pursue the idea of a musical documentary on film.

Charlie's adopted style was that of the troubadour – the folk singer as seer, telling it how it really was. Everyone loved a folksinger.

Wrap the message up in chords and it was easier to swallow – not exactly an earth-shattering concept but an effective and successful one. Music was another form of mind control, mirroring the significant power it held over the counter culture. Up on Spahn Ranch Charlie's songs kept the Family together and constant repetition of "The Message" in those LSD-sated sing-a-longs injected ideas deep into the consciousness.

Yet there was more to this love affair with rock music than that. Charlie wanted to become famous. In fact, never one to demand anything beneath the moon and stars, he wanted to be bigger than the Beatles – to have an audience far beyond his degenerate clan. He had been obsessed with the Fab Four since 1964 when Beatlemania was reaching its zenith in the US. The sheer side effects of fame and rock n roll – the slavish devotion and respect, the seriousness hung upon your every utterance – were more than attraction enough.

If ordinary musicians were inordinately feted, then The Beatles by comparison were Gods, ahead of the game and the benchmark that everyone, including Brian Wilson, was bound to follow. (Interestingly enough, The Process Church also saw them in such elevated status). Bearing little resemblance to the four mop-tops who had enchanted all America with "I Wanna Hold Your Hand", they were now instructing the youth to turn off their minds, relax and float downstream. Lennon and McCartney had plugged into the psychedelic revolution but to Manson these were *signs* – proof that music was the way to spread the word and that The Beatles were hip to his own far-out ideas. This was confirmed in December 1968 with the release of the *White Album*, which Charlie apparently divined as prophecy to prepare for Armageddon. As written in the *Book Of Revelations*, the Beatles were finally ready to take on their mantle as the four angels of the Apocalypse. Innocuous songs like McCartney's "Blackbird" or Harrison's "Piggies" now apparently foretold a coming to prominence of the angry black masses; "Revolution 1" that the time was ripe for chaos ("you can count me out....*in*"). The actual song "Helter Skelter" with its message of things "coming down fast" was adopted as a watchword, while Lennon's experimental cut'n'paste number "Revolution 9" was the actual sound of things to come – a Tower of Babel punctuated by machine-gun fire.

Whether he actively believed this lunacy is contentious. As with most questions on Manson who knows where the truth starts and ends – did he really believe that he was Jesus Christ or was this just a front to get his bidding done? The bottom line is that The Beatles were a useful and relevant smokescreen in 1969. Like Charlie they seemed to be operating in the same mystical sphere and on the same hidden wavelength. To be developing stronger and wiser through copious LSD use. Nor was he the only one seeing messages: the hype surrounding the *Abbey Road* cover in 1969 (Is Paul Dead?) or the controversy with "Lucy In The Sky With Diamonds" were all instances of how seriously The Beatles' work was taken. Similarly to invoking God, by quoting John, Paul, George or Ringo, some of their kudos naturally rubbed off.

The only problem was how to emulate such a band and follow their route to superstardom. Evidently telegrams and letters were sent to

Liverpool to make contact but all to no avail. For some reason there was a psychic block preventing reciprocal love and The Beatles would never know the extent of The Family's love until the murder trials of 1969/70 began. Charlie needed a Plan B and someone with connections to help realise his ambitions. That someone would be Dennis Wilson who, with the help of his immediate circle of show business associates, later devoted a considerable amount of time into getting Manson a record contract.

Charlie moved into the plush Wilson residence at 14400 Sunset Boulevard in late spring 1968. As already mentioned, the two had become acquainted a short while earlier. Parking up his black *Hollywood Productions* bus outside, he was to remain part of a pretty much open house (regulars along with Dennis were Gregg Jakobson, Bobby Beausoleil, Charles "Tex" Watson, Dean Moorehouse – the sexagenarian ex-preacher turned Family convert – and the Manson girls) until late summer that year. The unwritten living arrangements meant Dennis would have total access to the Family harem and its drug connections while Charlie lived the high life, meeting a significant proportion of the Californian music cognoscenti along the way and burning his way through Dennis' money, cars and clothes with a locust's abandon. In a bizarre contrast of quiet domestic bliss and carnal savagery everyone seemed to get along fine.

Roaming the small estate in robes and finery and expounding wisdom to one and all, Charlie settled in very nicely thankyou. Whether racing Dennis' Ferrari down the Strip or swimming in his pool, he swiftly appropriated the change from desert to mansion. As the girls wandered around in a state of permanent nakedness the Wilson house became enveloped by the same madness as Spahn Ranch. The orgies, the garbage runs, the communal love continued as before, only now the scene was attracting the very same Hollywood Pigs that Krenwinkel et al would soon be offing, eager to sample the excess of nubile young flesh.

In the words of Tex Watson: "People came and went, a peculiar mix of young drop-outs like me, drug dealers, and people in the entertainment business. It was a strange time in Hollywood. It had become chic to play the hippie game, and the children of the big stars partied with gurus like Charlie Manson and listened to them and bought drugs from them and took hippie kids to bed and let them drive their expensive cars and crash in their Bel Air mansions. Everybody felt aware and free. After August 1969, all that would change and those gentle children with flowers in their hair and tabs of acid in their pockets would suddenly seem menacing and dangerous. The Beverly Hills-Hollywood circuit would snap shut like a trap. Until then life was one big party. Rock musicians and hopeful singers like Charlie, actors and hopeful actors, girls who didn't do anything, producers like Terry Melcher (Doris Day's son), talent people, managers like Gregg Jakobson, and stars' children would all come over to the house and it would be a drug circus. Charlie always managed to show up for the parties. And he did it well, playing the free, spontaneous child, the holy fool, turning his self-effacing charm on a pretty young celebrity's daughter[1] with twenty different kinds of pills in her purse, giving her a ring and asking her to come join his Love Family. She kept the ring but drove home in her sports car with her boyfriend."

The whole package, the ultimate groupie experience ridden with danger, sated Dennis' need for kicks and hedonism. The subservient Family girls were going way beyond either the G.T.O.s or Plastercasters in services rendered. Upon Charlie's instruction it seemed they would do *anything*, the sin of ego apparently vanquished. And this of course raised Dennis' stock within Hollywood. Not content with picking up girls on tour or at the Whiskey like his contemporaries, he had the real deal waiting at home.

Some change this from life aboard the Beach Boys fast-sinking ship – it must have seemed that the Summer of Love, that bypassed the band completely, stepped right through Dennis' front door. Life had gotten pretty strange with the making of *Smile*, but the band had never been recognised as truly hip by the American public. Not like The Byrds or Dylan were. In macho America, The Beach Boys never attained the musical respect – beyond their peers and a few select writers – that was omnipresent in the UK. In retrospect, their failure to headline Monterey and maintain the momentum set by "Good Vibrations" doomed them at one stroke to play the same antiquated and irrelevant role as Elvis had before them. When Hendrix's guitar caught fire to the pay-off line "You'll never hear surf music again" the blueprint was altered forever.

This was a situation that must have irked Dennis in particular. Coolly aloof from the rest of the Beach Boys, he was, in Brian's absence, the only group member in tune with his surroundings. The sonic departure of his personal songs on the *Friends* LP had been proof of that – showing a willingness to flow with his own musical thoughts as well as contribute to the band's compositions. "Little Bird" and "Be Still" were statements of such individualistic and spiritual purity that they pushed far to the peripheral boundaries of what the Beach Boys were *supposed* to sound like. Immediately distinctive, they mirrored Dennis' personal standing: to the left of everyone else in the band and with influence to match. With Brian now starting to retire from experimental composition, his biggest supporter faced being shut out of their future.

This was central to the explanation of how rock star and soon-to-be-devil-monster hooked up. In 1968 Manson must have seemed the embodiment of all that Dennis wanted: his own personal guru, full of spiritual insights and with a busload of naked girls. A Maharishi with songs. A reflection of Dennis' own polarities: one moment Keith Moon psychosis, the next reverent and holy – like Charlie, Dennis had little conception of fear. In the recent words of David Dalton, Dennis had walked unscathed from numerous car wrecks and surfed through hurricanes. When Charlie famously put a knife to his throat Dennis would merely murmur "Do It" before the weapon was dropped. The madness of life on the road was transported to his own front room. Charlie

---

[1] Dean Martin's daughter, Deana.

represented the chance for Dennis to reclaim some of the credibility being rapidly lost. A step into the Now as opposed to surfing back to '63 like Mike Love would no doubt have wanted. Charlie was to be Dennis' first contribution to the Brother Recording label[2] – a venture established for each individual Beach Boy to nurture raw talent.

So, although curious bed fellows on first impression (and incomparable today – can anyone really imagine a member of one the world's biggest pop bands shacking up with such a person as Charles Manson?), the connections between the two were considerable and had little to do with the dark side for which The Family would gain their infamy. In the words of Gregg Jakobson: "Ultimately Dennis and Charlie went head on, because they both had the same energy. Only, Dennis was more heart-cultured. They attracted each other immediately and then immediately repelled." The reasons for the attraction were several.

Primary was Dennis' search for spiritualism. Brian had introduced religious overtones into the Beach Boys' music with *Pet Sounds* and *Smile*, profoundly influencing his middle brother in the process. It was Dennis don't forget who had first tuned the band onto the Maharishi, after meeting him at a UNICEF concert in December 1967 – "Live Your Life to the Fullest" was his wise counsel that he took so literally. Dennis' interest had waned long before then (though he still practised meditation with the rest of the band) and he was looking for new kicks and a new guru. His views on materialism, aired throughout various interviews of the time, showed his reasons for rejection to be the very same that attracted Mike Love so rabidly. "If I want money I come into the office and get it. I gave away everything, even my gold records. I don't have a car. If I need a ride I hitch a lift. All I need is a surfboard and a piano. I just don't dig marriage – though Carl does," ran a typical outburst. While Dennis seemed happy to keep his wallet as an open house, Mike, the eternal businessman, was drawn in by the combination of inner fulfilment and zero material sacrifice. Ultimately Transcendental Meditation was to become *the* big concern in the group and thereby confirmed their un-hipness. The subject of several pitiful songs, it was responsible for financial disaster soon after, and for one of the worst albums known to man in 1978.

According to Daryl Dragon, Dennis' chief collaborator between 1969 and 1972, his writing partner was well attuned with the existential part of his being. He may have exuded a primitive persona onstage but privately, and particularly when songwriting, Dennis radiated an inner longing for the unobtainable. "He could 'soul talk' if you were open to it. That's why with Manson he called him 'Jesus Christ,' and Manson called

---

[2] Set up by David Anderle, the purpose of Brother Records was to allow Brian the freedom to experiment denied by Capitol. When he stopped recording the emphasis changed. It became a vehicle for the other bandmembers to introduce new talent, akin to the Beatles' Apple Label. Along with Charlie other mooted releases were a post-Box Tops and pre-Big Star Alex Chilton (the Box Tops had toured with the Beach Boys in 1968), and the Flame, whose Blondie Chaplin and Ricky Fataar would join the Beach Boys in 1971.

---

himself 'Jesus Christ'. Those guys have taps. A guy like Manson is almost hypnotic. He had a way that attracted Dennis because he was always searching for extra spirituality, not knowing that it could be the Devil just as easily. It was all kind of weird."

In short, Dennis was a searcher. Always had been a searcher in fact, from his drag racing to his drug use. In late 1967 his recklessness was peaking to new heights – inhaling the nitrous oxide from numerous whipped cream cans and riding through Brian's house on his dirt bike. Interviews around the time seem to stress only his lack of surety and innate restlessness – "Once I wanted to be a gardener, I wanted to be the skipper of a boat, I wanted to join the Forestry Commission. I would like to be Elmer Gantry into his thing." This ceaseless energy and race for the prize drew Dennis towards anything that glittered. The Family merely represented a whole new thing going on and had to be investigated. Tackling obstacles headlong would lead to inevitable mistakes, but as David Leaf wrote in 1984, and only months after his death, Dennis "wanted to know everything through experience, and he attacked life with a combination of blind faith and childlike innocence." Never one to study the theory, he swallowed the whole package, seemingly without thinking and seemingly without fear.

A susceptibility to impulse was also accelerated by events in Dennis' private life. 1967 had been his *annus horribilis* with a foreboding trail of separation, plummeting popularity and depression. 1968 looked like it was going to be little better. Divided by his consistent womanising, his marriage to Carol was all but over and she had filed for divorce by the middle of the year. This was bad enough, but Dennis was also named openly in Mike Love's divorce settlement from his second wife Suzanne. Next to claims that she had partaken in illegal substances and "experienced hallucinations in which the devil had sexual intercourse with her in the presence of others" was an insertion that she had "committed adultery with Dennis C. Wilson". For a group whose last LP had charted at the dizzy heights of Number 126 this was another nail in the coffin they looked so eager to jump into. Combined with the ill-judged spectacle that was the aborted Maharishi tour, Brian's hibernation and the coming of acid rock, the Beach Boys' viability as a functioning pop act was bottoming out. Misunderstood and isolated, this was a group disintegrating into bitterness, with seemingly little future ahead of them.

In this scenario those dark inherent feelings of childhood unhappiness, kept at bay by the thoughtless fruits of success, looked set to return. No more hits, no sell-out tours. The riches of "California Girls" were spent, though the temptation to fritter money like the old days remained, to the horror of successive business managers. 14400 Sunset Boulevard for instance was a huge mansion, formerly the hunting lodge of Will Rogers, and complete with a Californian-shaped swimming pool. The artistic equilibrium of the band had now started to shift away from Brian to rest on Carl's shoulders, while business affairs (never a Wilson strong point), were being directed predominantly by Mike Love. Dennis, always the closest to Brian, was left in the cold. His lust for hedonism only fuelled opinions that he should not be allowed near a recording studio.

(According to engineer Steve Desper, "his brothers kind of thumbed him away. You know, 'Crazy Dennis doesn't belong in the studio.'")

Yet, as he revealed some ten years later, the ego bruising of sudden unpopularity hurt Dennis, always struggling for acceptance, immensely and as profoundly as anybody else. "There's no use denying it, we went suddenly from being a very large group into being a very small group again. It broke my heart. It hurt. It's no use me saying it didn't. Believe me, it really does hurt to suddenly realise that you're not what you used to be. And that people don't want to know." Consistently shunned as a musical talent by his fellow band members the free-falling inadequacy of Dennis' youth started to rear its head. While the echoes of Murry Wilson's put downs and "I-told-you-so's" ran riot in Brian's mind, Dennis too was drawn back to those loveless early years when he was a white punk and nobody listened.

And so here too was another cause of attraction. Charlie, as is well known, preyed on the dysfunctional and offered solace to the emotionally wounded. The Family was his vision of America's dispossessed white children – society's rejects living in the unwanted land of the desert amongst the coyotes and the rattlesnakes. The killers of August 9th and 10th were all portrayed as good WASP kids gone bad under Charlie's influence, yet they had all suffered a recent mental disturbance or personal upheaval, even before Manson got his claws into them. Leslie Van Houten and Patricia Krenwinkel were both well acquainted with LSD from their early teens, Susan Atkins a.k.a. Sadie Mae Glutz was a dancer for Anton LaVey's Topless Revue – LaVey being the founder of the Church of Satan – while Tex Watson combined a career selling wigs with extensive drug-dealing. The product of broken homes, these all-average American kids were all raking the debris for something outside the American Dream.

Dennis' vulnerability made him as susceptible as the others. He was only 24 after all. Drastic times demanded drastic solutions and Charlie seemed to have answers – his psycho-babble made some sort of sense. The idea of belonging to an Outlaw family living in the wilds of Death Valley seemed both perfect and romantic. As Gregg Jakobson wrote in 1970, "Charlie was certainly a fascinating Cat. He represented a freedom that everyone liked to see. He really was an active revolutionary of the time in that area. Like Castro in the hills before he overthrew the government."

Of course the utopia was illusionary. The reality being that Charlie wanted Dennis for his money and connections. And being naturally generous to the point of naïvete Dennis blindly succumbed – "He could never stand to see anyone who needed anything or anybody who had some kind of problem – he was right there" offered Audree Wilson as vindication for her son's choice of house guest. When the charity was no longer forthcoming then the death threats and ugliness began. Dennis would only learn the truth of Charlie's intentions sometime later at the expense of several cars, his wardrobe, his personal allowance, numerous gold records and the "largest gonorrhoea bill in history", when the Family's raging VD was extinguished by his private doctor. Manson's

"Sunset Boulevard period" would cost Dennis Wilson over $100,000. Yet as he told D.A. Bugliosi, "I'm the luckiest guy in the world, because I got off only losing my money".

The extent that Dennis came under Manson's "philosophy" was highlighted in his interview with the English pop magazine *Rave*. The piece – which was actually printed in the September 1969 issue, a month *after* the August murders – is exceptional in being one of the few open acknowledgements of Charlie's talents. Though Dennis was to later claim that Manson didn't have a musical bone in his body the article gave every indication that "the Wizard" would be appearing soon on the fledgling Brother Records. Sentences about fear being nothing but awareness and coming from within obviously came straight from the Master's mouth.

Look deeper though and there was more than just this overt and oft-quoted passage to indicate how far Dennis had fallen into Charlie's worldview. Many of his other answers also echoed Mansonite ideas. Most obviously was Dennis' vocal enthusiasm for the Robert Heinlein book *Stranger In A Strange Land* – one of only three he claimed to have read along with *Black Beauty* and Gibran's *The Prophet*. This futuristic story of an alien coming to Earth was entwined into Manson's magpie philosophy in much the same way as Scientology. Charlie identified with the telepathic hero, Valentine Michael Smith, who forms a religious movement, keeps a harem, "dis-corporates" his enemies and finally re-ascends to the heavens. As noted by Ed Sanders, in his book *The Family*, "Charlie was heavily into using many Heinleinian words like *Grok* and *Thou Art God* and *Share Water* and other Strange Land terminology, so Manson and the girls renamed Roger Smith (Manson's parole officer) 'Jubal' after the fatherly protector Jubal Harshaw in the novel."

Also relevant was Dennis' fervent anti-materialism ("I give everything I have away"), spread throughout the interview and presumably encouraged by Charlie. Dennis' personal allowance *was* bankrolling The Family after all. He had recounted similar opinions in an interview with the *NME* published on June 28th 1969. Admitting his current home was a one-room cellar in a friend's house (Gregg Jakobson's in Benedict Canyon) what he said was very revealing. Speaking at the height of his flirtation with Manson, Dennis rapped at length about the rock star "trial" of consolidating wealth with spiritual nourishment. The answer, befitting an inherently generous nature, must have been music to Charlie's ears:

"I live there out of desire. I'm living where I want. I look at the room as my mind. There's a piano in there, there's a bed in there and that's all I need. What do you need in a home? People have so much rubbish in their homes – clocks and watches, and they're scared of breaking them. I've lived in a beautiful home in Beverly Hills, in harems, in the mountains, with a family, but where I like best is where I am now. I want to achieve happiness.

"I love freedom and I love people who can express themselves. People have different ways of expressing themselves, some by hostility, some through love. I still give my money away. I give everything I have away. What I'm wearing and what's in that case is all I have. I don't even have a car, I have a 1934 Dodge pick-up somewhere. I can have anything I want anytime, it's just the way I want it. If I want anything I can send out and get it. I can even get it by smiling, but I don't."

At this point Dennis stood up on a chair, waved his arms about and yelled, "Yes I understand! There's only one thing you need in this world. I understand it all!"

The views certainly echoed Charlie's own take on materialism. Approaching the subject from the opposite end of the spectrum, he too had no time for worldly goods. Cars, guns, girls and money were given away as freely as they were received. A sure way to confound straight society. Gregg Jakobson remembered recording Charlie at Wilder Studios when the owner became concerned about his facilities being used by an ex-con. Manson just shrugged and left the scene, along with a number of guitars and amplifiers. As with any cult "what's yours is mine" was the Family ethos – particularly useful if you're hooking up with impressionable pop stars or young women with allowances or inheritance to burn – and day to day culture revolved around ceremonies of sharing. Though obviously Charlie remained at the head, the master of proceedings who directed every action.

Yet if Dennis did accept much of Manson's ramblings, and most writers suggest that he swallowed it wholesale, he was hardly a clone of the killers. He was never Charlie's slave on the level of Tex or Sadie – he had far too much money and independence for that. Their relationship in fact remained mostly reciprocal and Dennis, despite being reckless enough to invite the Californian underworld to share his home, retained a strong sense of autonomy. The most obvious example of this was changing the title of the song "Cease To Exist" to "Never Learn Not To Love" and the first line to "Cease to *resist*". This was Cardinal Sin #1 in Charlie's book, who hardly cared what the music sounded like so long as his messages remained unchanged. According to Jakobson, "Charlie had a big thing about the meaning of words that came out of your mouth. That is to say, to him all that a man is, is what he says he is; so those words better be true".

Charlie himself was a little more "distressed" about Dennis' lack of judgement: "They changed it, all the sound and the soul that comes off of prison and when it gets to your ears it comes off [all] *I been so lonely baby... heartbreak hotel*. You hear the bottom part of what's really happening on the top. Hollywood plays music for little girls. I don't play little girl music. I play music for God. I play music for myself. Then when I come up with a song and they change the words, I say, 'Don't change the words! If you change the words my shadows are running fast, man!'"

Despite this evidence, the TV movies and the gossip novels will forever depict Dennis and Charlie as the tightest of buddies – a black and white relationship with Charlie – the Wizard – holding sway over his naïve young apprentice. This simplistic picture continues to be fed by those who should know better. Indeed, following the most recent and shallow of fictional dramas about the band's travails, Mike Love would claim that Dennis wholeheartedly "invited" Manson into his life as a "house guest". The same programme would reveal Love as the Beach Boys' true genius.

The Rave

DENNIS WILSON is the walking contradiction in the Beach Boys, who provides the motor for the group with his powerhouse percussion and unlimited energy. Dennis Wilson is the gentle-savage, the intellectual primitive, full of wilful pride and enforced humility.

He lives his life at breakneck speed with scarcely a backward glance behind him, but tempers his own velocity with daily meditation which stops him burning up in the atmosphere as he defies the laws of gravity.

Here is a man who cares for no one and everyone with the greater part of his devotion directed towards his music. He cares almost fanatically about his work and the group's performance. When the backing musicians failed to measure up to standard in Berlin, it was Dennis who steamed off stage after the show and tore into the musicians' room to deliver a scorching sermon on profes-

sionalism and sack everyone in sight. Fifteen minutes later he had cooled down and reinstated them, but the warning was enough to ensure the group one hundred per cent effort from the men on the next show!

Here, then, are a few impressions of the Beach Boys' guided missile. You may read between the lines or over the lines or under the lines or through the lines but be careful not to tread on the lines because there is a train coming. Which you might be excused from thinking has nothing to do with Dennis Wilson unless you realise he is the train!

What other work are you doing independent of the Beach Boys?

"I am recording a friend of mine—'Medulla'—who is a singer-guitarist who played a long time ago on one of our tours as a backing musician. He writes all his own songs. I have completed an album with him and when Brother Records are

launched this year I hope to have him on our label."

What would you say for you was the happiest time you spent with the Beach Boys?

"Right now, because of the mere fact that I'm alive *now.* I live now—I can look back at the past and dig it, but there is more you can do about enjoying life now."

You live your life in an apparently fearless manner, but is there anything that frightens you?

"Fear is nothing but awareness. I was only frightened as a child because I did not understand fear—the dark, being lost, what was under the bed! It came from within.

"Sometimes the Wizard frightens me—Charlie Manson who is another friend of mine who says he is God and the devil! He sings, plays and writes poetry and may be another artist for Brother Records."

Do you think your marriage broke up because you were a Beach Boy—because you have to spend so much time

working away from home?

"Maybe—but that was just a small part of it. It was just a question of growing apart, changing taste, direction—growing out of a shoe. The fact that you are a part of a successful group means you can do a lot of things you could not do before for your family, so it balances out."

Is this story true that you are living in a cellar in California at present?

"Yep—it's a little room about half the size of this hotel room. I look at it as my mind. There's a piano in there and a bed and that's all I need. People fill their lives and their rooms with so much stuff that they don't need—watches, furniture, cars—and they pour their life into keeping and acquiring these things. They spend all their time working to pay for that car, which they keep in a parking lot all day long.

"I could live anywhere I want. I've tried living in luxury, living in the mountains, living with my family and my favourite place is that little room!"

**Subject
Dennis Wilson**

**Interviewer
Keith Altham**

**Situation
Beach Boys
Hotel**

Interview

How important is a hit single to you?

"Oh it's a lot of fun—it's all just for fun. It's good for your self-esteem. It's like bumping into a friend and saying 'Here's where I'm at'—I love it."

Why did you become involved in transcendental meditation?

"It's a very personal, fulfilling thing. It stimulates the mind and body and gives you a greater appreciation of life. It puts you in communication with something infinitely greater and more important than self."

Which people have most musical influence over you?

"I like parts of things—that is I can appreciate a piece of one thing or another for its chord structure, or its melody, or its lyric, but it's silly to nominate a whole thing which you probably only like in part. I very much admire Phil Spector, but I wouldn't say I loved everything he does.

"One of the most impressive groups to emerge from America in recent months is CTA—their whole structure is fantastic. They do everything tastefully, and progressively--boom! Mark my words!"

Why is it that the Beach Boys have never related to films?

"I don't think the Beach Boys are a visual thing in that way like the Beatles were. I can dig it for myself. The fun part of it—the glamour and the people. I'd love to play something like the Hunchback of Notre Dame or a Shakespearian role. I loved that Evelyn Waugh film, 'The Loved Ones'.

"Someone has just got to do a version of that book, 'Stranger In A Strange Land' and I think I know someone who has the rights to it anyway—he wanted Paul McCartney to play the role of the Martian. That is a fantastic book. I've only ever read three books, 'Black Beauty', 'The Prophet' and 'Stranger In A Strange Land'.

"I dislike censorship in films —art should be an entirely unrestricted medium in which the artist imposes his own limitations. There should be no boundaries."

What do you think has kept the Beach Boys together?

"A great love for each other and respect. The fact that we grew up together."

Are those stories true about you giving your money away?

"Sure—I give everything I have away. What I am wearing and what's in that suitcase is it. I don't even have a car. I have a 1934 Dodge pick-up truck which someone gave me.

"I could have anything I want. I just have to go out and get it. If it's worth having, it's worth giving. The smile you send out will return to you!"

Are you conscious of having moved away from the slightly philosophical content of albums like *Smiley Smiley* with your recent recordings?

(In mocking tones) "Philosophical—dat's heavy, man dat's really heavy, dat's de heaviest ting I ever hoid damn! Some people say we are tools and some people say we must polish the tool and others say we must use the tool. Who knows? It's all down to you."

How long can the Beach Boys go on being the Beach Boys?

"We can go on for ever—until we're eighty-three! Maybe when my son gets a little older—when he gets to eleven. . . ."

Would you like your son to be in a beat group?

"He can do anything he wants to do. He likes to play the piano and he likes to sing but he would rather wrestle or go swimming and fishing, hiking, get dirty or watch me race a motor cycle . . . who knows?"

Did you ever want to do anything else other than be a drummer?

"I wanted to join the forestry commission—have my own trees to look after, the peace of a piece of land. I wanted to be a gardener and skipper of a boat.

Who are the people who have had most influence over your life?

"Christ, Maharishi, Buddha, my Father, Brian and me."

Dennis was hooked on the girls and the drugs and the danger, he correctly recognised Manson as a powerful and individual performer, and he was certainly influenced for a time by concepts such as "Cease To Exist". But, and here's the rub, Manson came as a by-product of the sex and the drugs and not vice-versa. After Charlie's initial magic wore thin he was merely tolerated as the occupants of 14400 got drunk on pleasure and intrigue. According to Stanley Shapiro, who was there for the entire period, Dennis soon resorted to evading his new tenant at all cost. "Most of the time Dennis avoided him because he never passed up a chance to shake him down for money." Certainly Van Dyke Parks remembered the situation a little differently than Mike Love when interviewed in February 2000:

"One day, Charles Manson brought a bullet out and showed it to Dennis, who asked, 'What's this?' And Manson replied, 'It's a bullet. Every time you look at it, I want you to think how nice it is your kids are still safe.' Well, Dennis grabbed Manson by the head and threw him to the ground and began pummelling him until Charlie said, 'Ouch!' He beat the living shit out of him. 'How dare you!' was Dennis' reaction. Charlie Manson was weeping openly in front of a lot of hip people. I heard about it, but I wasn't there. The point is, though, Dennis Wilson wasn't afraid of *anybody*! Dennis was a total alpha male – something Mike Love wants to be but isn't."

The honeymoon period of early 1968 was soon past and their relationship seemed to wane. Dennis never did relinquish his rock star trappings for a new life up on Spahn Ranch despite the claims of Family member Sandra Good[3]. Out on tour with the Beach Boys for long stretches of time he actually abandoned no. 14400, leaving his house guests to be evicted while taking refuge with Gregg Jakobson in Beverly Glen – hence the talk of living in a one-bedroomed cellar. Dennis continued to plug Manson's talents (but without success) and pay the occasional visit out to Spahn, but he no longer lived in quite the same realms of intensity as before. For the most part he simply avoided him. The two characters were just too distinct to be mutually compatible in the long term. Charlie was still without a recording contract nine months after their meeting and was now cut off from Dennis' personal allowance. The changing of lyrics was the final straw. Realising that Dennis wasn't going to give up *his* world, Manson sent him a bullet. Apparently this was a gesture of love rather than a threat. As Charlie told *Rolling Stone* reporter David Felton, "His paranoia created the idea that it was a threat.

---

[3] Said Sandra: "Dennis Wilson wanted to live with us. He was gonna just drop everything and come and be with us whether it was living in a tent, or whatever. And his brothers basically said, 'You know, you're bound by contract, and if you renege we're gonna have you committed. We're gonna get psychiatric testimony that you've flipped your lid, and so you're a slave to this contract', and that was that. Dennis loved Charlie. Actually, I don't think his brothers cared too much for us. Their wives were kind of threatened by us. We weren't out to steal anybody's boyfriend or husband, but they were threatened by our overall lifestyle. But we got along with everybody, actually."

If you gave me a bullet, I'd wear it around my neck to let them see you love me. The only thing I'd want to do to Dennis is make love to him. You know, I used to say to him, 'Look at this flower, Dennis. Don't you think it's beautiful?' And he would say, 'Look man, I got to go.' He was always going somewhere to take care of some big deal. What it amounted to is that he couldn't accept my love. I love him as much as I love myself. I refuse nothing and I ask nothing. It all flows through me." With Charlie there was nothing less than 100% in the commitment stakes – you were either with him or against him.

Gregg Jakobson also noticed this deterioration in relations. By the spring of 1969 Charlie had "really changed radically from what he had been the former year." For Dennis the penny seemed to have dropped, through sheer financial cost or from one too many afflictions of VD. When Charlie held a knife to his throat with a little more conviction than before events were starting to get a little too freaky as all that talk of revolution spilled over into reality. Aggravated that the Beach Boys connection had not brought fame and that Dennis was proving no willing disciple, Manson disappeared back to Death Valley like an angry and desperate hornet. Other than that mere $100,000 extracted from Dennis' estate he received no credit or payment for his two songs, "Cease To Exist" and "Be With Me", that appeared on the Beach Boys LP *20/20*. He had no time for those who did not reciprocate the kind of love and commitments he was willing to make: "If Charlie said he would be some place at 4'o clock, he would be even if he had to walk. And it used to infuriate him that Dennis would forget what he promised immediately. So Charlie and Dennis never got along that well."

Even in the pop magazine interviews, despite the allusions to Heinlein and all the rest, there was enough of the pre-Manson Dennis to suggest he was his own man: stating that art should be unhindered by censorship, that the Beach Boys should continue until the age of 83 and playfully quoting the mantra from the band's great lost LP, "The smile that you send out will return to you!" He was just not your archetypal Family member. When asked which people had the most influence over his life he replied, "Christ, Maharishi, Buddha, my Father, Brian and me."

Dennis genuinely thought that Manson had a viable and definite talent. He was not only that Castro-like "fascinating cat", he also represented a chance to gain kudos within the Beach Boys, by providing Brother Records with a performer who was truly contemporary. An opportunity to make Hendrix choke on his words. And though few admitted to recognising Charlie's musical talents post-August '69 (least of all Dennis), during 1968 quite a few people heard and considered his music to be, at least, interesting. One such person was Neil Young, who purportedly recommended Manson to Mo Ostin, then head of Warner Brothers. Later to document his thoughts on The Family in the dune buggy-infested "Revolution Blues", Young considered Charlie to be a masterly lyricist and remembered well his brilliant spontaneity: "[He would] sing a song and just make it up as he went along, for three or four minutes, and he would never repeat one word, and it all made perfect sense and it shook you up to listen to it." He also imagined that, backed by a band akin to Dylan's circa "Subterranean Homesick Blues", Charlie might well have achieved the stardom he craved – except "there was just something about him that stopped anyone being around him too long."

Others too must have heard Charlie, either in passing at Dennis' house or during the recreational sessions at Brian's studio. John Philips of the Mamas & Papas certainly had – he was initially Roman Polanski's suspect for the Tate murders – while Mama Cass (whose boyfriend was the same Billy Doyle humiliated at Cielo Drive two days before the murders) bought her drugs through the Family. Terry Melcher, son of Doris Day and producer of The Byrds and Paul Revere and the Raiders, also had first-hand experience. Introduced to the Family by Dennis and Gregg, Terry was persuaded to hear Manson's music in its natural habitat of Spahn. The producer of the Byrds and Paul Revere & The Raiders was less than impressed but left a few food dollars as a parting gesture – leading a livid Charlie to make accusations of broken promises in the bitter aftermath of another rejection. At the time of course, Terry Melcher lived at 10050 Cielo Drive. Manson was aware of this since witnessing Dennis dropping Terry off there after a recording session while he sat in the back, playing guitar.

There were more than these few examples[4]. If you were well-connected with the LA drugs scene in '67 through '69 – and great swathes of the Hollywood machine were – chances are you would have stumbled upon Charlie or his associates.

So Manson was hardly unknown amongst the Californian entertainment business, but as Neil Young pointed out, most would deny their encounters with him now – much less be brave enough to praise his artistic talents. Dennis Wilson and Gregg Jakobson were left as the only scenesters to openly promote his music; Dennis the high-profile collaborator who, by calling Charlie "The Wizard" in print, was destined to appear suckered as a devout follower. So when the murder details filtered through he was easily tarred with the label of fool for allowing the Family entry to Hollywood. Even his own band members were not sparing – one anonymous Beach Boy was quoted in 1971 stating why they hadn't fallen for the scruffy guy they nicknamed "Pigpen": "Dennis was just divorced; I supposed the lifestyle appealed to him. Perhaps I have more sexual inhibitions, moral strictures. I wasn't into doing drugs at that point, which was Charlie's way of controlling his little friends... We've got several eight-track tapes of Charlie and the girls that Dennis cut, maybe even some 16 track. Just chanting, fucking, sucking, balling... Maybe we'll put it out in the Fall. Call it 'Death Row'."

These comments might seem a little hypocritical given the alleged existence of several master tapes of Charlie featuring backing vocals from the entire band. Certainly all the Beach Boys had met him when Dennis brought the Family entourage up to Brother recording studios. They may

---

[4] Alex Chilton, for instance, spent three days up at the house, nearly coming to blows with Charlie when he refused to join the Family.

---

have disliked this freaky individual who was a friend of their degenerate brother and cousin, but at the very least he recorded music in Brian's studio, with their equipment and their engineer.

Yet this is all hindsight. In the aftermath of murder, the black and white perception of Manson was as evil incarnate. Judged by the Hollywood furore, Dennis' foolhardy alliance seemed unwittingly to link many of the victims and the events of August. In this light his misdemeanours made a damning list:

Dennis introduces Manson to Charles "Tex" Watson and to Gary Hinman, the first victim of the murder spree.

Dennis introduces Manson to 10050 Cielo Drive. When Terry Melcher moves out, Watson stays there for a few weeks at the behest of Gregg Jakobson.

Dennis introduces Manson to Terry Melcher and Rudi Altobelli – elevating his status to artist and familiarising him with his victims.

Dennis funds the Family to the tune of $100,000 as they ransack his house and possessions.

Dennis records Charlie and puts his music into the hit parade – "Never Learn Not To Love" being the B-side to the Beach Boys' single "Bluebirds Over The Mountain" in 1968.

But the Manson Dennis knew well was not the crazed killer of August '69. He was a musician with the ability to rap lyrically on many different levels. A potential star. All these events – key events for that bloody August – happened prior to his being holed-out crazy in the desert awaiting Armageddon. The release of The Beatles' *White Album*, the supposed key to all this madness, was not until December 1968 – several months after Dennis had flown his own house.

Any flirtation with the dark side was most probably unintentional. There was some connection on a philosophical level but the primal attraction for Dennis remained the Family girls, and the drugs, and the thrill of the lifestyle. He was never going to commit his soul and was certainly not going to prove his love with a knife. If you want sinister it's best to look elsewhere to the other travellers of the era: Their Satanic Majesties the Stones and, in particular Mick Jagger, mincing his way round the race tracks of America and taking on the persona of the Midnight Rambler. Jim Morrison, singer in the most overrated band of the era (and now elevated to his desired status as son-of-Baudelaire by Oliver Stone and Danny Sugarman), calling for insurrection and revolution to the backing of Ray Manzarek's pitiful organ, and later marrying a white witch. Jimmy Page, and his continuing obsession with Aleister Crowley and sex magick.

The black arts were in vogue and for a good twelve months were *de rigueur* for any self-respecting pop star. The stuff was everywhere. Even George Clinton's Funkadelic used extensive testaments from The Process Church of the Final Judgement on their record sleeves – "Fear is at the root of man's destruction of himself. Without fear there is no blame. Without blame there is no conflict. Without conflict there is no destruction." Not that the rock press would worry themselves writing about that – Satanism and intelligentsia were for white artists only. The rebuttal of Manson was proof of how far the rock world was prepared to take this show. (Mick'n'Keef stood by powerless and impotent at Altamont as their Hells Angels attacked the very crowd they were hired to protect; Marty Balin of the Jefferson Airplane received a beating as he tried to pacify the barbarians). How pointed that Dennis, the rock star who really lived it for a while – who danced up close and personal with the most infamous devil of the '60s – was to remain virtually tight-lipped about his experiences.

The Rock Gentry's fascination with Satanism and its offshoots proved fleeting. A love of the mysticism was soon dropped by most of the above like a passing fad, as they explored new, less threatening avenues, like country rock, acting or poetry. After Altamont, Mick Jagger lost all "Sympathy For The Devil" and took to wearing a crucifix. In Marianne Faithfull's words, "I've forgotten exactly what it was we believed, but we believed in it fiercely".

But what of the music? Was Dennis' enigmatic protégé really in possession of the kind of talent that Neil Young so openly praised and that he and Gregg Jakobson felt so keen to promote? Or was Charlie's songwriting merely an excuse for Dennis to ingratiate himself to The Family through praise and attention? After all, the pairing completed two tracks worthy of inclusion on the *20/20* LP of 1969 – the Dennis-modified "Never Learn Not To Love" a.k.a. "Cease To Exist", and the full-scale collaboration "Be With Me".

20/20 would be the last LP of original Beach Boys material released by Capitol Records – their twentieth in seven years. Though as commercially unsuccessful as *Friends* was the previous year it now stands as one of the highlights of the band's career, and maybe the nearest to unravelling the essence of our continuing fascination with them. As a true reflection of the five disparate personalities that made up The Beach Boys and the schizophrenic realities of their fan base, *20/20* had it all – more than *Pet Sounds*, more than 1970's *Sunflower*, and certainly more than *Smile* would have ever been. From the back-to-the-surf hit single (it reached #20) "Do It Again" (Mike), to the Petsoundsalike "Nearest Faraway Place" (Bruce), to the Spectoresque "I Can Hear Music" (Carl), to the obligatory folk cover of Leadbelly's "Cotton Fields" (Al) – everyone in the band was represented. From Brian there were a couple of tracks culled from the riches of 1967 and some beautiful new pieces of nonsense that revealed the whereabouts of his current headspace: "Time To Get Alone" and "I Went To Sleep". The band's other genius was represented in abundance too, and for the first time Dennis' personal *and* musical influences was steeped in the grooves of an LP. The triumvirative aural glory of his "Never Learn Not To Love" followed by the *Smile* relics "Our Prayer" and "Cabinessence" is perhaps the highlight of any Beach Boys record – so far ahead of the game sonically and experimentally in 1969, and still unsurpassed today. The running thread of ideas and spirituality was just phenomenal. One can truly identify with Stephen Kalinich's regret that the Brian-Dennis axis was unable to gain full control of the Beach Boys and lead them towards the destiny of this blueprint.

According to Charlie, "Never Learn Not To Love" was given to the Beach Boys in order to quell simmering familial tensions. "They were fighting among themselves, so I wrote that song to bring them together. 'Submission is a gift, give it to your brother.' Dennis has true soul, but his brothers couldn't accept it. He would go over to Brian's house and put his arms around his brothers, and they would say, 'Gee Dennis, cut it out!' You know, they could not accept it." Under its original title "Cease To Exist", a straight reading of the song (just acoustic guitar with a reverb-drenched slide) was demoed by Manson during one of his late night recording sessions at Brian's home studio.

Given the song's lyrics however, such an explanation seems unlikely. It could be read as pertaining to the band, but the content was full of the symbolism and phrasing for which Charlie was soon to become infamous. The double-edged meaning (were they sinister, were they peaceful?) of couplets like "cease to exist", "I'm your kind", "give up your world" or "submission is a gift" sounded more like a clarion call. All were from the lexicography of Scientology and the song itself was a condensed testament of the teachings of Charles Millis Manson. If the lure of fame was a communication channel to release messages, then "Cease To Exist" sounded nothing less than a mating call to the youth of America, an advert to join the Family – "Give up your world, and come and be with me"[5].

That's why Charlie was so pissed when Dennis changed the words. His careful signalling had been tampered with. The alteration in the opening line from "exist" to "resist" gave off connotations of sexual submission rather than wholehearted ego surrender. That was nothing though compared with the transformation in the music.

From the lengthy intro of a cymbal playing backwards the song was light years away from Charlie's primitive folk version. It was also, given the dark emotion of the vocal and the bombastic production, a stand-out track on the album – considerably more sincere and twisted than the light-hearted standards. Layering on sounds and freaky effects from fuzz bass to timpani to ghostly strings it was more than obvious that Dennis was replicating some of his elder brother's finer moments. The sheer condensation of raw sound and driving rhythm combined with the incessant nature of the chorus was moving him into the alchemical territory Brian had explored with the mighty "Cabinessence" – though not achieving quite the incredible cauldron of ideas contained in that one song.

The vocals themselves, pitched by Dennis from a croon to a scream, were as gloriously imperfect and un-Beach Boys as always. This

---

[5] According to Gregg Jakobson's "Lance Fairweather" piece in *Rolling Stone*, one of the reasons he and Dennis were sympathetic to Charlie was his concern for down-and-outs washed up daily by the allure of a scene that no longer existed: "...he knew what the Haight had turned into and that these naïve, dumb, wide-eyed girls would be hopelessly lost in that jungle. He said that they'd be beaten up by the niggers, they'd be raped, they'd go onto speed, and so on. And he wanted to put a song out, telling them, 'Don't go to the Haight, come to me.' And that made sense to me."

was no "California Girls". Surrounded by tracks that veered into very easy listening (and that's a compliment as *20/20* is predominantly honey for the ears) there was something slightly malevolent in the nature of this song. Something unwholesome and perverse in its execution and in the incessant chanting of the message. The increasing howl of the word "closer" in the chorus, which finally collapses into a primeval cry, was pure garage punk. For a song purportedly about harmony it sounded remarkably discordant. The sighing mantra at the conclusion was actually a relaxation chant dreamed up by Charlie for the birth of his son Zee Zo Zosi Zadfrack.

Less lyrically overt was Dennis' epic lament (described by Brian as a "ballad with punch") "Be With Me". Genuinely sinister in sound, the production employed every symphonic device in the book set to stun: slow galloping beats paralleled by brass, eerie strings crossing through their scales, ghostly violins wailing discordantly in the background and yet another ragged vocal, buried like another instrument in the mix. The concluding passage where the drums roll over the trumpets roll over the orchestra roll over the vocal is an incredible piece of sound. More so coming after the chirpy cover of "Bluebirds Over The Mountain", that was inexplicably chosen as a single release. Compared to its sister piece this was a fully blown concerto, more in keeping with the idea of "feels" that Brian used in recording *Pet Sounds*. However, while "Never Learn" was the bastardised transformation of Charlie's raw blues, "Be With Me", according to Mansonite expert and writer Bill Scanlon Murphy, was a proper collaboration. Charlie wrote the words and Dennis the music – there were no alterations to the message this time.

The subject matter again could easily relate to a relationship, and I guess there is a danger of going OTT in looking for hidden messages in Charlie's songs – akin to his own supposed perceptions of The Beatles. As per usual with Manson "meanings" can mean whatever you want them to mean – "no sense makes sense". But the combination of spooked-out symphony, arranged by Van McCoy, and shadowy images of "walkin' round at night" do identify "Be With Me" as another glorified enrolment call. Certainly there was the usual freaky language (wondering if a girl is "nowhere"), the universal-one-as-everything-speak ("everything we will be") and obviously the title ("Come with me, be a part of me... BE. WITH. ME."). Scratch under the surface and the potential purposes of the song are legion – as the man himself said, "I may have implied on several occasions to several different people that I may have been Jesus Christ, but I haven't yet decided what I am or who I am." The last seconds of the fade-out are the strangest of all: with barely-there and out-of-tune "Ba-Ba-Ba's" merging into a hideous and semi-audible scream.

As some sort of counterpoint, Dennis' other contribution to the LP had a quite contrasting tag. "All I Want To Do", co-written by an un-credited Stephen Kalinich and sung by Mike "like a madman possessed" (Brian's words) was a dumb get-ya-rocks-off boogie. Against the fade was inserted the fully audible sound of some genuine bump'n'grind. Apparently Dennis had succoured the services of a Hollywood and Vine hooker in the pursuit of artistic authenticity. He even insisted that engineer Stephen Desper allow him a personal 2nd take before the song was put to bed – a fact evident on the LP which has a different recording in each channel. In any case it was a slightly more humorous reflection of the songwriter's libido.

If Charlie *was* hoping to unleash his vibrations on an unsuspecting public via Dennis then he picked an unfortunate time to do it. The *20/20* album spent only 11 weeks on the chart and peaked at a derisory Number 68. He also received no listed credit for his tracks nor any royalties for his lyrics. In a quid pro quo arrangement the cars, the clothes and the gold discs that Dennis so kindly donated were payment enough. The gold discs paid for the Family's tenancy at Spahn and Golpher ranch and proved useful trophies to impress parole officers. Ultimately though the Beach Boys were not big enough for his schemes. Dennis could get him so far in the entertainment business, but not, it seems, far enough.

The recordings that took place at Brian's home studio and a rented space in Santa Monica amounted to nothing. Beyond the fact that Charlie hated the sterility of the surroundings[6] and ignored Dennis' suggestions from the production booth, the sessions were hampered by an excess of recreational activity. Where Charlie went the girls followed and under the influence of psychedelics the combination degenerated too easily into a writhing mass of bi-sexuality. The resulting X-rated masters were "interesting" but unlikely to garner any interest other than the voyeuristic. (Dennis later claimed [untruthfully] to the D.A. that he had destroyed any tapes that might have existed since "the vibrations connected with them don't belong on this earth"). Light years away from Dennis' epic soundscapes, Manson's songs simply did not develop beyond the crudest demo stage, remaining just the singer and his acoustic guitar, with occasional backing from his girls. Gregg Jakobson's original plan to capture the whole Family on film would have been a far more successful venture than these wasted sessions – as Neil Young commented, "No-one was ever going to catch up with Charlie Manson 'cos he'd make up the songs as he went along." Terry Melcher and Rudi Altobelli, whom Dennis and Gregg strongly touted, remained unimpressed with the finished material. Any polite interest that had been initially expressed was quickly dropped. They simply made excuses and relinquished ideas to make a record.

Charlie would later claim that Terry *had* made promises of fame and that he'd gone back on his word. Offending his unwritten code of honour and brotherhood, this was supposed to be some justification of his hatred for plastic Hollywood – though it's doubtful this was the reason for the slayings of August 9th since the Family were well aware that Melcher had long since moved from Cielo Drive. In fact Terry had visited

---

[6] As he told David Felton and David Dalton in 1970: "I never really dug recording, you know, all those things pointed at you. Gregg would say, 'Come down to the studio and we'll tape some things," so I went. You get into the studio, you know, and it's hard to sing into microphones. Giant phallic symbols pointing at you. All my latent tendencies... [Charlie starts laughing and making sucking sounds]. My relationship to music is completely subliminal, it just flows through me."

Manson only a couple of times at Spahn, offering the Family some obligatory food dollars and maybe making some encouraging noises in the course of social niceties. Altobelli had not even offered that. There had been no talk of contracts.

Helter Skelter, whatever it was, was coming down. In conjunction with everything else that was happening up at Spahn in 1969 – the stockpiling of weapons and building of dune buggies in preparation for the impending apocalypse – Charlie's patience started to wear thin. His psychopathic nature could no longer be concealed and the guru of 1968 had now metamorphosed into "a caged animal". After the August murders he tried desperately to contact his showbiz friends again and exhort/extort one final sum of cash. Gregg Jakobson recalled seeing "the electricity pouring out of him". During one frantic visit, when asked of his recent whereabouts, Charlie merely rolled back his eyes and cackled, "I been to the moon".

The last straw for the Beach Boys had already occurred when engineer Stephen Desper voiced concerns about the knife that Manson liberally flashed around Brother Studios. After Charlie threatened Dennis that he would not see his adopted son Scott again, the writing was on the wall. A fact confirmed when Scott went missing for eight hours, only to turn up safe at a friend's house.

Whether they guessed who had committed the Tate murders is unknown, but in the weeks following 1st December 1969 Dennis and Gregg would realise how lucky they'd been. On that day Charles Manson, Leslie Van Houten, Susan Atkins and Patricia Krenwinkel were formally indicted by the LAPD for the killings.

Almost immediately after Manson was arrested Squeaky Fromme showed up at Gregg Jakobson's house demanding money from Dennis for the use of Charlie's songs. He refused to speak to her. Charlie was not listed on the credits – legally they were all Dennis' – and since his previous tenant had already fleeced him to the tune of $100,000 he was not about to contribute further to his "defence fund". This did not however prevent a thorough midnight audit of all masters in the Beach Boys studio by Dennis and Stanley Shapiro to appease the petrified Carl and Brian. Nothing was found with Charlie's name on it and they escaped to an isolated cabin 100 miles away at Lake Arrowhead to avoid the press. Dennis later admitted that if he did once have any tapes they would have been passed on to Terry Melcher. Since Terry claimed all ignorance their whereabouts remain unknown.

Dennis never testified at the trial. Somewhat surprisingly, considering his collaborations with Charlie and their time living together, the District Attorney was happy enough with interviewing Dennis privately. The reasons for this are still unclear: Bugliosi mentions the death threats – in addition to the bullet and the threats over Scott, the phone at Dennis' house was disconnected on September 23rd after a payphone call from Spahn – but anyone who gave evidence in court would need subsequent police protection. No doubt there was also pressure from the Beach Boys and their management to quickly nip the bud of this potentially embarrassing situation in the cause of damage limitation.[7]

In any case Dennis said remarkably little about his time with the Family after 1969: a statement in 1976 that this was subject non-gratis ("I don't talk about Manson. I think he's a sick fuck. I think of Roman and all those wonderful people who had a beautiful family and they fucking had their tits cut off. I want to benefit from that?") and then some teasing comments to writer David Leaf around the same period, "I know why Charles Manson did what he did. Someday I'll tell the world. I'll write a book and explain why he did it." Obviously the book was never written, but an unreleased song "Wild Situation", a lewd tale of groupie encounters originally slated for *Bamboo* in 1978 but actually written some 5 years earlier, apparently contained references to Charlie in its original draught.

Gregg Jakobson, Dennis' chief songwriting partner and one of his closest friends, was however a key prosecution witness. Claiming to have held over 100 philosophical raps with Charlie during his many visits to Spahn, his evidence was lifeblood to the D.A.'s theory of Helter Skelter. Manson's opinions on race, women, morality, domination and the Beatles were all synthesised for Bugliosi through Gregg's statements. If anyone had to fear for their life it was probably him.

Charlie's revolution never came: the wrath of the black ghettos did not spill over to Pacific Palisades and the Family never found their fabled hole in the desert. Armageddon was delayed for another time, but the killing of Sharon Tate did send earthquakes through the mansions and the avenues of the Hollywood Hills.

To those ends the events of August the 9th and 10th achieved their purpose – the world sat up and took notice. The "new celebrities" – those fashionable young things who hadn't cut their hair, sympathised with leftist politics and smoked a little weed – who had reached ascendancy throughout the 1960s suddenly felt the rug pulled under them. Since 1967 the hip elite had congratulated themselves for not being part of the old establishment; a new realism was ushered in as barriers of censorship were removed. The casual violence of films like *Bonnie And Clyde* and *The Wild Bunch* and the advent of "serious" rock music were supposed to reflect the turmoil of the times. Hollywood gave itself a mutual backslap and basked in the freedoms generated from the Summer of Love: sex, drugs and rock'n'roll.

The murders cast a dark cloud over this charmed life. It seemed that the realities of fascistic America had come home to roost and that no-one was safe. Only Charlie was not an outsider, he was supposedly one of them. And Sharon Tate was one of them too. Violence was no longer

---

[7] The whole of Hollywood was running scared after the murders and sales of firearms and home security escalated through the roof. Supposedly the Family had a "hit list" that included such luminaries as Frank Sinatra, Steve McQueen, Liz Taylor, Richard Burton and Tom Jones. Whether this was true or not enough Family members were still at large and vocal in their threats to high society. In 1974 Squeaky Fromme would pull a gun on Gerald Ford while Martin Scorsese became a target as late as 1977 after refusing to play Charlie in the made-for-TV movie *Helter Skelter*.

---

confined to the movies – it was here and it was real and terrifying. Beneath the illusionary language of free and easy brotherhood the sicknesses of racism, sexism, hypocrisy and murder, endemic in the US, were prevalent in the counter culture too.

The hierarchy of New Hollywood looked fallible for the first time. Momentarily ignorant that their Government was bombarding a developing country with napalm, the front pages were all focused on Sharon: the beautiful blonde actress snuffed out by evil. In one sense Manson was right when he commented, "If she hadn't have been an actress then nobody would have even worried about it." Beneath the polemic it seemed this society was little different from the conservatism of the white-collar suburbs it so openly ridiculed.

This being Hollywood the image would be appropriated back soon enough and Manson would provide inspiration for *Last House On The Left*, *The Texas Chainsaw Massacre*, and almost every other horror flick of the '70s. But in 1969, as home security and rifles sales escalated ten-fold overnight, the movie stars and canyon dwellers could not wait for the decade to end.

Like the survivor of an air crash Dennis walked away from the whole bloody mess unscathed. But the effects of an alliance to America's public bogeyman number one were to leave their mark on his life. With a significant following of Mansonites still based in California the fear of reprisal remained for some time – he had not exactly crossed the Family, but they had hardly proved discriminate in their choice of targets so far. Quoted in David Leaf's book was an unknown friend of Dennis': "It was really weird to see someone who seems in control of things get really spaced out by a noise in the bushes. He was very nervous. He couldn't sit for more than two minutes at a time." This opinion was quantified by Daryl Dragon: "Very few people know that the reason Dennis drove himself to destruction was the fear of Charles Manson returning into his life... should he get out of jail, or maybe hire someone to 'rub Dennis out'. It was really that bad." The Dennis Wilson who emerged from the 1960s was a changed man.

The dark and overtly sexual topics of his *20/20* songs would soon be replaced by lush ballads and upbeat soul. For the next three years, predominantly in collaboration with Daryl Dragon, he would hit an artistic peak with a collection of material that was shot through with deep-rooted melancholy but remained defiantly alive. Dennis was lucky and his songwriting seemed to discover a sense of humility previously lacking. He would retain the same foolish attitude to women and excess, but by 1971 he would again be married and inspired to create. The torpor of Manson lifted from his eyes, Dennis viewed the world with wonder and romance again.

SOUND OF FREE: FADE OUT/FADE IN

"Bad luck's all in the past / Now we'll grow at last / There's been a change / No bad luck no more"

Welcome to the '70s.

Musically and politically this was a far different landscape from what had come before, with none of that decade's sureties. As Mick Jagger was to inform one interviewer, "To use a cliché, the sixties never really ended until later on in the seventies. I sort of remember the album *Exile On Main Street* being done in France and also in the United States, and after that going on tour and becoming complacent, and thinking, 'It's '72. Fuck it. We've done it.' We still tried after that, but I don't think the results were ever that wonderful."

Since 1967, whether you were a straight or a freak (and let's face it the Beach Boys were a curious mixture of both), belief in something/anything just seemed to be sliding away. The likelihood of revolution emanating from the Panthers or the Hippies was diminishing by the day. Innocence was bought off the agenda as the hippy dream rolled over and succumbed to corporate US values. Of the bigger picture, the ongoing war in Vietnam was the most virulent cloud on the collective horizon. The Cold War logic of manifest destiny (the enforcement of "freedom" on other nations in the name of anti-communism) that seemed so obvious and correct and *American* in Kennedy's day was now just an exemplary symbol of all that was sick and divisive in society. To the draft dodgers and student protestors, to the young men being sent out to the slaughter, to the "Silent Majority" and the Administration, the world was being turned on its head. Everyone was having to face a different version of reality, whether that be an acceptance of US folly in South East Asia or that revolution in the streets would fail to materialise. A collective trip that left all heads truly shaken. Faced with a losing battle to win the "hearts and minds" of a never-existent South Vietnamese ally, the successive governments of Johnson and Nixon responded in the only way they knew how: to drop more bombs, to spin more lies and to ultimately send more, mainly black and poor, young American men off to die. By 1970 the US death toll was pushing 50,000 and the tonnage of bombs dropped that year exceeded all those dropped in WWII.

In those three insane years, in the wake of My Lai, the Democratic Conference of '68, the rioting in Watts, the assassinations of Bobby Kennedy and Luther King, and everything else, it seemed that America was turning in on itself. Listening to the prophets of the Haight you would have believed that rock'n'roll was the soundtrack to revolution and the harbinger of the chaos to come. "Blood on the streets in the town of

---

Chicago." And yet there was to be no change. Nixon got in, the system won out, and revolution, certainly for white culture, was off the agenda. The world was the same as before. 1968 was just a hazy memory – albeit one viewed with different, more cynical, eyes.

The Tate murders were just one sign that chickens were coming home to roost. In reporting on that other nail in the coffin of Hippy in late 1969, GP Csicsery wrote, "Altamont was America... Putting it all together looks like America's pulse 'now'. After all, not only do we make beautiful music, love and beadwork; we pay our pigs to exterminate Black Panthers, we fry Vietnamese in their homes and we elect Spiro Agnew to govern our lives." Paranoia replaced the trusting innocence of the early Bay scene and long hair was no longer the definable statement of peace and brotherhood, especially in the wake of the Manson murders. There was no "them" and "us" any more. "Out an' down. Ain't got a friend. You don't know, who turned you in" surmised Sylvester Stewart's *There's A Riot Goin' On*, in 1971.

The Beach Boys were of a product of the early '60s (their association with this era had branded them terminally in the role of "America's Premier Surfing Band"), that had mutated and stumbled into this scenario like B-movie voyagers to a strange new world. The leap from hot rods and surf boards, through the drug culture of *Pet Sounds* and *Smile* to acid burn-out, TM and Charlie Manson had been as immense as the changes in the world around them. Spector, The Beatles, the whole Californian scene, had just imploded as the decade wore on. Before '67 things had been so simple. Lennon and McCartney provided the competition as Spector did before them. America was the Free World. In 1963 Brian had written "The Warmth Of The Sun" in the wake of the Kennedy assassination. A poignant and beautiful hymn to lost hope in the wake of premature death. Which of them was going to write a song for the times now, as troops still poured into Vietnam and the truths of the Cold War became unravelled?

FUNERAL NOTICE
Hippie
In the
Haight Ashbury District
Of this city,
Hippie, devoted son
Of
MASS MEDIA

After Monterey the music industry "grew up" and Rock was born – the older and more serious cousin of pop and rock'n'roll. According to Barney Hoskyns the Festival was "the high moment of the hippie dream, which inadvertently opened up pop to every mogul in the record business" – the celebration of the scene in that moment was also its death knell. The dream was hijacked, as conservative record companies, used to covering up the excesses of their performers, now realised the profit potential in repackaging revolution. This was Hollywood after all. If music, fashion and drugs could change on a daily basis then the record companies would adapt to the pace. The Doors' eponymous debut was advertised with billboards on the Strip whilst Jefferson Airplane were promoting sales of white Levi jeans. Mo Ostin transformed Warners Brothers from the home of the Rat Pack to that of Neil Young and Frank Zappa, whilst faces on the scene became part of the establishment. People like David Crosby or David Anderle or David Geffen or Terry Melcher had become *players* – their influence and tastes to be transmuted into wealth and power bases. Warners, Capitol and Columbia all successfully bought into the FREE LOVE culture in the realisation that this was now the way to make dollars. "THE MAN CAN'T BUST OUR MUSIC" ran the ads.

"Can you take Grace Slick seriously," ranted Lou Reed from New York, "It's a joke! The kids are being hyped".

Rock music, despite its pretensions to high culture, was another commodity. A commodity with an audience whose resources ran beyond the 7" single that had been the staple of pop. When *Pet Sounds* was released pop musicians were not taken seriously, yet two years later they were linked with changing the political landscape. A "revolution" based on the commercial premises of pop music would pass through its inevitable full circle. So much so that even the scribes of *Rolling Stone* (the bible of the underground) were left in self-doubt – "We tell ourselves we are a counter culture", wrote Jon Landau in his obituary of Janis Joplin, "And yet are we so different from the culture against which we rebel?" The hippies thought Dylan was joking when he called Smokey Robinson America's greatest living poet. Peace and Love could be sold to the masses and, as in everyday politics, normal service was resumed. Cocaine had replaced acid, rock had replaced pop, and the prophets who wanted to free your mind were now locked up with their acoustic guitars counting the spoils.

Like a retreating army licking its wounds, the Californian scene moved out of the Hollywood Hills to the peace of Laurel Canyon. Hendrix, Parsons and Joplin were already casualties of the San Francisco Bay lifestyle while many more had touched upon at least the outer fringes of Manson's underworld. In this new millionaire's playground looking down over the city the incestuous rock aristocracy were able to come down and rebuild from the madness of 1969. Country and roots were now the definitive influence on the scene. Singer-songwriters were where it was at. Joni Mitchell and Sweet Baby James. Crosby, Stills and Nash. Music to mellow out to sung by the winners who survived. Music to reflect and bake bread to. The birth of AOR. This was not an exciting time.

God only knows what Brian Wilson, never mind the rest of the Beach Boys, could make of all this. For a start their music seemed archaic. When Murry Wilson sold Sea Of Tunes Publishing (aside from it being an act of revenge towards his eldest son) its market value was negligible. It was the sound of Kennedy and the Californian Dream, before the complexities of 1968 and beyond. A sound more relevant to McCarthy than the Yippies. A Cassius Clay rather than a Muhammad Ali. Even the name "Beach Boys" – no wonder this group of late 20s Californians had troubles, to the point where Mike Love (tongue-in-cheek) suggested halving the equation to plain "Beach". Even "The Beatles" was a better name than that! Since the glories of "Good Vibrations" the band had struggled to produce hit singles in America, their name too synonymous with striped shirts and teenage crazes. Though still a huge draw on the concert circuit the band had become more an institution than a healthy and creative entity. "The public thinks of us as surfing Doris Days," asserted Bruce Johnston correctly at the time.

Scorsese's post-modern use of Spector in *Mean Streets* was about the only chance for records like "Fun Fun Fun" or "California Girls" to be fashionable in the early '70s. Brian Wilson's music was, for the majority, the uncomplicated sound of Californian youth. The experimental era of *Smile* would be erased from history by record compilations of the era 1962–1966 that the public bought in their millions. Tracks like "Do You Like Worms?" did *not* make the track list of the *Endless Summer* LP, that anthology of huge hit singles which hit pay dirt in 1974, and confirmed The Beach Boys as both one of America's greatest bands and one with a future based in its own past. Maybe that's why discovering *Pet Sounds* is so special today. It was just such a departure to what went before, and, considering stuff like "Do It Again", what came after. For the uninitiated to unearth it's nothing short of a revelation.

With hindsight Brian would never write a song again to equal those of his golden period from 1965–1967. The dearth of ideas he proffered to the *Friends* and *20/20* albums was not a temporary glitch in his abilities, but pretty much as good as it would get from now on. With the notable exception of "'Til I Die" on 1971's *Surfs Up* and a couple of tracks on *Sunflower*, the old quality control just was not there any more. In self-imposed exile and without the collaboration of a lyricist of the quality of a Tony Asher or Van Dyke Parks to turn fantasies into words, his spirit lay broken and his hugely competitive ego vanquished. The creativity that blossomed in the madness of 1967 and the acid experiments at Laurel Way turned into inertia. The drugs that furthered Dennis' natural energy and exuberance would have the opposite effect on his brother – projecting his feelings inwards and fuelling an inherent immaturity. With the puppy love he bestowed upon his wife and his addiction to junk food, Brian was always prone to childlike tendencies. By virtually giving up on the band and on his music he was reaching for some kind of safety blanket by drifting into oblivion. "There's a place where I can go and tell my secrets to," he had sang on "In My Room" in 1963. Confined to the four walls of his bedroom and in a declining mental state, the antennae so attuned to making pop music from the experiences of others had stopped working. The songs would not come any more. "I was too concerned with getting drugs to write songs", he was later to confess in 1988. The inclusion of outtakes from the grand project of *Smile*, salvaged for the late 1960s LPs gave the impression of a creative force still at work, but the simple truth was that the golden goose had stopped laying.

This obviously raised issues of how the group was to function in the future. Particularly as their new contract with Warner Brothers was based on promises made by manager Nick Grillo to label head Mo Ostin that Brian would be actively involved in song writing. Ostin was a huge fan of the band. The $250,000 per album deal combined both his commercial and sentimental instincts, viewing the Beach Boys as a unique slice of pure Americana to be preserved. (Ironically Phil Spector would be signed to Warners in similar circumstances in 1973 to become the next "prize moose on... the office wall"). This had not been a problem with the band arrangement post-1965. Then the Boy Wonder Genius would present his messengers with the fully arranged hits in the studio, all concocted whilst they were on tour. The Beach Boys had been two separate parts: Brian composing with his army of session musicians while Dennis, Carl, Mike, Al, and Bruce handled the job of being pop stars. Despite the assured song writing of Dennis and the fact that all the Beach Boys were now composing, this illusion still persisted with the Record Company, the fans, and even within the group itself. Their very foundations of its existence were written in stone and, in Dennis' words, this is how it was and always would be: "Brian Wilson is The Beach Boys. He *is* the band. We're his fucking messengers. He is all of it. Period. We're nothing. He's everything."

This doctrine, bound tighter by familial loyalty, had been the key to success in the past. The Rolls Royces, the groupies, the Bel Air mansions and the burgeoning drug habits all existed because of big brother Brian. He had been the one stable factor amidst everything else. The creator of hit singles. The link to past glories and, when considering their new contract, the predominant reason that they had a future. No-one would suggest that there was a future for the Beach Boys without Brian Wilson. Yet whether Brian had any sort of future as a Beach Boy remained unanswered.

Whether anyone was fully aware of the gravity of his mental state at this time is open to question. Marilyn Wilson saw only the "eccentric" in her husband's increasingly bizarre behaviour. Mike would blame the drugs, whilst Carl could only offer a perfunctory, "Brian's Brian, y'know?" In open denial of the situation, and still proclaiming Brian as their leader, the group members shifted naturally into opposition with each other. Mike and Carl would compete to be the leaders. The former as a turban-headed showman, keen to give the public the hits of old that they craved. Since the live arena was becoming more and more the source of their reputation and finances, his forceful influence was to increase as the years wore on. Given that Mike's motto had always been "DON'T FUCK WITH THE FORMULA" this would essentially mean the end of musical experimentation and replicating the hits of 1964 with a hint of his beloved TM. He might have whined about Capitol mis-management of the group ("How relevant was *that* [promotion as America's No. 1 Surfing Band] after "Good Vibrations", *Pet Sounds*, *Smiley Smile* or Vietnam and everything else?") but Mike's ideas and style remained consistently unfashionable. Still following the Maharishi long after the Beatles, and even Donovan, had exposed him for a charlatan, his concerns would predominantly be driven by money. Carl meanwhile had wrested control in the studio, becoming producer and generally trying to fill the void of

---

Brian's creative vision. He remained the holder of an exquisite voice but lacked the consistency of his brother's songwriting. Nevertheless he would quietly hold the group vision together, waiting behind the scenes in the hope of Brian recapturing his talent. Bruce and Al would provide album filler with a schmaltz or folk-orientated slant respectively. With the family at odds, missing their natural leader, no individual could stamp their identity on the collective whole or bring any sort of cohesion. And so the group would continue along these lines for the rest of the decade: fighting over direction and promising "Brian's Back" whenever their survival was in doubt.

The cover of *Sunflower*, their first LP for Warners, and rejected initially when entitled *Add Some Music To Your Day*, would show quite clearly the fractures that now existed within the band. Released in August 1970, the sleeve presented six individuals about ten million miles away from the regulated image of striped shirts and smiles. Surrounded by their children, Carl looks spaced, Brian lost, Mike a mad Bodhisattva, whilst Dennis just scowls. Only Bruce and Al – the non-family members – pose for the camera. The others sit staring at the floor or into the distance, either totally disinterested, or totally embarrassed. There was no focus at all. And this was supposed to be their *Sergeant Pepper*, according to Carl Wilson "the truest group effort we've ever had".

The finished album was actually drawn from the best tracks of *Add Some Music* and another collection entitled either *Reverberation* or, according to a tongue-in-cheek Bruce, *The Fading Rock Group Revival*. At this point the Beach Boys were recording almost continuously with engineer Stephen Desper and able to draw on the results for the next few records regardless of chronology. *The Fading Rock Group Revival* was to be a kiss-off to Capitol Records to terminate the band's contract – among its proposed ten tracks were "Breakaway", an acapella version of "The Lord's Prayer", Al's psychedelic "Loop De Loop", and Dennis' "Forever", which Bruce hinted might be the new Beach Boys single. As it was, the contract was fulfilled by the *Live In London 1969* LP.

Everyone, particularly at Warners, was praying for Brian to come up with the goods, but it was Dennis' songs that both dominated and carried the album. If adversity killed Brian's talent it seemed to make Dennis stronger. With the traumas wrought by divorce, drugs and Charlie Manson, he had been as close as anyone to the dark side of the Californian counter culture. In the song "Celebrate The News" – his final recording of the 1960s – he sounded happy just to be alive. Not in the sense of Brian's youthful optimism but of merely surviving and coming through the madness that had claimed several of his contemporaries. The repeated refrains "THERE'S BEEN A CHANGE" "I GOT NEWS FOR YOU, THERE AINT NO BLUES" "BAD LUCK NO MORE", multi-tracked against the orchestral swirl, come across like Lennon's primal scream therapy-speak. As if the singer is trying to convince not the audience of redemption, but himself. While Dennis' previous songs were shot through with Manson's paranoia the only feeling here was of elation as the drums finally dropped into the mix to beat out the message. Throw in a John Cale-style bass line too and you have to wonder just *who* Dennis was getting his

influences from at this time.

Flip the 45 over to the A-side and you got "Break Away", written by Brian and father Murry (under the pseudonym Reggie Dunbar) and originally a gift to be recorded by Three Dog Night. Reaching only number 63 it was one of the great lost singles of the 1960s, and one of the saddest. Despite a sublime and lifting melody it was a heartbreaking and articulate statement of where Brian was going: to drop out of the present and find happiness someplace else. The sentiments of *Pet Sounds* in a package that sounded like sheer jubilation.

"Celebrate The News" was a collaboration with Gregg Jakobson and, as previously, Dennis continued to work with musicians and associates away from the band. Whilst Mike, Al and Bruce – particularly Bruce – were keen to be writing in the style of Brian and utilising the Beach Boys vocal talents, Dennis was taking his own direction, in the band's name. According to Stanley Shapiro he had become obsessed with the raw sexuality of The Doors – "Break On Through", "Back Door Man", "Light My Fire" – and sought to emulate their lyrical themes. Though songs were credited to him alone he was working increasingly with either Gregg or Daryl Dragon. The latter was the son of former American bandleader, Carmen Dragon, and had been part of the touring band for several years. He was later to find fame as the Captain of the duo Captain and Tennille. Pretty much out of the running to be unofficial leader, the signs were already there that Dennis was moving towards the idea of a solo career, operating outside of his elder brother's influence. For the purposes of touring and getting his music released and out there he was still a Beach Boy.

Yet despite the quality of Dennis' new material the inclusion of his four songs on *Sunflower* happened more by default than design. According to Stephen Desper factors of time and finance were the deciding issues in using his material. This is what he told me: "Although Dennis prior to that [the release of *Sunflower*] had worked independently and recorded a whole bunch of songs, he selected a number that he wanted to submit to the Beach Boys to see if they would include them on *Sunflower*. At the time of course Brian was not participating very much and the whole project was steered creatively by Carl Wilson. The Beach Boys are an economically driven group in that they over record and always have a lot of stuff on tape and they have contractual commitments to meet. They have to pay their bills and their alimony and their child support and everything. At the time *Sunflower* was due and first submitted to Warner Brothers in one form – WW7 album – it was rejected and Warner Brothers felt that the Beach Boys' effort was not up to par so they sent them back to the studio for a few months to get new songs recorded before they'd even consider the album. In the meantime the band were not getting any income, they were under the gun to produce.

Dennis had a lot of these songs in the can already almost finished. So they started considering more and more these songs because they were almost ready and they could get this album out and get some income. So Dennis then began to work more hand in hand with Carl and he brought in the Beach Boys harmonies much more. That's why there's so many Dennis Wilson songs on *Sunflower* compared to everybody else".

But however they arrived there, Dennis' compositions on *Sunflower* were to push the boundaries of production still further from "Celebrate The News". His four tracks included on the final cut were an extraordinary leap forward for a band lacking direction, and pushed them into territories never experienced before. In terms of sophistication this would be the equal of the move from *Summer Days (And Summer Nights!!)* to *Pet Sounds*, though hardly recognised at the time. If Brian could teach the band "holy music" against their wishes then Dennis would kick their dragging heels to play his own hybrid soul music.

And this was definitely and defiantly soul music. Though *Sunflower* was their best collective effort and the most pleasing to its makers (proving that they *could* compose and produce without Brian), the non-Dennis tracks were on the whole little more than pastiche. With the exception of Brian's "This Whole World", a pretty and hyper-melodic two minute piece that ultimately said very little, and the *Smile* out-take "Cool Cool Water", there was little input from the rest of the group that rose above the category marked average. Al and Bruce veered towards the middle of the road whenever possible, whilst Mike stuck to his strengths as lyricist and singer, only appearing as co-creditor on three of the tracks. Worst offenders in the trite songwriting stakes had to be either Al's childlike (that's not a compliment) story of a Spanish-speaking sparrow landing on his sill in "At My Window", or Bruce's very straight and solid "Tears In The Morning" and "Deirdre". Brian was a collaborator on all these, though in Bruce's eyes deserved scant credit for his contribution. "He came up with two lines, that was it. He was suggesting things like, 'My friend Bob / He has a job', and I was saying 'No Brian'. I was kinda disappointed." Such observations could only be reinforced by lyrics such as "pretty things like incense and flowers, I want to make them part of our sweet love", and the entirety of *Add Some Music To Your Day* which sounded like a Pepsi commercial in the making. Some of the tracks not included, and responsible for the LP's original rejection, were even worse: the truly awful "Take A Load Off Your Feet" turning up on *Surfs Up* in 1971 and "Games Two Can Play" and "I've Just Got My Pay" surfacing on the *Good Vibrations* Box Set in 1993.

The Beach Boys were at a crossroads, unsure whether progression should be determined on their own terms or from the foundations laid by Brian. It was a quandary they would never satisfactorily conclude. When Roy Carr of *NME* talked to the band in 1972 Mike was quite open in declaring "we get up every morning and water the Brian Wilson myth" while confirming that a release of *Smile* was imminent. This was a position countered vehemently by Dennis. In his opinion, a belated release of Brian's masterwork would have been totally counter-productive[1]. Not only was it never finished but Brian had forgotten what the set order was. "The best things they had done had actually come out on *Smiley*

---

[1] When the other Beach Boys cajoled Brian into ressurrecting his sacred "Surf's Up" for inclusion on 1971's same-titled album, only Dennis stood against them.

Smile and those LPs after. There was too much baggage with *Smile*. People were expecting some kind of revelation like *Sergeant Pepper* and they would have been disappointed. He said that the only thing he could compare it with – but I don't want to compare it – was the Beatles reforming. It would never be the same because the original magic had been and gone. If it did come out then a certain part of the mythology would have gone."

The appearance of the brilliant "I Like To Say Da Da" under the new title "Cool Cool Water" from the glory days of 1967 only highlighted the whole sad situation. The renowned studio perfectionist who pushed his band through nine months of rehearsals during the creation of "Good Vibrations" was now unable or unwilling to recognise the sublime from the ridiculous. Whilst his contemporaries Lennon and McCartney had split The Beatles at their zenith and emerged as solo performers with complete artistic control, here was poor Brian Wilson, still forced to play music at the beck and call of others. All in the hope of creating marketable product with that sunny Californian sound. Fun, Fun, Fun. Dennis summed up the whole ludicrous situation when lamenting "the attitude of a few mental dinosaurs intent on exploiting our initial success". "If The Beatles had suffered this kind of misrepresentation, they would never have got past singing 'Please Please Me' and 'I Wanna Hold Your Hand' and jumping around in Beatle suits."

The control, emotion, and joyful exuberance that emanated from the opening track "Slip On Through" had suggested so much more. If Brian had attempted to change public perceptions of the band during the middle '60s then Dennis was creating work that sounded like a different band éntirely. With the introduction of a few short bass notes the song progressed with short stabs of guitar and horns against a beat funkier than a Beach Boys record deserved to be. The production was crisp and the sound defiant. "Lots of people with no place to go / I know a place where you can go / You've got the ticket, come on slip inside / And let my song take you for a ride." This was a wake-up call for anyone who doubted Dennis' talent. By the song's conclusion, when the chorus builds for last time and he's tearing into the line "Oh can't you see what has come over me", sounding so justified against the backing mantra of "Believe... Believe", it is like the passing of musical knowledge from brother to brother. Brian had tapped a deep melodic soul but always through the thoughts and interpretations of others. His dream was expressed through musical feelings while lyrics were usually left to someone else. He never sounded this alive, this real or this funky, and that was probably the prime difference behind the two brothers. Dennis may have lived a life of excess but he sang from experience; Brian mostly created through the lives of others.

In much the same groove was "It's About Time", another triumphant song of self-recognition. Howling in on the introduction of a pounding bass motif combined with soaring strings (sounding for all the world like a John Barry spy theme recorded underwater) this was probably Dennis' greatest collaboration within the group and one of Carl's most powerful lead vocals. The track was underpinned by two different drum tracks courtesy of Daryl Dragon's brother Dennis – a solid James Brown backbeat and intricate percussive patterns. The driving uncluttered result reflected Dennis' love of jazz drummers such as Gene Krupa. With engineering genius Stephen Desper at the helm the Beach Boys were always keen to promote their mastery of studio technology, and the sleeve notes to *Sunflower* boasted, almost comically, the use of the "latest model Neumann computer-controlled mastering lathe, equipped with a Neumann SX-68 helium-cooled, dynamic feedback cutterhead". Whatever that was, it must have been in evidence on this track, such was the mastery of its production and content. The lyrics yet again dealt with the simple joy and consciousness of being alive while reflecting on events of recent history. The autobiographical opening verse confirmed the shift in Dennis' character from the one-dimensional hedonist of the early 1960s to the more humble (though no less hedonistic) musical genius of this new decade. If Dennis could sometimes have trouble expressing himself on record then "It's About Time" read like nothing less than a statement of intent and belief in his own ability:

"I used to be a famous artist proud as I could be / Struggling to express myself for the whole world to see/ I used to blow my mind sky high, searching for the lost elation / Little did I know the joy I was to find in knowing I am only me."

After hitting another mantra-like chorus ("I'm singing in my heart") the music dropped out to reveal the complex rhythm of conga drums underlying the whole track like a bubblegum Sly Stone. This again was beyond anything that Brian or the rest of the band had ever worked on. The prominent use of the Moog synthesizer and the possibilities this new instrument gave to the recording process highlighted Dennis' more avant-garde tendencies. "What I want to do," he revealed at the time, "is instead of renting a bell for $10, to try and get the bell sound with the Moog – or the sound of a snail crawling, or the noise a liver would make inside an alcoholic. But it takes time. I've only been at it a year." Stevie Wonder's groundbreaking use of proto-synthesizers on albums like *Music Of My Mind* and *Talking Book* has been well documented by pop historians, but Dennis and Carl Wilson were both proponents of this new technology back in 1970.

By the second verse and subsequent chorus the words were spilling out of Carl's mouth like a man possessed and the message of unity ("Serving out a love for everyone I meet in truth who are really me") was almost incomprehensible in the stream-of-consciousness flow. This was a rush of pure pop music and conviction far beyond the stylised emotions of the other album cuts. Whilst they attempted to copy Brian this was Dennis Wilson in essence. The final coda began with a one note bass line and a stuttering rap, as female gospel vocals threaded in and out of the mix. At the conclusion a heavily effected guitar solo was wandering all over the place and the youngest Wilson just screams "Lord Lord Lord Lord Lord Lord Lord Lord Lord" until the fade out. Like Iggy's cry of "Brother" in "TV Eye" or Lou Reed's laconic "It was alright" before the climax in "Rock N Roll" this was one of those transcendental moments in rock music, where words cannot express the feelings of the music. It was an extraordinary song, not unlike the unreleased pieces from *Smile* in its pieced-together construction but way beyond them in its emotional execution. While that album was still-born and numbed out in a marijuana haze, Dennis was singing and writing like his life depended on it.

"It's About Time" remained part of the Beach Boys live set for only two years – usually as the encore or set-closer. Domenic Priore (one of the few writers who has treated Dennis' latent talent with anything like the respect it deserves), described the crowd's reaction to its performance on the televised "Good Vibration From Central Park" concert in 1971 as "absolutely astounding". The supposed finale of "I Get Around", the sound that the band should have been working away from, the sound that Mike Love considered to be revolutionary ("I've got to find a new place where the kids are hip") held no comparison. Not that Dennis would ever become the dominant songwriter in the band. In reality he was being pushed to the periphery, to places where a Beach Boy was not supposed to go. The neglect of his talent that dogged his career would continue even after his death – the *Good Vibrations* box set of 1993 that covered some 142 tracks, centred almost entirely on Brian and allocated only 5 to Dennis. When considering the sub-standard material Brian churned out consistently since 1971, without a hint of his former greatness, this was a pretty absurd situation.

If any parallel can be drawn with Dennis' creative development and the constraints made upon it, the best comparison was away from California in Detroit, where Marvin Gaye was developing a style away from the formulaic Motown sound. Akin to The Beach Boys' relationship with Brian Wilson, the acts signed to Berry Gordy's empire were treated as little more than messengers for the songwriting teams of Hollier-Dozier-Holland or Smokey Robinson. As Mo Ostin and Mike Love wanted a "California Girls" or an "I Get Around" six years later, so the management at Motown wanted Gaye to be singing "I Heard It Through The Grapevine" and acting out the fantasy of his sex symbol image – in short, to deny the creative urge and continue giving the public what they supposedly wanted and recognised. Of course Gaye went on to create the masterpieces *What's Going On* and *Let's Get It On*, adding the sophistication of jazz arrangements with social and sexual commentary to Motown's oeuvre. (Ironically, sex and environmentalism were also to be the prevailing themes for the remainder of Dennis' work, though with the emphasis quite candidly on the former). The total honesty in Gaye's work – from his use of the voice as an instrument, to his subject matters (the sleeve notes on *Let's Get It On*, quoting T.S. Eliot's "Birth and copulation and death, that's all the facts when you get to brass tacks" hardly pussyfooted around the subject), to the LP *Here, Here My Dear* that was an open invitation to view the dirty laundry of his divorce from Anna Gordy – all draw striking similarities with the way Dennis projected himself.

He too was a soul singer in frustration (and by that I mean he sang from the heart on the instinct of his feeling) able to conjure moods through a combination of intense orchestration and the power of his wracked voice. Mike Love may have claimed that his cousin was "not verbally facile" yet the sheer emotion and belief he gave out overcame any shortcomings in his lyrics. Like Marvin, Dennis made records that said "Let's Get It On", or "I Love You" or "I Want To Spend My Life With You" and it sounded like he meant it. He did not fuck around with the message. That was the power of pop music (of Elvis singing "Heartbreak Hotel" or Aretha singing "Respect") as opposed to the self-indulgent whines of the rock musicians up in the Canyon, too cynical and knowing to actually relate human feeling. In another dig, his cousin would assert that "the one thing you must understand about Dennis is that Dennis does not understand". And yet that was the whole point. This was music that came from within. Dennis told the truth via his music and it gave you the whole man, flaws and all. He was a contradictory character, who could cheat on his wife and then write declarations of love that verged on the obsessive. Songs became a vehicle to communicate his innermost feelings and pent-up desires.

This was certainly true of his other compositions on the *Sunflower* album and on those that were excluded from the project. "Got To Know The Woman" was a more throwaway straight-ahead rocker that dealt with lust for a groupie but never took itself too seriously. Midway through describing how his woman was going to make a man out of him, Dennis starts collapsing with laughter. Underneath the honky-tonk piano ran a strange psychedelic bassline like the electric jug in Roky Erikson's Thirteenth Floor Elevators. A positive horny blast, it was a companion piece to "All I Want To Do" from *20/20*. The line "I just met a woman on my way home, she just blew my mind" may or may not have concerned the picking up of Manson followers Patricia Krenwinkel and Ella Jo Bailey in 1968. Backing vocals were supplied by Julia Tillman, Carolyn Willis and Edna Wright.

"Forever", another collaboration with Gregg Jakobson, and a gift to his second wife Barbara Charren, was to become arguably Dennis' most famous song. Mournful, evocative and sensitive, it remained his party piece in the Beach Boys live set over the next few years. This simple and touching ballad with an opening line – "If every word I said could make you laugh, I'd talk forever" – that could have been just *too* sugary if not for the yearning voice that sang it, offered us another side to Dennis. The devoted husband. The spectre of Charles Manson, the discovery of LSD and the decline in Brian's health had been important factors in Dennis' song writing development, and the stability that marriage brought in April 1970 was another no less crucial one. The security of their union fed Dennis' newfound optimism and Barbara became a figure of worship he could relate his songs around.

He met her in the summer of 1969 when she was 23 and working for the Hamburger Hamlet. A year later they were married in Hawaii – their first son Michael was born in February 1971. While Dennis' immaturity had wrecked his first marriage Barbara gave him a sense of stability lacking since childhood. He had grown considerably in the last few years, and his songs reflected this with their grace and maturity. (In comparison Brian was unable to enjoy a healthy adult relationship with

Marilyn Rovell, the girl he had married at 16 and was now almost dependent on to mother him).

For so many of the people in his life, it was Dennis' contradictions and sense of the unexpected that made him so attractive. The constant friction between the soulful lover and the macho rock star would cement his appeal between both sexes and direct his life any which way. The loves of his youth ("I was into carburettors, cars, peeling out, cruising, A/W root beers. I was also into tit, nipples, dirty pictures – I loved dirty pictures, magazines, Tijuana, surfboards on top of the car. Even if I wasn't going surfing that day, I'd put 'em up there anyway. Anything to do with that – with having fun") sat side by side with romanticism and devotion. Seemingly he was unable to disconnect the spiritual from the earthly. Murry could be a monster one moment and soothed to tears by the sound of music the next, and Dennis too was capable of acting on impulse in two different directions. Barbara and Karen Lamm (his third *and* fourth wife) were to comment that marriage to Dennis was a maelstrom – perfect at first with the "crash landing" coming later. Yet both, despite being put through the extremes of his behaviour, would hold few grudges and look back with something resembling fondness: "Dennis taught me that you treat a person in the gutter the same way that you treat people in the White House," reflected Karen. "He was the same with everybody... I had a great three-year stint. The other five years I got my butt kicked!"

When the band appeared on a David Frost's US chat show in 1971 it was not "Forever" that they played but another Dennis composition, "Fallin' In Love" (along with a hilarious version of "Vege-Tables"). Finally recorded solo as "Lady", "Fallin' In Love" (introduced bashfully on film by its writer as "for my beautiful wife, she's an... inspiration") was a hymn to their marriage. "Flowers come in the Spring / All the love I can bring / I bring it for my Lady." The "Moon In June" lyrics were hardly inspired, but took on deeply personal sense with Dennis' yearning vocal. His image may have been the swaggering dumb cocksman (the formation of "The Golden Penetrators", a men-only club whose other members were Gregg Jakobson and Terry Melcher, and his notoriety for affairs on the road saw to that) but these were open love letters to his wife. The period 1970–71 saw Dennis writing a succession of these ballads; their innocence and contentment in distinct contrast to the brooding and dark voice he would reveal later in the decade. "All Of My Love", "I've Got A Friend", and more obviously "Barbara", also came under this banner. Unreleased, until its inclusion in demo form on *Endless Harmony*, the latter was a virtual studio-jam between Dennis and Daryl Dragon. Their intertwining piano lines apparently acting out ideas for potential string sections whilst the actual song was another child-like and personal ode to love. "Everyday is a special day for me living with you, just being with you. My love, for all my life. I love to sing songs just for you." Musically reminiscent of "Imagine", the reading of the song was reverential and the final bridge quite beautiful. The effect was akin to eavesdropping on an intimate lover's conversation.

Perhaps Dennis' most audacious move musically at this time was

---

the release in December 1970 of the single "Sound Of Free". Another collaboration with Daryl Dragon (with Mike Love, of all people, getting a co-credit for lyrical assistance), and released under the name Dennis Wilson And Rumbo, for the first time he showed the will to promote his talents alone. *Pet Sounds* may arguably have been a solo Brian Wilson record, (certainly the single "Caroline No" appeared under his name only), and Dennis had collaborated with Gary Usher on the Four Speeds side project, but "Sound Of Free" signified the biggest challenge yet to Brian's dominance over the band. As with his contributions to *Sunflower*, Dennis was again breaking away from the sunny but constricting themes of Beach Boy records to create a sound that was as modern as it was personal. Recording with such spontaneity, for the first time an entire solo project was planned. At his physical, and arguably musical peak, stardom in his own right surely would have beckoned[2].

In the vein of "Slip On Through" or "It's About Time" the A-side was another one of Dennis' upbeat classics with an almost religious zeal to its message. "Children of light in darkness all around. Born without sight and shackled to the ground. Drawn always toward the sound of free." Almost gospel or hymnal ("The mountains are high, the valleys are low. I know the way through...") the exuberant vocal on the pay-off line "Come Baby listen to me, I'll whisper the sound of free" suggested some sort of higher knowledge. As a pure pop single, without cynicism or wastage it was a promising start to test the waters. The production, from an underlying harpsichord to the fuzz guitar on the fade out, together with the stop/start construction that segmented the song, highlighted Dennis' advances in the studio. Another passing of the musical torch between himself and Brian.

The song was backed by the version of "Lady" that had failed to make the final cut of *Sunflower*. Performed as an acoustic strum on the David Frost show, the song was now a mini-symphony. (From the fragments left behind, we can only guess how Dennis' other recordings from this era would have sounded given his obsession of drenching the finished product with strings.) While the opening lines were sung acappella to a drum machine (another pioneering act) with the voice mixed claustrophobically to the fore, the sound expanded in one sweep to a full orchestra. A real sense of melancholy ran through the entire song despite its subject matter.

The reasons why this single alone was released, and why it was only released in Europe and later Australasia on the subsidiary label Stateside, still remain unclear. Public reaction to the band in Europe and the UK since 1966 was probably paramount. In the words of Dennis' co-writer Daryl Dragon, "The bottom line is: Europe is more evolved, more sensitive, and more romantically aware. Period." Since *Pet Sounds* the band had always garnered serious interest in the UK, their changes in direction followed with rabid enthusiasm. While *Sunflower* garnered little

---

[2] Bruce Johnston at least seemed to have recognised this – remarking in interview on his own future plans to record unilaterally that "Dennis Wilson's solo album would prove far more commercial in its appeal than mine".

---

interest with US record buyers the UK press was hailing it as the Beach Boys' answer to *Sergeant Pepper*. To Dennis, who wrote the bulk of that LP's material, this must have seemed the perfect market place to gain artistic credibility and recognition. In addition was the plain fact that, in the new democratic-style Beach Boys, Dennis was writing songs at a greater rate and of greater quality than anyone else. If all six members, with their frightening egos and conflicting tastes, demanded representation on their collective finished product then there was simply no room for the amount of material he had. This certainly explains the addition of "Lady" as the B-side.

Indeed, a *Melody Maker* article from September 15th 1971 under the headline "A Beach Boy Says: 'I'll Never Tour Again'" did more than suggest a solo project. Interviewed after pulling his songs from the *Surfs Up* project and in the wake of ditching live commitments (à la Brian) in the wake of an argument with Carl, Dennis was his usual candid self when talking to journalist Al Aronowitz. "I have a belief in my music. And it sounds nothing like it should on the album – it should have a flow on it from one song to another. Well it didn't, it didn't sound like the Beach Boys. They thought it did. I said 'Bullshit' and pulled my songs off." After criticising the price of concert tickets ("I wanna stay close to the people") Dennis revealed he was looking forward to returning home and recording with Daryl Dragon. "...we're partners, he's my buddy... his whole being is connected with playing the piano. We're going to work together, aside from what we do in the Beach Boys. We almost have a full album recorded already." This proposed venture was confirmed by the band's recording engineer, Stephen Desper, who claimed "90% of it was 90% done". The working titles *Hubba Hubba* or *Poops* were light-heartedly considered for use.

Had the project reached completion then most likely it would have been recorded in 3D. This technique, utilising a matrix now called a "Spatializer" was pioneered through the efforts of Stephen Desper using Dennis and Daryl as his guinea pigs. So-called "Quad Symphonies" – essentially the two artists jamming together – have appeared in recent years on various bootlegs but these were not designs for future material. Reciprocating the long hours put in behind the desk Dennis had merely sanctioned the use of these musings and some of his other songs to further Desper's sound research. This was sometimes in a spirit of generosity rather than progress, as according to the erstwhile engineer, he had to "practically pull every note out of [Dennis'] gut", while the donation of "Barbara" towards the same ends was submitted only when Dennis was bored working on it. "'Barbara' was just an old track that Dennis let me use to demonstrate Quad recording techniques. He had already OD'd on the production and had lost interest in finishing the song. The piano segments were recorded live for the paper only and were as far as Dennis got in the writing." After *Sunflower* every Beach Boys LP would be encoded with this process, though only a version of "Loop De Loop" on the *Endless Harmony* compilation and a coupe of tracks on the re-issued *Ultimate Christmas* would end up released in 3D sound.

The "Sound Of Free" single was a good indicator of what could have been expected (uplifting pop one side and string-propelled ballad the other), though Dennis' prolificity ran far beyond the few tracks that did see the light of day. According to Desper, Dennis, like Brian, would over-record in the studio, discarding tracks at the rate of three to one. For the time being though Dennis returned to the fold and the tracks remained unreleased or were donated to Beach Boy albums over the next few years. The single "Sound Of Free" remained a testament to what might have been.[3]

Any decision to work solo would have reflected those of '60s contemporaries like The Byrds or Buffalo Springfield, who were now operating either as individuals or creating music far removed from that which made them initially famous. Like The Beach Boys, most of these bands had peaked commercially in the late-mid '60s and were now searching for new styles for the audiences who had grown with them. With his propensity for drugs and rock'n'roll, the free-spirited and liberally minded Dennis was already a strange bedfellow for a band with predominantly conservative instincts. His rough and cracked voice, his lifestyle, (even his haircut) were way out of synch with the traditional Beach Boy sound and image. This was ironic since, with his sense of adventure and preparedness to take risks, he provided the closet thing they had to the spirit of Brian. Certainly he recognised in himself the spirituality of Brian's music and underplayed his own contributions, in genuine awe of what his eldest brother had achieved – "...look around you, he's everywhere," he commented in 1970 when asked about Brian's whereabouts. And while they too hailed the proven talents of Brian they were less quick to acknowledge Dennis' work. "(He's) into strings and things. He wants to do classical things," commented Mike with typical faint praise in 1972. As with *Pet Sounds* and *Smile* there was a lack of empathy with anything that did not fit the typecast or produce instant hit singles. It was surely no coincidence however that Dennis brought out the best in Mike or Al or Carl when they did collaborate together. His songs that were the epitome of soul and passion had become instantly distinguishable from their more anaemic efforts.

Melody Maker was the only UK publication to pick up on "Sound Of Free", though even then it seemed something of an anomaly. The review on December 19th 1970 stated that the single was interesting primarily because it was the first solo release by a Beach Boy (a fact in ignorance of 1966's "Caroline No" which appeared under the name of Brian Wilson) and the mystery surrounding the name Rumbo. In typical late '60s lexicon the critique offered was hardly strong in any direction – "Absorbing because of the swinging beat and fascinating vocal textures" but equally lacking hit potential since "it doesn't have a memorable melody line". The reviewer did concede however that this was a

---

[3] For instance the Wilson-Jakobson number "San Miguel", penned in 1969. Describing a trip down to Mexico looking for the ladies of love' it was one of Dennis' favourite numbers according to Fred Vail. Though he considered the song to have hit potential it only made the final cut of the rejected *Landlocked* LP – finally seeing the light of day officially on the 1993 box set.

"worthwhile debut from Dennis". Given the low key nature of its release "Sound Of Free" would have been some consolation to its maker and further proof of a vision and creativity beyond the Beach Boys.

1970 would also see Dennis create even more distance between him and his band members. Film director Monte Hellman was casting for another actor to join James Taylor in his new road movie, to be called *Two-Lane Blacktop*. Despite a lack of acting experience, Dennis' audition for this sought-after part was successful and he was given the part of "The Mechanic". From drummer to songwriter, he was now going to be a movie star.

NO SPEED LIMIT

"He never sold out. Sometimes he never sold at all."
—Harry Dean Stanton on Monte Hellman,
director of *Two-Lane Blacktop*

"Dennis Wilson's two songs are both delivered in an irritating nervous tremolo which isn't at all helped by Brian's big-toned symphonic accompaniment to his troubled brother's heavy-handed lyrics and rudimentary piano playing. The more trite and tortured the lyrics, the louder the strings become, until both 'Make It Good' and 'Cuddle Up' are swallowed up in a lugubrious Mahleresque crescendo."
—*Rolling Stone* gets it wrong on several counts
in June 1972 – *So Tough* review

*"A pity that Dennis Wilson is missing. He's been coming into his own ever since 'Little Bird' on **Friends**, and on the last few LPs he's been making music that has all the Wilson talent without the Wilson psychosis. Perhaps it was only Warner Brother's promotional machine that made this a hit – or maybe it's a question of 'Vive La Difference'".*
–While *Creem* gets it right –
Surf's Up review from December 1971

Returning to Hollywood from a trip to Italy in 1970 Monte Hellman, the "Great American Auteur" and should-have-been-feted film director, was introduced by his agent Mike Medavoy to producer Michael Laughlin. Hellman had not directed a feature for nearly three years, but Laughlin had two scripts in the pipeline he might be interested working on: *The Christian Licorice Store* and *Two-Lane Blacktop*. The former was an unlikely tale concerning the search for the meaning of life of a Hollywood tennis player. The latter, written by character actor Will Cory in 1968, was the tale of a cross-country race between two 17-year old kids: one black, one white; one driving a '55 Chevy, the other a souped-up Pontiac GTO. In the wake of *Easy Rider*, the movie that dragged the counter culture to the big screen and the mainstream – in addition to starring his long-time friend Jack Nicholson – Hellman chose to make the road movie[1]. In the golden age of modern Hollywood it was to become one of the most-hyped but little seen flicks of the era.

Hellman himself had a background in filmmaking little different to the other great directors of the 1970s. A student of schlock master

---

[1] Hellman would however play a small cameo role in *The Christian Licorice Store*, which was eventually directed by James Frawley and starred Beau Bridges.

Roger Corman his first picture was a 1959 B-Movie creature-feature *Beast From Haunted Cave*. Work on *The Wild Ride* followed a year later and in 1963 he worked as one of five directors, the others included Francis Ford Coppola and Jack Nicholson, on Corman's *The Terror*. Shot over a weekend when Corman's main picture *The Raven* finished slightly ahead of schedule, with its star Boris Karloff owing a couple of days extra work, the result was a triumph for inspiration and resourcefulness over budget. Despite a destiny as drive-in fodder, *The Terror* contained scenes of striking tranquillity and imagination that belied the hurriedness of its execution. In 1965 Hellman travelled to the Philippines, again with Nicholson, to make *Back Door To Hell* and *Flight To Fury*.

Thus enlightened in the process of making film on the hop, Hellman would take these experiences onboard and further them with his next pictures *Ride In The Whirlwind* and *The Shooting*. Shot concurrently to save money in 1966 these westerns were the making of his reputation – though in Europe and France rather than the US, since both films were incarcerated for three years after his studio went bankrupt. Subversive and existential, both movies – and *The Shooting* in particular – were genuine classics of the genre. Both starred Jack Nicholson, who also scripted *Whirlwind*, but in vastly differing roles. The former was a tale of innocent men gone bad when they are mistaken and hunted down as stagecoach robbers while the latter, and more interesting of the two films, had an embittered Millie Perkins dragging a cowboy and a bounty hunter through the desert to an allegorical hell. In common with *Two-Lane Blacktop* both would feature the Hellman trademark of a bizarre, unresolved and open-ended conclusion. Throughout the 1970s he would successfully utilise this combination of arid humour and unreserved bleakness.

Among the other players involved were Harry Dean Stanton and Warren Oates, who would both feature prominently in future Hellman projects. Indeed Oates, a brilliant but unsung character actor, despite decent roles in several Peckinpah movies[2] and playing the title role in John Milius' *Dillinger* in 1973, would feature in all Hellman's subsequent directions[3].

With his films locked away, Monte Hellman's future as a director would remain on ice until receiving Cory's script. Eager Parisians might have queued around the block to see his westerns but in 1969 his career had seemingly stalled. Back home nobody could see his films and he busied himself with other people's projects, including The Monkees' *Head* in 1968. *Two-Lane Blacktop* offered a perfect opportunity to rectify this situation.

The years of 1970 and 1971 also promised a watershed for the

---

[2] Most famously in *The Wild Bunch* (1969) as Lyle Gorch. He would later star in Peckinpah's macabre road-to-hell movie *Bring Me The Head Of Alfredo Garcia* (1974).

[3] "Definitely one of the greatest actor-director teamings of that period. It's definitely on par with Scorsese and De Niro." (Dennis Bartock, *American Cinematique*).

career of Dennis Wilson. With the inclusion of his songs on *Sunflower*, talk of a solo record and the actual release of the "Sound Of Free" he had achieved a degree of autonomy hitherto unknown within the band. Put down upon for so long Dennis was eager to seize the moment and consolidate this position. When the notion of appearing in *Blacktop* was thrown up it seemed the ideal opportunity to flex his competitive muscles further. The decision to travel to Burbank to screen test for the part of The Mechanic was not taken without forethought – this was a chance to work with an emerging director in a genre that was becoming a dominant movie type. The decision was not accidental. Fred Vail remembers driving to Dennis to the studio and his excitement at the prospect – "I can remember Denny being nervous and worrying if he'd do wrong or if he'd do right or if he'd blow it. He was almost thinking about turning around and going back".

Hellman had been auditioning for the role for some time now. In actual fact he had seen and rejected literally hundreds of potential candidates. With four days until shooting commenced he was already pushed to testing the abilities of local garage attendants. The other major parts had already been filled: the faithful Warren Oates as GTO, an unknown seventeen-year-old, Laurie Bird, as The Girl and James Taylor taking the part of The Driver. Taylor had been enlisted after the director saw his face on a billboard advertising the album *Sweet Baby James*. Recovering from a heroin addiction that had blighted his time on Apple Records Taylor's star was now in the ascendant, and he was stepping out with Joni Mitchell.

Dennis was offered the chance to play The Mechanic after the shortest of auditions – he had no experience per se but Hellman, always keeping an eye out for the extraordinary, noted other qualities: "Dennis is the only actor I've ever worked with who completely forgets he's on camera. A couple of times he just laughs because he was just caught up in the scene. Totally natural. Just amazing." Yet, even more immediately relevant to a director obsessed with realism was Dennis' car-crazed youth – "he had lived the part, taking apart autos and putting them back together." Hellman recently stated: "I think just that he had lived that role, that he really grew up with cars. It was almost as though he were born with a greasy rag in his back pocket." In short, there seemed little point employing an "actor" when you could have the real thing.

By the time filming began in the early autumn of 1970 the script had undergone a major re-working. Cory's basic plot line needed greater depth and so the help of Rudy Wurlitzer was enlisted. Fresh from the success of his surrealistic 1969 publication *Nog* (lauded by Thomas Pynchon with "The novel of bullshit is dead") Wurlitzer was a darling of America's literary underground. Having this one renowned "road novel" under his belt, but no great knowledge of car culture – "I didn't know a car from a cow" – he embarked on a short road trip with Philip Glass, then a plumber rather than composer. The trip resulted in a considerable degree of metamorphosis for *Two-Lane Blacktop* with the creation of GTO, the film's prominent character, and some sharp dialogue. The central precepts of a cross-country automobile duel for "pink slips" remained, but Wurlitzer had twisted the story line around Hellman's desire to portray an overwhelming loneliness. GTO, the aimless fantasist so brilliantly portrayed by Oates, was akin to the nameless narrator of *Nog* as his character transformed itself chameleon-like with every roadside encounter. The buzz surrounding the project was enough for *Esquire* magazine to name *Two-Lane Blacktop* their film of the year before it was even completed, while the script was described as "the most brilliant and idiosyncratic" to come out of Hollywood that year. So good in fact that the entire screenplay was published in their edition of April 1970.

This was one of the factors behind Universal Pictures' decision to plough $900,000 into making the film. Though not a great sum it was considerably more than the $75,000 used to make *both* Hellman's Westerns back in 1967. More important to the director though was the levy on artistic freedom, which was tipped 100% in his favour. Along with Milos Forman's *Taking Off*, Peter Fonda's *Hired Hand* and Dennis Hopper's *The Last Movie* he was a beneficiary of Universal's Youth Division, set up in 1969 and run under the stewardship of Ned Tanen. Sensing they could be riding the same successful path as Captain America and Billy only a year before, the studio left Hellman pretty much to his own devices to produce what they thought would be *Easy Rider II*. "Contractually, they said they would not touch a frame of the film as long as it was under two hours. We didn't have any of the usual problems of a studio coming in and saying to cut out this or add that. We were left completely alone during the shooting and editing. Even producer Michael Laughlin, who was very supportive, did not come on location." This was a scenario indicative of Hollywood at the time: the barriers momentarily lifted, as they had been for pop music between 1966 and 1967, in what had previously been a predominantly conservative industry. According to Tanen it was a frightening time for the ageing studio heads: "They looked at a movie like *Easy Rider*, and they said, 'What in the hell is this?' It's against everything they thought was a value in this country; they were still worshipping the grand ol' flag. But suddenly they were looking at these movies where everyone was dropping acid, was fucking in the park. Even I, who was much younger, didn't know who was a star any more."

The establishment stepped aside to usher in the mavericks and the business of making movies changed nearly over night. The Director gained equal billing to their stars. And while these freedoms and benevolences were due to a generational gap as much as anything else (Tanen again – "They viewed *them* [the "New Hollywood" Directors] with absolute dread. It was like they wanted to send them to a concentration camp. But the studio left them alone because they thought they'd screw up if they interfered, and the movies didn't cost anything") they were freedoms nonetheless. This was a point conceded by Hellman over twenty-five years after his film's untimely demise: "They really wanted to let us make the movie we wanted to make. They hated the movie after it was made, but even after they hated the movie, they didn't try to change it."

For Hellman, realism and existentialism were everything – his maxim, ingrained from the '60s, was, "Whatever you do is right." Far from being the action-packed adventure proclaimed by the trailer and movie poster ("Their world is a Two-Lane Blacktop... No Beginning... No End... No Speed Limit!") his vision was an open-ended trip populated by characters as lost and directionless as the times. Distinct from other road movies of the era in that it did not refer directly to the counter culture, he portrayed a journey around the numb backwaters of America's Southwest. To these ends tactics and methods were employed that exemplified nihilistic feelings of the ordinary. Filming was undertaken chronologically and on location from California to New Mexico through Santa Fe to Oklahoma in direct correlation to the actual journey. Oates, one of the few professional actors on the set, was the only player to see the script in its entirety while Dennis, James and Laurie were fed the action day by day. The intention was for the story to unravel naturally and for the occupants of the Chevy to build relationships naturally, as they would had the cameras not been present. (As in life, who knows what comes tomorrow?) The majority of characters encountered along the way were portrayed in their actual jobs in their actual workplaces. Certain segments, particularly at the race meets or when Laurie Bird wanders around Santa Fe, took on a documentary feel as the actors blended in with genuine members of the public unaware they were being filmed.

The emphasis on improvisation and Hellman's desire, as a self-confessed control freak, to recreate normality with this combination of professional and virgin actors evidently pleased some more than others. For James Taylor the experience was a nightmare – he detested playing a part in someone else's grand design and at one point refused to continue until Hellman relented with the script and showed him the whole thing. Holing himself up with Joni and a guitar for much of the shoot he had still not seen *Two-Lane* in 1973, the very thought of it dredging up bad memories: "Monte really wanted to control us without letting us be creative in ourselves. He wanted to use us. I think rather like John Ford used John Wayne. Ford did the best stuff with Wayne. But Hellman was into using us. So that by then time the movie was started, with no acting experience I was totally dependent him for any sort of training or any sort of suggestions that he might give me. I needed him so totally but he never, ever tried to talk to me on a personal basis. He's the most incommunicative cat I've ever met. It was excruciating."

The seemingly one-dimensional persona to all characters aside from GTO ensured that Dennis too was not beyond disillusionment. Required to say nothing that did not include monosyllabic references to "the points", "the valves", "the jets" and "the carbs" his role was spent mostly under the hood. Long days on set, unhealthy hours and regimentation were all too familiar to someone who had recently announced a wish to follow Brian's lead away from the monotony of the road into the permanence of the studio. Journalist Shelley Benoit, who spent several days on set for a piece in *Show* magazine, noted that Dennis had a cocktail piano moved into his room, while between sets he organised shooting competitions with the crew after picking up an old BB gun – "His energy is continuous, astonishing. He will not tolerate a void." A *Rolling Stone* article from October – which like *Esquire* claimed the film would be an "instant classic" – showed pictures of Dennis horsing around on a kid's mini motor bike, pulling wheelies to relieve the tedium. When the interviewer mentioned all those great Beach Boys car tracks he became increasingly pissed-off, bemoaning the fact that the musical score, including the Doors' *Moonlight Drive* and Kris Kristofferson's *Me And Bobby McGee*, was not contemporary enough: "They're using all existing music which bores the shit out of me. They ought to use something with a Moog, something you can get into." Like Taylor he seemed to drift through the whole alien experience unsure of the how it would result, and when interviewed by David Frost in 1971 Dennis too had not seen the finished movie.

But unlike Taylor, Dennis did try and concede to Hellman's ideas. While his co-star had gone cold on the idea of filmmaking, even before shooting began, and sauntered around hunched and scowling, Dennis proved at least adept at improvisation. This was well highlighted by the final cut. The interplay between the three non-actors remained stifled and uncomfortable, befitting that of strangers cooped up on the road, but at times Dennis seemed to lose himself in the action – momentarily forgetting that his actions were destined to appear on cinema screens. Hired primarily on aesthetic appeal, his unaffected nature – the odd wry smirk or intent stare – transcended many of the scenes. This desire to immerse himself in the process was noted by Harry Dean Stanton who had a small cameo role as a gay cowboy hitchhiker: "He [Dennis] talked about how the actors and everybody should change during the making of a film. That it's another part of your life. I was impressed with his perception of that."

Ultimately though, Hellman's wish was to portray a sterile emotionless America. The Driver, The Mechanic and The Girl as reflections of the desolate post-60s fall-out were only vehicles to portray a message. Here we are, three years after the Summer Of Love, and nothing but conservatism reigns. Like the pre-Watergate characters in Ang Lee's *The Ice Storm* these were individuals living in a vacuum, unable to express feeling or to even communicate with each other. The heart of the film was perhaps best exemplified by the hippy who is Oates' penultimate passenger, cutting short his bullshit monologue with the words "It doesn't matter" before it's even begun. The race, the competition, the relationships, were all without apparent meaning – heading towards an extraordinary conclusion where the actual film seemed to catch in the camera grate and ignite. Not one issue had been tied up: GTO was still living out his dreams, the Chevy was still racing and The Girl was still hitching to nowhere. *Two-Lane Blacktop* remains one of the bleakest cinematic depictions of the era.

Certainly it was vastly different to the panoramic beauty of *Easy Rider* or the action-packed vistas of *Vanishing Point*. Mostly nocturnal, wet and mute, Hellman dealt in confounding expectations not meeting them. The meaning was in the void, since the action itself was meaningless. The use of two cool high-profile rock'n'rollers acting so ordinarily was all part of this ploy. There was no glamour or notion of celebrity in any of the roles with the exception of the film's true star: Warren Oates. He alone provided warmth, humour and a sad sense of

humanity, albeit as a product of self-deceit. Stealing every scene in which he appeared, Oates was one vote away from capturing the New York Film Critics' best actor award from Gene Hackman's Popeye Doyle. In a quieter year than 1971 we would surely have been talking Oscar nominations.

Yet *Two-Lane Blacktop* was a failure at the box office. In contrast to the hyperbole that greeted the script, the reviews were mediocre. A *Rolling Stone* article, printed almost a year after the same paper had affirmed Hellman as "an American director of major importance", described the overall picture as "moody" and "self-conscious". Most others were less kind and it was viewed as a cinematic oddity in a year that produced *The French Connection, Carnal Knowledge* and *The Last Picture Show*. According to Hellman the blame for this could be footed directly at Universal, and to company head Lew Wasserman in particular: "...he didn't promote any of the pictures and in particular *Two-Lane Blacktop*. It opened in New York City on July Fourth weekend without one single newspaper ad. People didn't even know it was playing. The excuse was that it was Fourth of July weekend and nobody would be in town, so what's the point in advertising? But then if nobody's going to be in town, then why open the picture?" Essentially Wasserman had closed the door on Tanen's Youth Division after seeing Dennis Hopper's *The Last Movie*. Finding that film personally repugnant he decided that Universal should distance itself from the rest of the program. Subsequently *Two-Lane Blacktop* was viewed as something of an embarrassment and its chances for success were sabotaged at birth.

Universal were clueless on how to market the film they originally anticipated as mopping up the burgeoning youth audience. Dennis and James were ridiculed – which sort of missed the point since they were supposed be epitomising a drift of impotency. Hellman's gamble had failed and *Two-Lane* was allowed to limp off into obscurity, its costs never recouped. Lost for years because of wrangles over musical rights it did not even appear on video until over twenty-five years later.

Perhaps it was too perfect an allegory of the early 1970s to connect with an audience hung over from the '60s. The optimism of that decade was fast draining away to be replaced by a sense of failure and nothingness. *Two-Lane Blacktop* was a mirror held up to the America of conservatism and the America of liberalism: both were repelled by what they saw. The dream was over and this reality of isolation and selfishness was the last thing the AOR-loving masses wished to turn to now.

Hellman returned to his low-budget roots making *Cockfighter* (1974) and *China 9, Liberty 37* (1978) with Warren Oates before a decade-long hiatus of only intermittent activity. Laurie Bird became a photographer, James Taylor resumed his career as a bed-sit poet and Rudy Wurlitzer went on to write the screenplay for Peckinpah's *Pat Garrett And Billy The Kid*.

For Dennis the experience was one never to be repeated. *Two-Lane* had not furthered his ambitions of independence and he remained stunted in his role as a Beach Boy. The financial spoils were minuscule compared to making records or playing live and he had spent them within weeks. The rest of the band, jealous when Dennis was given the role, could now bask in self-satisfaction. In future he would have to achieve individuality through his music.

In the meantime the Beach Boys were continuing their dramatic change both musically and stylistically. The pure pop of *Sunflower* (as Bruce Johnston rightly described it, the Beach Boys' own *Pet Sounds* – a final approximation of their '60s, not '70s, sound) and the clean-cut image that accompanied it was slowly making way for issues and politics. Beards and anti-war sloganeering were finally in, as were songs about ecology and the Kent State shootings. This new direction and about turn could be summed up in two words: Jack Rieley.

Rieley was a program director on the underground LA radio station KPFK and had candidly interviewed Brian in July 1970. Forming some sort of mutual appreciation he devised a dramatic plan of bullet points to resurrect the career of the Beach Boys and make them popular again. Rieley loved their efforts on *Sunflower* and correctly recognised that the band were suffering a problem of image rather than musical creativity. Collectively they had kept abreast of technological change and produced wonderful sounding records, but their brand name had to be re-established. It was time for the Beach Boys to mature and gain a new audience. Rieley's diagnosis was simple – the band must adapt their lyrical approach away from the clichés that bred them and start playing to the hipper crowds yet to realise how funky they had become. Rather than skating round the counter culture they would have to jump in feet first and embrace it.

In actuality Rieley had blagged his way onto the Board with spurious claims of being an award-winning NBC journalist. He was nothing of the sort, but his fast-talking demeanour was impressive and the Beach Boys quickly promoted him to management. From here the influence he exerted on the band was vitally important in that it filled the creative void left by Brian's continued absence. They would finally catch up with the rest of the world lyrically as the rest of the world tried to catch up with them musically. (In fact, the Beach Boys were actually moving towards Rieley's intended direction anyway – they had just got a little lost with TM – but without a dictator they were incapable of making the collective change. The songs that appeared on *Surf's Up*, the first LP where he exerted influence, had mostly already been recorded in the rolling and continuous sessions that continued from *Sunflower*).

One of his first moves was encouraging the band to play the Big Sur Folk Festival in October 1970[4]. Monterey had been *the* symbol of their commercial failure – where the Beach Boys had lost their credibility only three years earlier. That night though they earned rave reviews for a superb live show based predominantly on material from 1967 onwards. The only pre-*Pet Sounds* number they played was a triumphalist version of "California Girls". Given their lack of record sales in the past three

---

[4] Dennis' place behind the kit, while he filmed *Two-Lane Blacktop*, was taken by Mike Kowalski.

---

years the band had played constantly in a desperate bid to make money and had subsequently been honed into a formidable force in concert. As Stephen Desper in his role as live engineer remembered, it was pretty hard work; "They ran two shows a day simultaneously in different cities. They ran two different sound crews by telephone and radio. When the Beach Boys went on the first act would drive or fly to the next venue and start the show while the Beach Boys were doing their bit. At weekends they would have three shows going at the same time. They made a lot of dollars but they were running ragged. Carl was taking medication until finally he developed polyps. That was a gruesome time."

Big Sur was followed by a succession of key profile-raising concerts at the Whiskey A Go Go, as guests of the Grateful Dead, and on May 21st 1971, at the Washington Anti-War Rally. It seemed as if the Beach Boys had finally grown up. Under Rieley's direction the band were suddenly opening up to new influences and it was paying dividends: their credibility was back.

Not that he stopped there. The new manager was also keen to involve himself creatively, a fact immediately evident on the release of the *Surf's Up* album. Rieley became the guiding force in deciding that Beach Boys songs should contain conscious lyrics to reflect their new stance as guardians of the planet. Al contributed a hobo's lament with "Looking At Tomorrow" and a slight anti-pollution ditty with Mike in "Don't Go Near The Water". Carl produced his finest music for which Rieley provided some beautifully spaced-out lyrics. Most tellingly of all he also sang on Brian's "A Day In The Life Of A Tree", another somewhat bizarre tale of man against nature. The album was released without any involvement from Dennis, which was a shame since he also had recorded some great music with Rieley. An argument with Carl over the track listing ensured that his "4th Of July" and "Fallin' In Love" were removed from the final master and kept on hold for Dennis' proposed solo album.

The conception of "4th Of July", which was finally heard on the 1993 box set, had been openly mentioned in a *Rolling Stone* interview of 1971. When Tom Nolan dropped in on the Beach Boys camp Van Dyke Parks was already openly praising Dennis' latest music compared to the rest of the band – "I think that's nice, you know? I think he deserves his shot. At least he's not doing Charles Manson. And that's a very thin line, you know." He then encountered a conversation with Rieley and a visibly unimpressed Brian. The manager proposed the idea of juxtaposing American Independence with the current controversy involving the Nixon Government's suppression of the *New York Times* after their decision to print the Pentagon Papers[5]. Days later he had written his song with help

---

[5] These were Defence Secretary Robert MacNamara's 47-volume report from 1967 of how the US had become embroiled in Vietnam. Sections of these confidential documents were then copied by Daniel Ellsberg, a former Defence Department economist, and published by *The Times* on 13th June 1971, accusing the Government of lying to the American people. Nixon responded by serving an injunction on the paper for publishing "leaked" papers and kick-started a debate on the rights of citizens to know.

from Dennis rather than Brian. The achievement was then relayed to Al Jardine: "'Listen to this lyric I wrote for Dennis' song, Al,' Jack called. He read it through once aloud and then repeated it, explaining each line to Jardine. The lyric does not leap readily to mind, but had the words been Francis Scott Key's anthem, the explanation would have been: 'The bomb's bursting in air' – explosions going off; 'the rocket's red glare' – lights given off, when the bombs explode; 'given proof to the night' – showed the people were watching that... Al nodded dubiously, with energy."

Dennis' production and backing track bore all the hallmarks of his symphonic collaborations with Daryl Dragon. Drawing on his love of Wagner he created a slow bombastic background of multi-tracked strings and cymbals, before swerving to a lone piano and flute in the coda. Carl sang an impassioned lead. Rieley displayed in full his skill of penning lyrics that evoked emotion rather than overtly describing it. His work on Carl's hymns to positivity, "Long Promised Road" and "Feel Flows" ("white hot glistening shadowy flows") was sheer poetry – more emotive and less "clever-clever" than Van Dyke Parks' equally complex wordplay; Rieley was among the best lyricists the Beach Boys ever had. "4th Of July" would have made a worthy inclusion to *Surf's Up* and had it replaced "Student Demonstration Time" or "Take A Load Off Your Feet" would have made a strong record even stronger.

As it was *Surf's Up* was released to excellent reviews on both sides of the Atlantic, trumpeting a renaissance of America's forgotten sons – "You can come home guys, all is forgiven," ran one memorable line. Riding on the back of their newfound popularity as a concert act, the record was accorded a reverence that its predecessor never had and reached a peak of Number 29. This was no doubt helped by the inclusion of two tracks from Brian Wilson – especially the title track, a reworked version of the legendary *Smile* song that Brian alone had previewed on the Leonard Bernstein television show. The world had waited five years to hear this and it did not disappoint. Sung beautifully by Carl, with another 1967 fragment, "Child Is The Father Of The Man", tagged onto the ending, "Surf's Up" was simply a breathtaking four minutes ten seconds.

More exciting than this though was the inclusion of a second, equally great song by Brian. "'Til I Die" with its "How deep is the ocean?" refrain was beyond all expectations. It was everything *Pet Sounds* fans could have wanted: concise, introspective, chilling and as beautifully blue as ice. Lyrically, not only was it as perfect as anything on that record but it also hinted at a self-realisation from Brian of the mess he was in. Aeons away from the juvenilia of old the suggestion was there that "Brian was Back" with his creative juices intact. For the faithful who had sat for too long waiting it seemed the moment of resurrection had arrived.

But this apparent phoenix-like rise was illusionary. True, Carl and Brian had produced two great songs apiece and even Bruce had contributed what sounded like a potential hit with his homely "Disney Girls". True also that Jack Rieley had provided the sort of impetus to change tact and grow up that no individual member seemed capable of.

Certainly, over half of *Surf's Up* was brilliant, up with the best that the Beach Boys had ever produced. The only problem being that it this was not a realistic picture of the band in 1971. Under the veneer of progression things were still very wrong indeed.

As it turns out Brian had not even wanted "Surf's Up" included – the misery of *Smile* still raw in his mind – why were the band so keen to centre an album around what was dismissed as ego music a few years earlier? True to form he had to fight for the inclusion of the glacial "'Til I Die", considered a real "downer" by Mike. Like Dennis, Brian was still finding the Beach Boys a difficult outlet for personal emotion. And these were not even recent compositions – "Surf's Up" was obviously five years old while "'Til I Die" was rooted in sessions from 1969 and then mixed down in 1970. The signals emitted to Warner Brothers and to the press were of a functioning band with their original leader back on track but this was simply not the case. Brian had been crushed again and the treasure chest that had filled out previous LPs was fast emptying.

Beyond these tracks the picture was even less optimistic. With Dennis' material absent (a fact recognised and mourned by Arthur Schmidt in his *Rolling Stone* review) there was little depth to the scraps that remained. The most prominent example being "Student Demonstration Time", an ambiguous comment from Mike Love on the Kent State shootings, that was based musically on Leiber-Stoller's "Riot In Cell Block #9". The chorus of "There's a riot going on" to the sound of wailing sirens suggested an affinity with Neil Young's "Ohio" but the underlying message was to stay home and avoid the bullets. A live favourite throughout the early 1970s, its dubious message was highlighted when sung after to Merle Haggard's "Okie From Muskogee" (another concert choice) with its reactionary lines about not smoking weed or taking LSD. The irony seemed to be lost.

The only real progressions had been made by Carl whose songs were truly a revelation, easily the match of Dennis in the multitude of instruments used and the quality of production. Here at least the momentum of *Sunflower* was pushed onwards and upwards.

The hidden fractures were laid bare when Bruce Johnston left the band after consistent arguments with Rieley. He realised correctly that the band were "writing and arranging in the style of Brian Wilson, because he wasn't really actively involved": "To me, *Surf's Up* is, and always has been, one hyped-up lie! It was a false reflection of the Beach Boys, and one which Jack engineered right form the outset. Jack was just very, very smart in that he was able to camouflage what was actually going on by making it look like Brian Wilson was more than just a visitor at those sessions. Jack made it appear as though Brian was really there all the time."

The cycle of misery was complete when Dennis, who had actually played drums on much of the album, severed the nerves in his right hand after smashing it through a door of sheet glass. "I got drunk," he later explained, "walked into the house, threw off my wife's clothes, ripped mine off. It was cold, and I went to slam the door, only we'd just moved and I'd forgotten that the door was made of glass, and I put my hand

right through it. You know how it is when you're drunk?" Whether this tale was true or not, he was unable to even play the piano for six months and was replaced behind the drum kit by Ricky Fataar of South Africa's Flame.

For the next few years Dennis would just wander the stage like a spare part – contributing the odd vocal and occasionally taking to the keyboards to sing one his heartbreaking ballads. He was even given Al's role as the lead on "Help Me Rhonda". Bored by the whole scenario and playing an increasingly superfluous role, his energies drifted away from the live arenas that had been his domain. As noted by Stephen Desper, "There was a period when Dennis didn't do very much. He got involved with girls and drugs and stuff. He hurt his hand also and he was in pain a lot from the drugs he was taking. He was spaced-out a lot. Dennis would just come along and do his two songs and other than that there wasn't much need for him to be around. Sometimes he would turn up drunk and sing them. Nobody cared. Whether he was drunk or not they still sounded the same."

At Rieley's behest, Ricky Fataar was joined by his ex-band mate Blondie Chaplin as replacement for Bruce Johnston, while the touring band was reinforced by the ever-present Daryl Dragon, Carl's brother-in-law Billy Hinsche, and session bassist Ed Carter. Over the next few years the "whitest" American rock band was transformed by Rieley to include a variety of different, multi-national players – so much so that by 1974 they were named "band of the year" by *Rolling Stone* for their live shows alone.[6] The infrastructure remained hopelessly weak however and it would be for the next record, 1972's *Carl And The Passions – So Tough*[7], to provide a more realistic snapshot of the band's ragged condition – and of how far Dennis had moved ahead of his band mates.

Running in at a minuscule eight tracks, a number of facts were immediately obvious when needle departed groove. Firstly was the now almost total absence of Brian. While his ghost had run throughout *Surf's Up* he featured here on only two tracks, both of which were laughably sub-standard. The best that could be said of "Marcella", the LP's chosen single, was that it was charmingly naïve. With hindsight this lightweight tale of Brian's masseuse dragged his career back ten years to the land of teenage cotton candy. "'Til I Die" had been the sound of *then* but this, unfortunately, was the sound of now. If nothing else, "Marcella" was proof that genius in pop is fleeting.

Even less subtle were Mike and Al's fundamentalist rantings in praise of the Maharishi. To be fair, "All This Is That", their yogic broadcast on the eternal oneness of being, did contain some decent harmonies but "He Come Down" was just execrable. Combining "mystic" kindergarten rhymes against a mock gospel revivalist setting the only conclusion drawn was "just what were they thinking?". And just to confuse the fans a little more Fataar and Chaplin made an instant contribution with two lazy

---

[6] According to Carli Munoz – who joined the Beach Boys as a percussionist before replacing Daryl Dragon on keyboards when he went on to form The Captain and Tennille – the addition of Fataar and Chaplin combined with his own Caribbean influences brought a whole different flavour to the band: "Everything was radical during those three or four years. Also with me I brought along an African-American percussionist, Kenyata, from the Wilson Pickett touring band, and two other musicians who were LA jazz bassist Putter Smith and another drummer/percussionist, Mexican-American Bobbie Figueroa who remained with the group also for many years. We were something like the United Nations at war! There was no doubt that the group was hot. The level of musicianship was extraordinary, and we often felt embarrassed for the opening act, whoever that was. We were simply making a very powerful musical statement, and we knew it. If we were band of the year, it was not an overstatement; we earned it."

[7] As the title suggested, this was Carl's album and a reflection of his level-headed leadership qualities that had steadied the Beach Boys through their recent trials. Since *Wild Honey* his voice and productions had dominated their records.

R'n'B numbers, replete with considerable doses of lap steel. Quite what audiences were to make of this disparate mess was never mentioned. Warner Brothers must have feared the worst and, hoping to limit the damage, the record was released as part of a two-vinyl set with the original *Pet Sounds*.[8] The words "pearls" and "swine" were mentioned in several reviews in the same sentence and the album was savaged in America. Back-to-back with *Pet Sounds* the evidence of decline, particularly Brian's decline, was more than evident. That *So Tough* reached Number 50 on *Billboard* was a minor miracle.

In Britain, it was a slightly different story. For on two tracks of *So Tough* there was evidence of another course being plotted. Dennis, working away from the other Beach Boys with Daryl Dragon and Stephen Desper, was busy recording symphonic soundscapes for his proposed solo record. Rather than reviving the past or replicating the flaccid sound of The Eagles, Dennis was experimenting in the studio as Brian had years earlier – multi-tracking entire orchestras or his voice until something incredible and otherworldly resulted. The parallels with the lush textured sounds of *Let's Get It On* or *What's Goin' On* again make comparisons with Marvin Gaye uncanny.

Perhaps justifying the decision to designate "Sound Of Free" a Europe-only single, Dennis' new music won much praise over here. Chris Bergson in *Creem* compared his latent spirituality with a haunting Methodist hymn "for those in peril at sea". *Melody Maker* simply ran the headline "Dennis Steals The Show":

"...his two songs here demonstrate a new direction: 'Cuddle Up' and 'Make It Good', both penned with the assistance of Daryl Dragon, are quiet, passionate ballads with fragile melodies balanced atop yearning string arrangements. 'Cuddle Up' particularly is 5:42 of aching emotion – Dennis sings with great delicacy and feeling, guaranteed to turn the toes just the way 'Kiss Me Baby' and 'Girls On The Beach' used to. Here is real development."

The *NME* provided an even more interesting insight, with Bruce Johnston reviewing the album in the same week that his ex-band mates were playing at Crystal Palace in the pouring rain. Johnston provided a sense of realism to the group's current plight, criticising production techniques and highlighting the cold fact that Brian was an absent leader – "I spoke with Brian a couple of weeks ago and he told me he didn't really have much to do with this album... I'm hoping that if he does come to Holland to meet the guys and get involved in recording in the summer we'll hear some more Beach Boys hits like we used to hear, but not repeating the old success formula, and we'll hear some 1972 Beach Boys with 1972 Brian."

The few wholly positive comments emanating from the Beach Boy's most diplomatic ex-member were reserved for Dennis and Daryl's new music. "Make It Good" has an "incredible arrangement" and

---

[8] Originally *So Tough* was going to be doubled up with a version of *Smile*. When this failed to materialise Warners demanded back $50,000 from any future advances, knowing full well that they had an almost unmarketable LP on their hands.

"musically knocks me out more than anything on the album" while the sublime "Cuddle Up" is only criticised because "I don't think the song is quite up to some of the other songs that he has hidden in his closet – which he'll play for some time and then hide them away for a year."

"Make It Good" was a dramatic surge of minor-key strings and horns that simply defied the categorisation of "song". Noting that Dennis had a tendency towards the grand sweeping gesture Daryl Dragon had suggested to him several LPs by Wagner and the results were obvious here. Dennis considered himself and the German composer to be "kindred souls". Dragon's arrangements managed to be both bombastic and affective while the caverns of sound Dennis had experimented with in 1970 on fragments such as "All My Love", finally reached their fruition. Without beginning or end, or chorus or verse it appeared out of place on a record of such mixed styles. The results however were astounding: his rough cracked voice mixed alone against the maelstrom, accentuating his lonesome tones, was quite, quite beautiful. A towering performance of passion and grace, the Dennis Wilson voice would never sound better than on *So Tough* – before the attritional effects of coke and alcohol finally took their toll.

And lyrically, though "Make It Good" dealt with Dennis' usual themes of the heart, there was an almost unbearable sadness in his delivery. It might have read on paper like a hymn to love – or more specifically to Barbara – and to the healing powers of the spirit, but the sadness in his voice transcended any meanings. The subject matter was romantic but the execution was desolate and tense. The lines, "All of my life I haven't known much, all I know is what I feel," as the orchestra swelled to a climax were simply devastating. Sung like some obscene apology they might well have read as testament to the way Dennis lived his life and approached his music. While the other Beach Boys reached out for any passing fad to find resurrection, Dennis went deep inside and dredged up these feelings.

Unsurprisingly his marriage to Barbara, that had provided such stability after the Manson episode, was starting to unravel acrimoniously. His consistent infidelity and the disruption of touring took their toll on what seemed a perfect union. Consequently there was little romance in these exorcisms of despair and the difference between Dennis' *So Tough* songs and the likes of "Forever" was marked. Rather than professions of adoration they sounded like barren cries for help. As Barbara herself was to comment just over a decade later, in the wake of her ex-husband's death, "Dennis was just so empty inside, he just never realised what a unique person he was. He tried to fill that need any way he could. When we were living together, he loved the sense of family. The only problem was that he couldn't stay long. He always had to leave and come back." As any of his wives would later testify, marriage to Dennis was doomed from the start – sooner or later the macho persona would fade to leave a confused and complicated individual, still wracked by the turmoil of his youth. The source of attraction would turn too easily to destruction.

These traits were highlighted further in the album's best moment and one of Dennis' most beautiful songs, "Cuddle Up". Another declaration of love and the desire to find love ("waking to find... we're still one") it was another perfect ballad that should have graced his solo record. Based around a piano line not unlike that on 1971's "Barbara", Dennis again poured out his vulnerable soul in a display of genuine emotion, quite distinct from the passionless exercises treading water around it. It made ridicule of the one-dimensional character portrayal he was forever fighting against – comparisons are difficult, but if Kurt Cobain had loved Wagner and Brian Wilson in equal measures he might have sounded something like this. It was also one of the most frightening expressions of love ever committed to vinyl.

Again the protagonist is on the verge of falling into a state of perfect romance that is both unbelievable and startling in its intensity – the sweet musing of the lyrics bearing little relationship to the pained and intimate performance (despite the title and elementary nature of the subject, Dennis Wilson sounded unbelievably sad). Though more conventional in structure than "Make It Good", these factors made "Cuddle Up" the more disturbing song overall. A disquieting sense of something awry, something not quite right, pervades its entirety. The ingredients – the Spector-like backing, the angelic Beach Boys' choir, the sublime melody – suggested lightness and joy, not this *bleakness*. This was more than an ode to love. This was desperate.

The polarities left an aftertaste that was both unsettling and bittersweet. After the last line "I know a man who's so in love" (the fatalistic change of tense implying that the intended listener doesn't reciprocate this) a lone cello returns with a grating and lasting sweep. Daryl Dragon's symphony of gorgeousness reduced to nothing. It sounded ominously like a tear; reminiscent of the closing seconds of *Pet Sounds* with its barking dogs and passing trains.

Had they not been given to the album, "Cuddle Up"[9] and "Make It Good" would almost certainly have appeared on Dennis' proposed solo LP and are probably the best indicator we have of how it might have sounded. A whole record of this neo-classical soul music, perhaps combined with Motown-like numbers à la *Sunflower*, would have been closer in spirit to the heights of *Pet Sounds* than anything else released under the name of the Beach Boys since 1967. And just as *Pet Sounds* has hardly dated in over thirty years, neither has the music of Dennis Wilson from these prolific years of 1970 to 1972. True emotion is timeless.

This is what the other Beach Boys, with the exception of Bruce Johnston, never understood. To dramatically start singing about TM or Vietnam as a last gasp effort to consciously attain popularity was only to gain another albatross – another surf board, another 409. "Student Demonstration Time" or "He Come Down" were nothing more than marketing tricks, or at least that is how they sounded. Dennis, like Brian before him, was proving consistently that the Beach Boys did not have to stand before an "image" – surfing, cars, Maharishi, whatever – to make

---

[9] As it was "Cuddle Up" did make the status of B-side, in a slightly remixed form, on the flip of "You Need A Mess Of Help To Stand Alone" in May 1972. Dennis also sang the song at a small number of concerts in 1971 and 1972.

Dumb Angel

good music or be successful. He knew that the band was at its most affecting and powerful during the latter 1960s when experimentation and introspection was pushed to the forefront.

A case in point here was the unreleased song "Carry Me Home" that Dennis had written in 1972 for inclusion on the *Holland* album. More desolate even than his *So Tough* compositions, it described in moving detail the last moments of life from the perspective of a dying American soldier out in the Vietnamese jungle. "I got the image of a soldier – me – dying in a ditch, and I ended up doing a song about it. The soldier began feeling, 'Why the hell am I here?' Then the coldness started to move up his body, from his feet to his legs, to his chest... until he was dead." With a slow country backing, all steel guitar and rolling piano, and an emotive lead vocal sung by Blondie Chaplin, the results were wholly believable. There were no embellishments in the recurring cries of "carry me home to my daddy, carry me home to my ma," and then there was a simply incredible performance from Dennis. Immersing himself totally in the role of the wounded he takes over the centre of the song in a voice seemingly on the verge of tears. The line "My eyes are getting tired, I guess I won't grow old" has obviously taken on a more significant resonance now, but a couple of minutes in the music suddenly halts, and Dennis is alone at the microphone pleading with God not to take his life. Even as the band, after decamping to Baambrugge, were on the verge of releasing their last record of any consequence it was an astonishing track for a Beach Boy to be involved with. A finished version never graced *Holland* or any other LP – "It was too negative... how could I put *that* on a Beach Boys record" – but the song was covered by Primal Scream in 1992[10]. As Dennis' last vowels fade away on the demo and the song shudders to a halt, someone in the studio audibly draws breath and utters, "That, was a motherfucker."

"Carry Me Home" also marked a period of reconciliation between Dennis and his father, almost the first they had known. Desperate to experiment outside the constraints of the family that was stifling his creativity, Dennis had approached Murry for cash on several occasions in order to fund his own independent recording sessions. When Ricky Fataar came in as cover while Dennis recovered from his hand injury various press reports claimed he was actually thinking of setting up a production and publishing company with his father. Two unheard and unreleased songs, "Behold The Night" (written with Daryl Dragon) and "It's A New Day" (written with Dragon and Stanley Shapiro) were even assigned to Bri-Mur Publishing – the company Murry had set up with Brian in 1969 to administer the royalties for "Breakaway", one of only five songs in the

---

[10] Primal Scream's Bobby Gillespie would later comment (*NME*, January 25th 1992): "It's devastating. You know 'Knocking On Heavens Door'? The feeling in the song was something like that. It was really hard for me to sing that, because when you actually hear him going 'Life is meant to live/And I'm afraid, to die... please God' it sounds like somebody that's completely fucked... *devastated* is more like it. His voice is so beautiful and homeless. It's experienced and ragged – not like a falsetto Beach Boys voice... He was a good man, a beautiful lookin' guy."

catalogue.

Murry refused to fund this "new direction". He had always viewed Dennis' wayward behaviour as a liability to his strict codes of professionalism. He had always been out of control and recent events with Manson, the hand injury and a more sensual direction did little to revise this opinion. Dennis himself had been seeing a female psychiatrist, ostensibly to come to terms with his childhood and a guilt complex brought on by fame – though he also claimed to have slept with her – which resulted in an urge to seek therapy by confronting his past. Subsequently by the time Murry died in June 1973 he was closer to Dennis than any of his offspring – the two would meet regularly to watch boxing, and it was Dennis he phoned when realising his heart condition was terminal.

Lacking the financial backing to break away, Dennis and Stanley Shapiro (who was now contributing lyrics to most of his songs) even pursued the idea of breaking into the advertising market to raise funds. A "close friend of the group" was quoted in a September 11th 1971 issue of *Disc And Music Echo* saying that Dennis was preparing to strike out on his own: "Dennis contends that he has left the group once and for all, and is setting up a production and publishing company with his father, Murry Wilson. Dennis is quite into writing and producing commercials for various products. He was in New York last week to finish negotiations with a major company." This was certainly the case with "It's A New Day", concocted by Shapiro as a sales pitch for Bristol-Myers. Sung by Blondie Chaplin to a Dragon-Wilson melody, Dennis attempted to persuade the company's sales executives to use the song as part of a tie-in commercial for Brylcream, to the tune of $1,000,000. Unsurprisingly the proposal was rejected[11]. The song was eventually deemed good enough for the whole band to record, but Shapiro refused to relinquish his publishing rights and so it was shelved. (Similarly, they were thwarted on another occasion when at dinner with an unnamed movie producer to discuss the idea of recording a film soundtrack. Dennis was questioned on his driving ambition and replied that he wished to sleep with the producer's new girlfriend, who he could not tear his eyes from. Announcing that he could not be held responsible for his actions in the next thirty-minutes, so strong was his desire, Dennis took her back to his pool house when the producer passed out from one joint too many. Needless to say, they didn't get the job. Another defeat in the face of commercial America).

Yet just when it seemed that the Beach Boys might finally implode with a whimper, they embarked on a trip to Holland to make their last great LP. Dennis and Brian's[12] side projects were put on hold

---

[11] According to Shapiro, Dennis was given ten seconds to leave their sight or they were going to throw him out of a sixty-storey window.

[12] Brian's creative energies had been concentrated on producing the *American Spring* album for his wife and sister-in-law. Among this collection of Beach Boys covers and classic songs was a sweet version of "Forever". A single, "Shyin' Away", was backed with a take on Dennis' "Fallin' In Love".

as the entire band and entourage relocated from California at Rieley's behest. The hope was to resuscitate their career and provide Warners with the hit album they so craved. Logistically a disaster – new engineer Steve Moffitt had to construct and then ship an entire state of the art studio from Santa Monica, only to reconstruct it in mainland Europe – the exercise was one of supreme '70s rock indulgence. The band had decided to record in a converted barn in Baambrugge only because Dutch audiences had received their new image so well. With them they brought wives, children, dogs, and cars. As Jack Rieley noted ruefully in the sleeve notes, "Some day accounting will face a column just called 'Holland'."

Setting aside the differences that had been revealed on *So Tough*, they finally, amazingly, worked as a band again to produce a entire unified suite of songs. A definite thread of sound ran through the entire record. To Warner's dismay Brian was yet again a mere spectator in proceedings – his last great song, "Sail On Sailor", that had been co-written with Van Dyke Parks, was reworked by Jack Rieley and Tandyn Almer and sung by Blondie Chaplin. His other major contribution was the fairy tale about a magic transistor radio entitled "Mt. Vernon And Fairway Theme" and issued as a bonus 7" EP. For the rest of the band though it was time to set aside differences and work together. As a record constructed almost totally of collaborations, *Holland* now stands as easily their most mature and adult work.

Carl, as on *Surf's Up*, came into his own again. Producing the majority of the record in his brother's creative absence his "Trader" was a real highlight, as was Ricky and Blondie's "Leaving This Town". The former was a condemnation of imperialism through the ages while the latter was an elegant rock star blues. Mike and Al provided the centrepiece trilogy "Californian Saga" which was by turns pretty and pretentious – a meandering landlocked homage to their home state. The third part, "California", despite some shocking wordplay ended in harmonies as rich as any Brian Wilson composition. *Rolling Stone* summed up "a special album" as follows: "Like the finest Beach Boys' work, *Holland* makes me consistently smile, as much at its occasionally unnerving simplicity of viewpoint as at its frequently ornate perfection".

Dennis' "Carry Me Home" did not make the finished product, but his "Steamboat" and "Only With You", written with Rieley and Mike Love respectively, did. That the latter was involved writing with Dennis at all only highlighted the paradoxes that existed within the band. There was little love lost between the naturally competitive pairing of Dennis and Mike, but here they combined on an exceedingly soft and tender ballad. "Steamboat" was a slow-burning chug of a song for which Rieley provided his usual esoteric lyricisms, ostensibly as an "adventure of sound as life's recreation". Both sung by Carl and as solid as anything else on the record they were good, but far from Dennis' best songs.

They would be his last works to appear intentionally on a group album. After *Holland*, Dennis would be the only Beach Boy to keep alive the flame of experimentation.

The band also reached the end of the line with *Holland*. Returning from the nadir of 1972, not only with a very good record of original material but also one that did not lean heavily on their Brian-dominated past, they were ready to be reborn once more. The money and risk poured into their Dutch relocation looked to have paid off and they were at last equipped to compete with the likes of Chicago and Little Feat and all those other cocaine-numbed giants of FM radio. In short, a balance seemed to have been struck between the Beach Boys of the 1960s and the 1970s – a fact evident from their phenomenal live shows that sandwiched swathes of the new material between Brian Wilson classics, before ending with the obligatory "Surfin' USA".

Yet eighteen months down the line, and with no follow-up in sight, the surfing songs and the car songs were on their way back. A typical Beach Boys concert was becoming more and more a celebration of the past, and anything from 1968 to 1973 was gradually phased out. Audiences were treated to what they apparently wanted – a group of grown men singing about teenage love. By deciding to go back to the future the Beach Boys skipped a generation and began performing for an audience who had either never seen them or who had grown through the pain of the late '60s and wanted their innocence back. But regression was (financial) progression. Turning their back on over five years of musical exploration the Beach Boys walked back laughing all the way to the bank.

So what happened?

Firstly, Warner Brothers hated *Holland*. The Beach Boys had been a nightmare to market since day one – and they were showing few signs of any great commercial renaissance. Despite the critical plaudits for *Sunflower* and *Surf's Up* the band remained a financial black hole, still living and spending like it was 1966. Yet the Beach Boys had almost totally cut themselves off from those heady day and the record company simply did not know what to expect any more. They had become a maverick outfit, changing direction and style at will.

The only thing Warners *did* know for sure is that they did not want this record. Hyper-wary since the abortion that was *So Tough*, they feared this new collection seemed to lack an obvious hit single, while Brian's chief contribution... well, it sounded like some kind of joke. The man was meant to be a genius, the selling point of the group, and all he could produce was a children's fairytale. There was something faintly disturbing about this gargantuan recluse concocting fantasies about a magic transistor radio.

Only when they heard "Sail On Sailor" did the company give *Holland* the green light. Backed by Dennis' "Only With You" the single rose to a measly 79 but was big enough of an airplay hit to push the album into the Top 40. This was not a great return on the thousands of dollars poured into the project. The bottom line remained as it was since the start of the decade – the Beach Boys were a great and popular live band, with one of the best-loved catalogues in pop, but fewer and fewer punters were buying their records.

The departure of Jack Rieley in 1973 was another signifier of change. Though disliked by many within the Beach Boys management his hands had been firmly on the wheel for the last three years – changing personnel, adjusting image and shaping the music. Generally all the tasks

that Brian should have been undertaking had he been in any way fit. The battle lines between Dennis and Carl on the one side, and Mike and Al on the other were too entrenched for any one personality within the group to assume leadership. Dennis was blazing a trail in the quality songwriting stakes but there was no way the rest of the band was going to follow him – that road was too close to the one chosen by Brian in 1967 when emotions over-ran business. Rieley had massaged the conservative tendencies of Mike Love and Al Jardine and channelled their love of the Beach Boys pre-1966 – when they had been happiest – away from the current music. Better they sing about TM than surfing. The addition of a multi-ethnic backing band and his own conscious lyrics had gone a long way to making them hip again.

Rieley's dismissal in the wake of *Holland*'s failure swung the power balance firmly in the favour of the Love-Jardine axis[13]. Not only did Mike's brother Stephen replace him as manager, but also within the year Blondie, and then Ricky, were gone. Dennis was back on drums and away from the microphone by the end of 1974 – his one regular contribution in concert was a cover of Joe Cocker's "You Are So Beautiful", reworked as a hymn to California, to kick off the encore. In that one year, the Beach Boys became a far less exotic proposition.

The real clincher though was the release of the Capitol compilation *Endless Summer* in June 1974. That was the event beyond all others that altered the course of Beach Boys' history, as much as *Pet Sounds* had in the 1960s. At one sweep the band were suddenly the biggest in America once again, their reputations staked upon a stash of records that were about ten years old and spoke of another more innocent time. While the four preceding LPs had fared averagely *Endless Summer*, containing nothing beyond 1965, launched them into supernova status again. Heavily advertised on TV, the record tapped into the expectations and psyche of the American public. It was a huge Number One that summer and remained on the charts for an amazing three years.

Maybe it was a fluke – a lucky coincidence, post-Watergate and with the Vietnam War grinding to an ignominious conclusion, that these twenty tracks of wholesome and unbridled innocence were unleashed on the population. The fortunes of the country had mirrored those of the band and perhaps they needed each other. A veil of sunshine, masking a vile and corrupt decade. As Dennis himself perceived: "I think we represent to people in other countries, and even in America, something that they imagine that we do. Everyone has fantasies. People use the Beach Boys for their thoughts of America, or what America should be, or the beach. A place for people to let go and kind of drift, to enjoy themselves."

The soundtrack to George Lucas' *American Graffiti* had already associated the band with a bygone age in 1973, and when *Rolling Stone* made the Beach Boys their "Band of the Year" in 1975 it seemed that Mike's 1966 mantra of "Don't fuck with the formula" had become a self-fulfilling prophesy. It was like the intervening years had not happened and the band and the country had woken up to find themselves still in love. The sell-out concerts and the influx of royalty dollars confirmed that America did not want the Beach Boys to be anything else than a product of escapism – a celebration of belonging to the Greatest Nation on Earth. A celebration of California. In a decision of lucrative pragmatism the band ditched their pretensions to making original records and grabbed the lucre. Their Vegas Years beckoned as the Beach Boys became the biggest show band of them all, a guaranteed hit-fest.

With experimentation and soul off the agenda this would leave the music of Dennis Wilson in an extremely precarious position. Since *Holland* he had been continually recording and preparing new songs for

---

[13] The exact reason why Jack Rieley was sacked is still unclear. The poor returns on *Holland*, that he was gay, that he was too autocratic or perhaps a combination of all three are possibilities.

the band. Among these was an ambitious piece called "River Song" that had been previewed live on a few occasions[14], with Blondie taking the lead, and "Pacific Ocean Blues", a funky Stevie Wonder-style ecological protest for which Mike had provided lyrical assistance. With Dennis now perched back on the drum stool, these songs would have to play an incidental role to the job in hand and would certainly get no space in the new set. The new-look old-look Beach Boys required that Dennis become the idiot drummer he was as a twenty-year-old. There was no time to be Wagner. And not content with snubbing one genius they also required

---

[14] Indeed, the band were seen rehearsing "River Song" on a KABC television feature in 1973.

that Brian come back and start writing the hits again. It was a series of decisions based in delusion.

It was time for the true personalities of the band to show through.

Dumb Angel

SURF CITY SOUL

"I take full responsibility. I want to meet with everyone in the field, want it to be different. I think music belongs on a personal level, instead of the mindless corporation ordering the artist to 'do this, do that, do this'. People have to meet, discover, grow, build."
—Dennis Wilson in interview with David Leaf, September 1977

"If these people want to take this beautiful, happy, spiritual music we've made and all the things we stand for and throw it out the window just because of money, then there's something really wrong with the whole thing and I don't want any part of it."
—Dennis Wilson, September 1977

"If there was ever a real lover in my life, it'd be Karen Lamm and music."
—In interview with David Leaf again, September 1977

It was early Spring 1977 and Chuck Kirkpatrick was busy working at Brother Studios on his LP *Crane*. Aside from the Wilson brothers, Ricci Martin and Helen Reddy, he was the only musician booked into the beautiful Santa Monica building, all stained glass and wood. Chuck had met Dennis briefly a few nights earlier and been introduced by house-engineer Earle Mankey. The Beach Boys' drummer – a musical hero – had been warm and complimentary towards his guitar playing and even suggested they record something together.

That night Dennis, slightly drunk, returned to the studio and barged into the control room. He requested that Chuck should come and listen to his new music. The erstwhile guitar player agreed and followed him out. "I went out into the studio and sat down next to Dennis on the piano bench. He closed his eyes and began playing these hauntingly beautiful chords which sounded a lot like Brian's kind of chord changes. I didn't know what Dennis was singing or even trying to sing because it just sounded like he was moaning." Then, taking a breather, the impromptu session was put on hold until a drinks order – some $150 of Jack Daniels, gin and vodka – was dispatched.

"Dennis proceeded to drink a little of everything while I sipped a styrofoam cup of Jack Daniels. An hour passed, and Dennis was really getting ripped. He started playing his songs again, first the beautiful chord changes with the moaning, and then suddenly he was beating the keyboard with his fists and yelling obscenities. At least that was what it sounded like, although I think it was probably just a Dennis Wilson song about love gone sour. Not wanting to appear impolite, I continued to be Dennis' audience long after Earle had gone home and Steve had fallen asleep on the control room couch. When Dennis finally ran out of obscenities and the piano went out of tune from his pounding, he looked at me and quietly said 'Oh I'm sorry, man. You were working and I interrupted.' He then went into the control room and tore up our bill for that day's studio time. 'Today's on me... don't worry about it.'"

A few nights later the scenario was repeated. Dennis played drums to one of Chuck's songs, breaking every skin on his kit in the process ("He was so out of it he didn't realise what he had done"), before returning to the piano to play his "love song". This time the session was interrupted by the appearance of Dennis' lover Karen Lamm. Only Dennis didn't want to speak with her that night, he merely muttered some obscenities before growling at Chuck to remain where he was ("Sit down, we're working. Don't pay any attention to her") just as an almighty domestic storm was set to ignite. Karen wisely turned on her heels and departed leaving things to continue as if nothing had occurred. "With another evening's work on my album interrupted, Dennis again tore up the invoice. He gave me a big bear hug, said goodbye, and left."

In 1977, as he worked on completing his masterwork, it was a typical Dennis Wilson session.

The cover of *Pacific Ocean Blue* held few clues to its contents. Barren and sombre there was no song listing, just a title and a photo of its maker that dominated the jacket. For those who had come back to the Beach Boys since 1974 there was nothing to link this blue austerity with the shiny happy fun promised by *Endless Summer*. Staring out from beneath the bold legend of "WILSON" was an unsmiling and bearded face that was no longer the sex symbol of *Two-Lane Blacktop*. Now 32, Dennis was showing the signs of his lifestyle. The photos inside the gatefold sleeve illustrated a man flexing his muscles, preening on the beach, or working in the studio. But that front cover was of a stone-faced individual, his eyes strangely old and weary through a mass of hair.

A year earlier the Beach Boys had released *15 Big Ones*, their most eagerly anticipated record for nearly a decade. The successes of 1974 had been replicated in 1975 with *Spirit Of America* (another compilation of early hits, this time constructed without input from any of the band[1]) and the world was again keen to know if the fire of genius still burnt within Brian Wilson.

Their contrasting appearances could not have been stronger. The cover to *15 Big Ones* – as in "15 Hits included and 15 years in the business and still here" – was confident and glossy. In a total reversal from the impressionistic watercolours of *Surf's Up* and *Holland* or the bright Warhol-like *So Tough* it really was back to 1964 and all five Beach Boys circled in their airbrushed, tanned, white-toothed glory. The "adult" concepts brought in during Jack Rieley's short tenure were dismissed as the new songs, what there were of them, concerned themselves with nothing loftier than the teenage dramas of boy-meets-girl. The reversal of image to meet the expectations of Middle America was hardly subtle and as a depiction of reality it was utterly ridiculous. The truth, as always, was somewhere between the two extremes.

---

[1] When asked if he approved of this Mike Love replied, "I approved of the fact that it sold a million."

To put it mildly, the background to recording *15 Big Ones* was far from harmonious. The personnel that helped produce such beautiful records in Brian's absence (Desper, Dragon, Rieley, Chaplin, Fataar) were now mostly absent. Without their support and good influence it was time for the true feelings to be aired of where each member envisaged the Beach Boys to be going.

The changes since the start of the 1970s had been successful only in artistic terms. From the personal depths of 1968 the band had proved themselves in the field of battle, that their songwriting could adapt and compete with the best of the new decade. On the whole the LPs since *Sunflower* had met critical favour. But commercially it was nothing on the 1960s – a fact hammered home by the mega-sales of *Endless Summer*. In the US, the Beach Boys had not had a top twenty hit, never mind a top ten hit, since *Do It Again* some eight years ago.

Therefore the decision to return to the Beach Boys circa 1964 was met with a collective cry of "Eureka!" from both the band and Warner Brothers. The answer had been there all along and they had been fighting it. The statistics and the sales suggested one logical truism: when Brian wrote the songs the Beach Boys had hit records. In a dramatic volte-face the decision was made to return him to songwriting duties. Money was to be poured into a dramatic "Brian's Back" campaign at the behest of Stephen Love and Mike, Al, Carl and Dennis were to resume the roles they led in 1967: as the California King's messengers.

This was a notion that appealed to all four of them. It represented a return to the good old days and some sort of structure within the organisation. With Brian as chief and over-riding tunesmith it would stem the divisiveness evident on *Surf's Up* or *So Tough*. The others could reaffirm their territories in the touring band as before. Mike and Al would front the live show and supply those proven "Beach Boy" lyrics while Dennis and Carl would be happy to see their beloved brother, the creator of their current lifestyles, back where he belonged. It was a time to put egos to bed. As Dennis succinctly put it, "The Beach Boys are not a superstar group. The music is the superstar of the group."

The plan was to nail some classics such as "Blueberry Hill", "Peggy Sue" and "Chapel Of Love" to get the creative juices flowing once more and re-acclimatise Brian with the mixing desk. After half a decade in bed he was going to be a little rusty after all. In January 1976 the band entered Brother Studios and recording commenced with Chuck Berry's "Rock And Roll Music". The Beach Boys Mark 3, the *Endless Summer* years, was launched in a blaze of glory.

"Lately I have found it difficult as heck to finish a song. It's a funny thing. Probably not much of a song left in me... if any."

It was immediately obvious that Brian was more than a little rusty. The parts were not moving properly. Some were not functioning at all; and not because of his five-year hiatus, they were clogged with drugs, paranoia and mental sickness. A cocaine habit, that had been no more than a dalliance at the start of the decade had taken over his life while his weight, due to those years spent in bed, had reached 240 pounds.

When asked what he had been doing for the last few years he simply replied, "Drugs and hanging out with Danny Hutton." On top of that Brian was being nannied by Stan Love to prevent self-harm and had just begun his association with "psychiatrist" Eugene Landy. He was far too vulnerable for exposure to the in-fighting that was now part of daily life in the band.

The decision to place all bets on him coming through with the goods, whether taken in good faith or through greed, had simply not taken into account that it was not 1965 any more. Brian had already moved far beyond all that once in his lifetime and here he was forced to do it again – snippets of original material that slipped through like "Still I Dream Of It" or "It's Over Now" suggested his head still yearned for the melancholy of *Pet Sounds*, even if he could not replicate the music. Lacking concentration or self-belief the warm-up material that was meant to provide stimulation ended up comprising half the album. *15 Big Ones* was rushed out in July 1976 to mass derision but was, inevitably their most successful "original" record of the 1970s, peaking at number 8.

"Rock And Roll Music" became the much sought-after hit and crashed into the top 5.

The finished product was more undignified even than *So Tough* and the Beach Boys took on the appearance of performing monkeys. From promoting themselves as serious artists here they were again bop-ditting and shoo-bee-doin' in a candy-coated world. Every factor that had made them a great group was brushed under the carpet like a dirty secret. The new music was perhaps best encapsulated by "That Same Song" with its forewarning that the band were going to take their rock style just one more mile. Mike Love, now dressing up for gigs in gold lamé and a turban, was ecstatic.

Dennis and Carl were furious. Dennis in particular – he had carried on recording and experimenting but in a spirit of brotherly kinship left his accomplishments on the backburner while Brian re-established himself. However the idea behind *15 Big Ones* had been to ease his brother back gently, not regress for the sake of money. In other words the finished album was a complete misfire. And while Mike and Al's standings as concert frontmen were boosted by the resurgence in popularity and subsequent mega-tours, Dennis and Carl's positions within the group had been severely compromised. As Dennis told Timothy White in *Crawdaddy*, "The album should have been 100% original. We had enough Brian Wilson material to do it... Steve Love, Mike Love and Al Jardine were pushing to get it out – it was just a big push. They'd rather just get it out there than take time and develop it. Carl and I were really upset."

This was a position reaffirmed by his younger brother: "We were heartbroken. People have waited all this time, anticipating a new album – I hated to give them this. It was a great mistake to put Brian in full control. He was always the full producer, but little did he know that in his absence people grew up. We became as sensitive as the next guy. Why should I relinquish my rights as an artist? The whole process was a little bruising."

Dennis had spent the years between 1974 and 1976 honing his craft and had bag of songs that could readily have been contributed to the album. The concentration on "oldies but goodies" (Brian's terminology) meant they simply did not fit in. In 1975 Dennis had hooked up with his original writing partner Stephen Kalinich to start several songs and plan future projects[2]. Among these unheard and unreleased numbers were "Our Love Remains", "Grateful Are We For Little Children", "Mona Kana", "Helen Keller", "Marble Sittin' At The Kitchen Table" and (great title) "Don't Want Much Just A Country Or Two Maybe A Planet Before It's Through". An innate positivity, traceable back to "Be Still" or "Little

---

[2] Interestingly Stephen also started providing lyrics for Brian around the mid-1970s. Together they wrote "You're Riding High On The Music", "Lucy Jones" and one of the better unreleased songs from this period, "California Feeling". Stephen kindly played me his copy of the poetry album he planned to release with backing from Brian. As well as supplying organ to the extended "Be Still", Brian provided some great vocals (not harmonies, more spontaneous sounds) to some of the other poems.

Bird", always surfaced when the two collaborated. This was especially so with their most fully realised song from this period, the upbeat and innocent "Rainbows". The penultimate number on *Pacific Ocean Blue* it provided a welcome glow on the album, the mandolin driven melody perfectly at ease with the "celebration of nature" theme of the lyrics.

The two also made sketches for an ambitious project entitled "Life Symphony" that would never become realised. Based around a series of poems reflecting life from childhood to death it was to be backed by orchestral movements courtesy of Dennis. "We're searching for a blending of words and harmony/Darkness comes before the dawn, sorrow before the song/Make your life a symphony and we'll all sing along," ran one segment. Again though, it remained fragmented and unfinished – there was simply no outlet for it within the Beach Boys of the mid-1970s. The words exist but Stephen is still waiting for someone to put music to them...

Dennis had also been busy with other projects. In late 1975 he had been producing sessions for a young songwriter called Jim Dutch – his whereabouts are now unknown though he did receive part of the writer's credit for Dennis' "Thoughts Of You", sung a duet called "Miller Drive" with America's Gerry Beckley and apparently hosted some joint sessions with Van Dyke Parks.

Aside from "Rainbows" and "Pacific Ocean Blues", the former recorded at the time of the Dutch sessions, he had a host of other songs ready for possible inclusion on the album. Some of these remain unheard ("Holy Man And Slow Booze", taped on 12th February 1975 or "Barnyard Blues") while others such as the driving, rhythmic "10,000 Years" were previewed to journalists and then dropped. Dennis actually wrote the germ of the latter song with Mike Love in 1974 before they both laid claim to it and reworked their own versions over the next few years. The lyrical theme would not have sat easily with "Susie Cincinnati" or "Palisades Park": "(It's) about how man has changed and not changed in 10,000 years; the only real change is that we have roofs over our heads and we have toilets. We're still murdering and lustful and all that crap, still paying to see *Deep Throat* over and over again."

The divisions that had come with democracy, and that *15 Big Ones* was supposed to eliminate, were to return ten-fold. Brian's supposed renaissance had succeeded in complicating an already difficult situation and his sad figure became a pawn in successive power struggles as the decade wore on. Since Al Jardine had become a full-time member of the corporation the question of direction was split 50/50, with Mike Love joining him in opposition against Dennis and Carl. The advocates of TM and the status quo versus the advocates of artistic expression and growth with Brian playing the part of figurehead and – more importantly – the deciding vote in any business-related matters. Given that Mike was far more *au fait* with industry matters than any of the Wilsons and his brothers Stephen and Stan were band manager and "protector" of Brian respectively, it was his faction that gained dominance. Dennis remained bonded to his brother emotionally and in awe of him artistically but this was a weakened currency in the cold light of commerce. A weak and malleable Brian Wilson, on paper by far the band's most important member, meant a weakening of Dennis' own influence. By binding himself obligingly to a powerless figurehead he was pushed into the background, his role limited to playing the drums.

It was a classic situation of Catch 22. Dennis had gambled everything on Brian to resurrect the Beach Boys to the glories of *Pet Sounds*. He spoke only of Brian's talent, how nobody on the band could touch him, how he was a master and how music rather than personalities should define the group[3]. He had no problem in becoming Brian's tool once again and he laid down his own future refusing to even mention his own songs. As with Carl this was an admirable but, in hindsight, rash decision. The Beach Boys had effectively become the Mike and Al Show. The forces of blandness had assumed control and Dennis would have to lump it.

The irony being of course that it was Dennis who possessed the greatest musical talent in the band. Since 1970 it was he who concurrently had dominated the albums and suffered the indignity of having his songs dropped from successive projects. Brian had the past, that's unarguable, but Dennis had the present and held the vision to the future. The likes of "River Song" or "Pacific Ocean Blues" were far beyond the imagination or capability of the others. In slavish devotion to his brother he had underestimated his own talents and ultimately discarded them. The reality was a reaffirmation of the situation in 1971 – the Beach Boys were too conservative a vehicle for Dennis' music and because of personality clashes his suggestions were undervalued. To fully realise any personal ambitions he would finally have to work outside of the Beach Boys and release a solo record.

Central to this realisation was the support of Gregg Jakobson and James William Guercio. Gregg, as Dennis' most constant companion, had been there since 1967 offering advice, lyrics and occasional guitar. Guercio – the producer and driving force behind Chicago and owner of Caribou studios in Colorado, where the likes of Badfinger and Elton John recently cut albums – had assumed bass playing duties for the Beach Boys when Blondie Chaplin departed. (Chicago, despite a somewhat staid image, even back then, represented the epitome of the American mainstream. They were the competition of the time and Dennis, Carl and Al had provided backing vocals on their 1974 hit "Wishing You Were Here"). Already immensely successful and powerful his presence helped galvanize the touring band, and in Rieley's absence James Guercio was one of the few individuals who could straddle the inherent divides of the Beach Boys. It was with his backing that the band would sign to the CBS subsidiary, Caribou Records, in 1977.

And it was Guercio's suggestion to Dennis that he pick up the thread of his solo career and pursue unfinished business from earlier in the decade. Initially he hoped to collaborate personally, but after hearing

---

[3] "There's not one person in the group that could come close to Brian's talent," was pretty much the gist of Dennis' comments to journalists in the period preceding *15 Big Ones*.

the strength of material already recorded Guercio stood aside. Predating the Beach Boys' own move[4], Dennis was granted leave from Warner Brothers to produce an album on Caribou to the tune of a $100,000 advance. This was tied to fairly stringent restrictions that no other Beach Boys could be involved with the record and, conversely, if any songs were played live they would have to be played with the band. A confusing situation, and one that granted Dennis the total freedom to create but little scope to promote his efforts. All the conditions for a "Great Lost Album" were in place.

Back in 1971 when Dennis should have released his first solo record there had been no such Guercio figure fighting for his corner. His importance to the project was highlighted by the final credit on the inner sleeve that simply read, "Thank You Jimmy G".

That was the background to the release of Dennis' finest moment – the conditions that made it inevitable. (He still loved the sense of being a Beach Boy and the hedonism and adulation it entailed but he also had his own things to say). There were other relevant factors though.

In 1974 Dennis met Karen Lamm, the former wife of Chicago keyboardist Bobby Lamm, and entered into a life-changing but tempestuous relationship. A beautiful blonde actress and model, Karen was also a kindred spirit – when Dennis was bad she could be badder. "We were both dynamos. When you put two dynamos together you get dynamite!" If songs like "Forever" and "Fallin' In Love" had documented the early idealism of his marriage to Barbara Charren then the bulk of what ultimately became *Pacific Ocean Blue* described the travails of his new love. In what became a series of highly personal statements there were songs inspired by Karen, about Karen and ultimately written with Karen. Marrying twice in the space of two years they seemed to be either fighting insanely or in the process of an intense and blissful reconciliation.

In the first throes of their on-off relationship Dennis gave up a dependence on cocaine that was starting to rival his brother's fierce intake. By the mid-70s the entertainment industry in LA was literally fuelled by white powder and its influence was apparent everywhere. In the thin white sound of session player sterility, just about every other song on the radio reeked of it – that lazy unfeeling indulgence of FM rock, a reptilian sound as lifeless as a lizard on a dry rock. The city was becoming hard, drained of emotion and literally eaten away. The 1970–79 roll call of death through indulgence was unprecedented before or since: Tim Buckley, Lowell George, Al Wilson, Danny Whitten, Janis Joplin, Gram Parsons and Hendrix were only the most prominent casualties. Perhaps the physical state of Elvis – who had descended from leathered guitar God to heavyweight parody in the space of a decade – provided the most fitting embodiment to the times.

The drug was another lever to wrench apart the Wilson and Love factions – Mike and Al never touched the stuff. And for a while neither

---

[4] Indeed, it was the strength of Dennis' demo material that was one of the primary factors in CBS chancing their arm and signing the Beach Boys.

---

did Dennis: the two lovers were presented in the media as the idyllic Californian couple: healthy, wealthy and happy. "He'd get up in the morning and catch halibut for our breakfast, he'd go out and dive and surf, we'd run on the beach every morning. It was so good, he didn't think he deserved it," was Karen's assessment.

Yet the instances of their mutual insanity were legion. Dennis happily torched a brand new Ferrari in a typical fit of jealousy – Karen responded in kind by firing holes in his Mercedes. Dennis resumed his philandering ways even before they were married – after a bust-up in Australia Karen attacked him with a stiletto in an airport lounge. By 1976 Dennis was running on coke again – when Karen found a huge bottle sitting on the mixing desk after an all night recording session she spilled the lot onto the carpet. Dennis responded by changing the locks to their house, whereupon Karen gained access via a brick through the window...

Dennis' other obsession was his sailboat *Harmony*. Purchased in 1974, he poured thousands of dollars into refurbishing the Japanese vessel that had once been a wreck. The 50-foot boat was customised to accommodate an electric piano, a drum kit and recording facilities; the interior was draped in oriental and fur rugs and, while berthed at Marina Del Rey, served as a home from 1976 to 1981. As labour of love it was perfect for Dennis: filling his hours productively and satisfying his wanderlust. "Whenever the mood is upon me," he commented, "I can capture the feeling. My greatest passion, after my music, is the sea. I love its mystery, its high adventure, and its peacefulness. It's the only place I can truly relax." When business affairs became overbearing Dennis could disappear up the Californian coast, sometimes accompanied by Karen or Gregg Jakobson and sometimes alone, travelling as far as Hawaii or the Baja peninsula of Mexico.

Harmony would prove as relevant a symbol to personal freedom for Dennis as the surfboard some fifteen years earlier. It offered a fleeting vision of escape and purity. While the old material had informed the teenage world of the beach, Dennis' new music was drenched with imagery of another kind: turmoil, faith, love, freedom, fame. He sounded like he wished to grow up: the bright lightweight sound of the 1960s that Brian was busy replicating was replaced on *Pacific Ocean Blue* by dark and brooding overtures of great power. While Brian was scared to even paddle in the shallows his brother was diving into the fathoms. Consequently the ocean was an almost permanent backdrop to these haunted songs of love and loss. Those numerous trips away from shore had returned Dennis full-circle to his roots – only now he viewed the horizon through the damaged eyes of an adult.

The sessions proper for *Pacific Ocean Blue*, or *Freckles* as its working title was known ("right now I like *Freckles*, 'cause they're nice – especially freckles and red hair") began in September of 1976. Working eighteen-hour days at Brother Studios or from the temporary mixing board at his modest beach house, Dennis enlisted an impressive array of backing musicians to achieve his vision. Joining him on drums were his touring deputies Ricky Fataar and Bobby Figueroa while, as a mark of respect and reverence to the man who had worked while he played all those years ago, Hal Blaine was drafted in too. Similarly he used a trio of bassists: Ed Carter who had played live with the Beach Boys since 1973, and seasoned session players Jamie Jamerson and Chuck Domanico. Jamerson was the son of Motown's own bassist who had played on literally hundreds of hits[5], while Domanico had worked with artists as diverse as Chet Baker and Scott McKenzie. Carter also contributed guitar with Ed Tujela, Earle Mankey (ex of Sparks and soon to play with The Cramps), John Hanlon [see Appendix] and an un-credited Billy Hinsche. The horn section was led by classy players like Bill Lamb, Lance Buller and Charlie McCarthy. Akin to Brian's mid-60s experiments, Dennis sought out the cream of Californian talent, both rock and jazz musicians, to achieve the sound and textures in his head – this would be his own *Pet Sounds* steeped in the sounds of the 1970s as opposed to those of a bygone era.

Aside from Dennis' own voice – now stripped bare by the cocaine to a hoarse one-octave croon – backing vocals were a mixture of friends (Karen, Gregg, Jim Dutch, Billy Hinsche, Trisha Roache), gospel (The Double Rock Baptist Choir), ex-Beach Boys (Bruce Johnston) and un-credited Beach Boys (brother Carl's distinctive tones could be heard audibly on "River Song"). Production duties were shared with Gregg and the sleeve was designed by Dean Torrence of Jan and Dean.

But this was unmistakably Dennis Wilson's record. It was his thoughts, feelings and moods that inhabited the grooves. Combining a fusion of Little Feat, Brian Wilson, Motown and the live sound of 1973–74 he was to create a masterpiece unlike anything in the Beach Boys' past and certainly unlike anything in their future. While Brian was watching his musical life flash before him and undergoing some sort of therapy/humiliation in public, Dennis had come up with the goods. The Beach Boys might have been labouring in auto-pilot towards a sound of anodyne MOR but *Pacific Ocean Blue* was raw.

The songs could be placed into three categories that often interlinked. Songs about the ocean, about Karen Lamm and about rock'n'roll. Of the ecology themes, "River Song" was the most successful. Inspired by a trip to the High Sierras the recurrent and rolling piano riff reflected the water's journey from source to ocean. From an opening trickle it grew organically to a bombastic display of choirs, keyboards and thumping drums. The shifts of energy conducted from a lone voice in the verse, cursing the state of the city, to the majestic drama of the chorus in praise of nature was breathtaking and a far cry from the one-dimensional compositions Brian was churning out. The sheer capacity and dynamism of the sound was simply awesome, an absolute ten miles high vortex of melody. And, if it was lyrically simplistic, then at least it was heartfelt –

[5] As dynamo of the Motown house band James Jamerson had driven over 30 number one pop hits. That he had already played on "You Keep Me Hanging On", "My Girl", "Uptight", "I Heard It Through The Grapevine", "I Second That Emotion" and "I Hear A Symphony" makes him one of the most remarkable characters in modern music history. In the 1970s *Let's Get It On* and the Temptations' excursions into psychedelic funk were added to the list. He died in the August 1983 of pneumonia – broken, alcoholic and forgotten.

as always with Dennis Wilson the justified delivery equalled any amount of verbosity; he sounded like he truly believed. For an opener it was a real statement of intent – its uncluttered power highlighting Dennis' excellence behind the mixing desk and his desires to escape the smog of LA. To literally run away and find the river. The belief in redemption was all encompassing: "I'd like to donate everything I make and do to the environment and ecology. I'd like to get a list of them. We've been thinking and talking about it but I'm tired of just talking. I wanna do free shows, get rid of the pollutant in the cock, in the mind, everywhere. From syphilis to smog."

Thematically "River Song" could be paired with another pre-1976 number, the title song "Pacific Ocean Blues". Mike Love's heavy-handed lyric ("The flagship of death is an old whaling trawler") was less esoteric than the rest of the album but it at least reflected his own golden period around the start of the decade when "Big Sur", his rumination on the physical beauty of California, was written. It certainly compared favourably with his dumb contributions to *15 Big Ones*, for which the track was originally intended. Heavy on the Moog and the sound effects, its ecological themes wrapped up in a Lowell George white-boy funk, this was where the Beach Boys should have been heading in the mid-70s.

The most effective music however was very much different from the Beach Boys. The overtly environmental songs might have been considered for group recordings but it was a collection of very blue and tender ballads that defined the record. Highlighting a subtlety and grace unheard since Brian's heyday the lonesome spirit of the sea was a constant presence. It was the introspective laments that made *Pacific Ocean Blue* a masterpiece.

"Who made my moonshine, intoxicating me." With those words the listener was transported back to the territory of "Forever" and steeped in the romantic drama that Dennis had specialised in for ten years. Entitled "Beautiful Play" during the sessions of 1977, "Moonshine" was the first of four incredible songs that documented his relationship with Karen Lamm. It was a painful cry of loss in the past tense – a realisation of love gone astray so climactic and powerful that it was as if viewed through the eyes of a cinematic audience. The scene of parting was so dramatic that viewers "thought they would die". Its fatalism was an aftermath to the satisfied warmth of "You And I" – the latter song being a shuffling tale of infatuation for his wife with a recurring statement that there would be no more blue songs and no more lonely nights.

This would prove to be wishful thinking. During the creation of these songs Dennis had married Karen and then decided on divorce within a six-month period of 1976. In the first few weeks of the following year they would reunite and attempt to wed a second time. A bizarre and tangled soap opera. Whatever the endurance of their love it was too volatile to last.

The opening track of Side Two, "Time", written in the air when floating back into LA was blatantly confessional. Over Bill Lamb's beautiful trumpet lines Dennis crooned along in unison that he was "the

---

kind of guy who loves to mess around – know a lot of women, but they don't feel my heart with love completely free". His voice was immense and filled the speakers. It was pure rock star blues – a comedown to on-the-road adulation when the ovations ceased and the music was over. A startling admission of infidelity, it was actually a collaboration with Karen. Having already been married to one musician she understood the unwritten laws of the road: "I know Dennis loved me with all his heart. Guys will be guys, boys will be boys. It's all about the male ego and has nothing to do with the woman in their life. I'm not saying I applauded it, but I understood it. When you perform in front of two hundred and fifty thousand people, you get it. When you come offstage you think you can go to the hotel, call your wife and go to bed? The energy, the adrenaline is pumping, people are telling you how great you are, and it's lonely on tour." One of the most brutally honest assessments of his contradictions and failings – especially when the Beach Boys were writing simplistic boy-meets-girl nursery rhymes – it was let down only when huge slabs of processed synthesiser invaded the ending.

However, the track that preceded it was something else. Everything about "Thoughts Of You" was perfect. A by-product of the 1975 Jim Dutch sessions, and co-written by him, it was a song of two parts. Beginning with Dennis alone at the piano, quietly walking his fingers around the minor chords of the keyboard and ruminating on fleeting spells of happiness ("Like the sunshine, love comes and goes again"), it segued in mid-stream to a turbulent piece of awesome power. On signal of the phrase "I miss you" the music started to rise, the notes suddenly repetitive and bass driven and the vulnerable lone voice multi-tracked to infinity. It was an audacious piece of studio trickery but the results were devastating. The pay-off line was "All things that live one day must die, you know – even love and the things we hold close..."

Comparable in achievement with something like Alex Chilton's "Kangaroo", "Thoughts Of You" pushed Dennis Wilson's songwriting into the ether. It remains probably his best performance – the perfect balance between the spontaneity of raw emotion and studio mastery. After the storm of the mid-section the fractured voice of the beginning was reprised and against groaning strings choking back the lines, "Loneliness is a very special place, to forget something that I've never done. Silently, silently you touch my face". In the background the waves and sea sounds were audible. There could be little doubt who the song was about: the working title had been "Thoughts Of Karen".

Other highlights were the majestic grandeur of "Farewell My Friend" and the closing "End Of The Show". The former was a touching tribute to Otto "Pop" Hinsche ("My best friend died in my arms, and I came to the studio... When my father died, Pops saved my life in a way"). The septuagenarian father of Billy Hinsche had helped Dennis come to terms with Murry, and his passing in May 1976 was one of the reasons for a hasty first marriage to Karen in the same month. The album closer was a small epic of expanded strings, cavernous guitar noise and Moogs, filled with truisms that were by turn positive and resignations of failure. In interview with David Leaf, Dennis claimed "End Of The Show" was a farewell to world conflict and a farewell to his wife. The final words drifted away over the sound of applause from a Beach Boys' concert:

"Thank you very much for everything you've ever dreamed of. It's over."

Even the three songs about rock'n'roll, which did not fully pay off, had moments way beyond the average. "What's Wrong" was slight musically but contained some slyly amusing observations about fame while "Friday Night" was a more energetic description of Dennis' youth as a white punk. They were throwaway in the manner of his earlier compositions "Got To Know The Woman" or "All I Want To Do". By contrast "Dreamer" was musically never less than interesting, moving from electronic funk to sweeping melody to jazz cacophony. Concerned with achieving your desires (by getting to heaven or sleeping with a rock star) the lyric was less than subtle in conveying its message, though the slow passage about letting the wind carry your blues away was lovely. Ballads, not straight-up rock, remained Dennis' forte.

These were not the only songs recorded by Dennis during 1976 and 1977. It had been an extremely prolific period and the final tracklisting had been juggled around on several occasions. Most interesting had been updated versions of both "Lady" from 1970, now entitled "Flowers Come In The Spring" after the opening line, and a take on "Only With You" from *Holland* where Carl's lead vocal had been originally used. Another track, "Tug Of Love", had been taken off the album at the last minute while other completed songs were "I Didn't Mean To Make You Worry", "I Don't Know", "School Girl", "Time For Bed" and "Taking Off", as well as the previously mentioned "10,000 Years", "Barnyard Blues" and "Helen Keller" plus other tapes labeled with working titles like "Carl's Song" or "Mike's Song"[6]. Of these only "School Girl" was held over for inclusion on *Bamboo*, the proposed title for Dennis' second album, while the others are still missing in action. The fact that they probably reside in the vaults of CBS/Caribou rather than Capitol or Warner Brothers may mean that they are never heard again.

That *Pacific Ocean Blue* was the best thing to come out of the Beach Boys camp in the 1970s was highlighted by its towering presence over 1977's *Love You*, the real "Brian's Back" album. This all new synthesiser-drenched collection was the record that the band had envisaged appearing in 1976 in that it contained 14 new and original Brian Wilson compositions[7]. Indeed, if *15 Big Ones* had been the sound of the recluse touching base with his past then *Love You* was the result: the sound of

---

[6] The contents of the latter two are unknown – it is more than likely they contain versions of songs already known about since Dennis collaborated with both Mike and Carl.

[7] As well as writing the songs, Brian also handled the bulk of the instrumentation – at least eighty percent calculated co-engineer Earle Mankey: "Mike was teaching TM, Al & Lynda raised bees and horses, Dennis was busy with his own album and a huge sailboat, Carl was producing a singer."

Brian Wilson in 1977, schizophrenic and lost, trying to recapture the essence of what made him so great. That this was to mean thirteen lightweight and inane pop songs plus one glimmer of his former greatness was due to the combined pressures of the Beach Boys and an audience clamoring for the simplicity of yore. They presented Brian with the order form and he processed it from memory. This meant *Love You* was a deeply disturbing record for all the wrong reasons: a 34-year old man singing through the eyes of a teenager. The sense of wonder that had once been an unbridled joy of warmth and sensitivity was now grotesque, and sometimes downright creepy. Middle-age was not the place for songs about the amazing talents of "Johnny Carson" or "Honkin' Down The (Gosh Darn) Highway", while observations that the solar system was indeed big or cars looked small from the seat of an airplane were the expressions of a child, not a fully-grown adult. For a man who had written "I Just Wasn't Made For These Times" and "God Only Knows" it was nothing short of criminal.

The record coincided with Eugene Landy's decision that Brian should once again play concerts as part of his rehabilitation program. He was dragged out of the bedroom into the studio and onto the stage, his presence proof that the good old days would soon be back. The world was consequently treated to the sight of an extravagant greatest hits show with the Beach Boys dressed in white and gold, the Stars and Stripes draped everywhere and a forlorn figure in the shadows, his keyboard not even plugged in. The lank-haired giant with the thousand-yard stare was a depressing contrast to the glitz and showbiz that surrounded him. When introduced to the crowd during the encore he barely responded to their applause. It was as if one of the patients from *One Flew Over The Cuckoo's Nest* had escaped and slipped unnoticed onto the stage. Nobody seemed to notice.

Brian could still produce a pretty melody but recording with cod-disco keyboards and electronic drums meant *Love You* was dispatched with all the subtlety of a lesser glam rock band. Coupled with facile lyrics, with all the dexterity of "cat-rat-mat-sat" and an unhealthy fascination with adolescence it was a half-baked conception at best. Brian had been back to college and apparently forgotten more than he had learned. The thought of these aging, bearded "boys" singing with gusto about "sittin' in class" or "makin' sweet lovin'" with a rollerskating child was truly pathetic. On the unintentionally humorous "Johnny Carson" and "I Wanna Pick You Up" or the deeply pitiful "Mona" it seemed that no-one concerned could even be bothered. The latter was nothing more than a '50s rock'n'roll pastiche replete with lyrics that were less stream-of-consciousness than made up on the spot. What was even sadder was the unmistakable growl of Dennis Wilson that sang it.

Indeed Dennis' voice was all over the record. In addition to "Mona" his voice dominated "I'll Bet He's Nice" and "I Wanna Pick You Up", all equally throwaway. If Brian was firing blanks then by default Dennis, as his self-confessed tool, would be dragged into the mire with him. Surely this was the ultimate expression of his love for his brother, that the year his own sublime solo record was released Dennis was willing to squander his talents for the sake of the Beach Boys. The inherent contradictions of the band meant that he would have given it all up just to have his brother reinstated and functioning like it was 1966.

Only a single track on *Love You* might have justified such a decision. "The Night Was So Young" on Side Two was an undeniably gorgeous song, with a trademark Brian Wilson chorus of heart-swelling harmony. Though hardly on a par with anything on *Pet Sounds* it was an isolated moment of beauty and as such it remained an anomaly. Not that this affected unduly the sales of an album which reached number 53 on *Billboard* and garnered some reasonable reviews. Nick Kent described it as the best Beach Boys LP since *Sunflower* while Lester Bangs, never a huge fan, wrote that *Love You* was "almost more juvenile than their original stuff, it's not self-conscious, and it sounds right up-to-date. It's joyous, roller-rink-in-the-sky sound that always made them the real American Music... and as far as I'm concerned it might be their best album ever."

Pacific Ocean Blue also received considerable accolades from the US Press. In *Rolling Stone*, Billy Altman praised Dennis' contributions to previous Beach Boys records and described the album as "truly wonderful and touching": "...though the tunes are often little more than fragments, they have a way of taking hold of your emotions. 'Farewell My Friend' and 'Thoughts Of You' demonstrate the intensity of Wilson's songs, although both avoid the verse/chorus/bridge structure of most pop songs. And even on such up-tempo numbers as 'Friday Night' there's a sensitivity and vulnerability that is almost irresistible." By contrast the UK weeklies, consumed by the summer of punk, were less than complimentary. Ian Birch in a combined *Melody Maker* review of *Pacific Ocean Blue*, Blondie Chaplin's eponymous debut and Bruce Johnston's *Going Public* wrote of a "sort of miscalculated Spector Wall Of Sound with ethereal choir swamps... Dennis is no great shakes as a singer. His strained vocals are often (and unwisely) submerged in the mix. The overweening sentimentality of the lyrics are best left alone."

A 45 of "River Song"/"You And I" did nothing, but *Pacific Ocean Blue* was a minor triumph, selling an impressive 200,000 copies and reaching a peak of number 96 after entering the US charts at 166. This was a higher charting than the next two Beach Boy LPs managed and remains by far the most successful solo venture by any individual in the group. Caribou's failure to promote the record sufficiently and constrictions from within the group probably scuppered the chances of further success in 1977. As a subsidiary of CBS the album was not a priority, according to Fred Vail "it got lost in the major label shuffle. I knew early on that CBS were not going to latch onto it – they had Neil Diamond who was hot and Streisand who was hot – they had an enormous activity going at that time. I think they were penny wise and pound foolish."

The restrictive nature of Dennis' contract was also a hindrance. Despite clauses stating he was not allowed to perform without the Beach Boys a solo tour was actually organised and dates arranged for November with a full orchestra at venues including Avery Fisher Hall, Pine Knob

Music Theatre, the New York Academy of Music and Hofstra University. Support was to come from Ricci Martin for whom Carl had recently produced an LP. These were abandoned following a band meeting where Mike Love and Al Jardine issued an ultimatum to Dennis: either do the tour and leave the group for good or remain in the Beach Boys as drummer. For financial reasons he chose the latter option. The only songs off *Pacific Ocean Blue* that would get aired publicly were "River Song" and, on a couple of occasions, "Friday Night" and "What's Wrong"[8].

Mike and Al were more than a little irked by Dennis' success. That the figure they considered to be the least deserving, least talented member of the band should find critical acclaim (and be given a $100,000 advance) was a considerable affront – and Dennis proceeded to rub their noses in the fact whenever he could. The bogus image of a harmonious family took another dive. The deep resentment caused by *Pacific Ocean Blue* would lead directly to the extraordinary incident of early September 1977 when the Beach Boys nearly disintegrated before the eyes of *Rolling Stone* reporter John Swenson.

Following a huge free concert at Central Park and on the eve of their signing an $8.5 million contract with CBS, the tensions over artistic direction and over Brian's well-being finally boiled over. Apparently Mike and Al, buoyed by the backing of various Love brothers within the Beach Boys management, had already discussed replacing Carl and Dennis in the band – "I heard Buddy Miles mentioned as a possible replacement for Dennis, and I suppose they felt they didn't need to replace me with another guitarist," bemoaned Carl. The wholly commercial bloc of the band felt the time was right to split from the artistic; if they could drag Brian along then Dennis and Carl would be superfluous. They could concentrate on their solo careers if they didn't want to be a full time part of America's favourite band... and didn't the audiences only want to hear the greatest hits of the '60s anyhow? When Brian was constrained by the Love contingent from leaving his plane and joining Dennis and Karen overnight in New York tempers ignited. Dennis turned on Al and the white-stetsoned guitarist responded audibly: "We don't need you. We can make it without you."

From thereon the scene degenerated, all being noted down by Swenson, with Dennis encircled on the runway and Stan Love screaming that he had was only riding on Brian's coat-tails. It might well have been a scene from 1962 with Dennis still considered the no-talent drummer, his station dependent on his mother's wishes[9]. A family argument over fifteen years entrenched and the subsequent tug-of-war over Brian

---

[8] "River Song" was not played beyond 1974, while the other two were played on only a few occasions during Canadian dates in October 1977. After that, nothing.

[9] As Dennis quite rightly contested, he and Carl had been the keepers of the flame since 1968: "Stan Love thinks it's a big deal that he's been taking care of Brian for a while. He says I'm quitting on them. What does he think I've been doing all these years? Carl and I kept this group going through all the hard times. At one point or another they were all out of the group, but we kept it together."

ensured that Dennis' talents would never be fully recognised: "They kept telling me I had my own solo album now, like I should go off in a corner and leave the Beach Boys to them. The album really bothers them. They don't like to admit it's doing so well; they never even acknowledge it in interviews."

Brian too was fearful of what Dennis had achieved. "When my record was finished Brian was the first to hear it. In the middle of some tracks he'd say, 'I can't stand this' and walk out of the room. Sometimes he'd laugh. Sometimes he'd cry. I guess he was thinking that he'd seen me grow up as a musician."

By late autumn Mike and Al had decamped to the Maharishi International University Institute in Fairfield, Iowa to start recording the last Warners album – a follow-up to the Christmas record of 1964 – and the first Beach Boys effort for CBS. Now in full control of the band, both projects were worthy testament to their combined talents. The *Christmas Album*, rejected out of hand by Warners, was twee and cornball containing a mixture of old tracks – Brian's "Child Of Winter" and "Winter Symphony" – with the likes of Al's take on "Christmas Time Is Here Again" and "Santa's Got An Airplane". The *MIU* album, the final Warners release on Brother-Reprise in October 1978, was even worse. Recording at the Maharishi's behest, Mike and Al took Brian's lead from *Love You* and regressed even further. *MIU* had it all: a song about the rain called "Pitter Patter", a song entitled "Hey Little Tomboy", and an ode to the weather in Hawaii. It was a single most embarrassing release of their career – a prostitution of the Beach Boys name and their talents. The crowning glory was a cover of Buddy Holly's "Peggy Sue" that was also released as a single. It was the anaemic epitome of soul-less and ball-less – a terrible idea sucked dry. It was an album that belonged in the sterility of the 1980s.

Dennis and Carl wisely stayed home and continued working at Brother Studios, seeing no reason to promote such an abortion. What Mike Love and Al Jardine had done in the Beach Boys' name was unforgivable: "I hope that the karma will fuck up Mike Love's meditation for ever. That album is an embarrassment to my life. It should self-destruct."

Only Brian's "Diane", a statement of desire for his sister-in-law, rose above average. Predictably enough that included an impassioned lead vocal from Dennis that was his sole contribution to the record. As Richard Williams wrote in his scathing review for *Melody Maker*, "Should you choose to ignore the rest of the album, at least hear 'Diane' and be reassured that the spark still glows". Had the *Christmas Album* been released in tandem then the gulf in class and artistic superiority would have been even more pronounced. For amongst the contractual fluff was the truly gorgeous "Morning Christmas", otherwise known as "Holy Evening" or "Holy Holy", a sombre hymn for the season that was as good as anything Dennis ever wrote. Employing orchestra bells, a bass harmonica, and an ARP string ensemble – all processed through the mixing board – as a basis and counterpointing them with a delicate piano melody that ran up and down the scales, he created a sound that was purely spiritual – perhaps closer to the ghost of *Smile* than any of the Beach Boys had dared tread. "Holy, holy. Halo glowing. Candle burning. Christmas evening". It sounded like the eerie unwinding of a musical box.

The fate of "Morning Christmas", overlooked due to inclusion on a novelty record, emphasised the crossroads that Dennis Wilson found himself at by the conclusion of 1977. During that year he had fulfilled his bizarre dual existence as unreconstructed Beach Boy (drummer, bit-part, sex symbol) and solo performer (visionary, soulful, pioneer). A deep-seated love of Brian Wilson ensured he was happy to sing both "Mona" and "Thoughts Of You". Like Carl, Dennis believed the group's existence could only be guaranteed if they operated as a fully functioning creative force. The Beach Boys was an umbrella term that would cover every spectrum of the emotions; Brian would be the leader but each disparate individual would contribute so that the resulting harmony was more than the sum of its parts.

This was the antithesis of what Mike and Al saw. For them the Beach Boys future was in their past – lived out every night in the packed and ecstatic stadia of America. The public wanted *Endless Summer* and that's what they were going to get 365 days a year. The musical ideals of Dennis and Carl were nothing but a deviation from the plan; more than that, combined with their wayward lifestyles the Wilsons' were a threat – a danger to the newfound dollar prosperity. All they needed was Brian Wilson, and even his empty shell poking around inaudibly at the piano was good enough.

With hindsight maybe Dennis should have left the Beach Boys in 1977 with his dignity intact. *Pacific Ocean Blue* was proof enough that his promise could be fulfilled without the others, while the sequence of infantile group efforts from *15 Big Ones* to *MIU* only threatened to obscure his talents further. Alone and free he seemed on the verge of something great; with the Beach Boys he was abused artistically in much the same way as his brother.

Indeed, as Brian had discovered a decade earlier, it was almost impossible to reconcile the conservative and experimental elements of the band. Only with "Good Vibrations", when the commercial melded seamlessly with the ground-breaking had all sides been happy. Without significant sales the questions of image and audience perception would always be over-powering – the easy option to fall back on the hits would ensure advantage always tipped to the straight faction that did not fuck with the formula. By gearing his own music towards emotions and the soul Dennis emerged in a position of irreversible weakness. He was caught in no-man's land, between a loyalty to the band and the opportunity to flex his genius. Something had to give.

And so it did. 1977 would prove to be his last good year before everything started to slide. It was like Dennis had reached the top of the mountain and there was nowhere to go but down. In frustration and anger he pressed the self-destruct button and slowly started to fall. There was nothing else to do. On the eve of 1978 Dennis and Karen tried heroin for the first time. His love was turning from white to brown.

HOLY MAN AND SLOW BOOZE

*"The next album is a hundred times what **Pacific Ocean Blue** is. It kicks. It's different in a way. I think I have more confidence now that I've completed one project, and I'm moving on to another..."*
—Dennis Wilson to David Leaf, September 1977

"Dennis has thrown me into the deep end, literally and figuratively."
—Christine McVie, *People* Magazine, November 26, 1979

"Cocaine, cocaine, running round my heart running round my brain... Ah, Bittersweet."
—Fred Neil, *Cocaine Blues*

So, all but avoiding the antiseptic group sessions at Maharishi International University, Dennis prepared work for his follow-up to *Pacific Ocean Blue*. The short distance from his modest Santa Monica beach house or the *Harmony* to Brother Studios was perfectly suited to an increasingly instinctive method of recording. Like Brian in his prime, Dennis worked on several different ideas at once and would constantly erase segments until they were reworked and remodelled to his satisfaction. Steve Desper recalled that even back in the late '60s Dennis would "start so many songs or have so many musical ideas he wanted to explore that we simply ran out of 2" tape to record them onto. He would select a song he may have started to work on several weeks prior and discard it, forever, so that the multi-track of that song could be erased and a new song (which he felt was the better song of the moment) could be started."[1] A prime example of this was "River Song" which retained Ricky Fataar's original drum track from 1973 sessions but was transformed four years later into the layered and complex symphony that kick-started *Pacific Ocean Blue*.

The new record was to be called *Bamboo*. Simple and plain. A stripped-down title to reflect a new musical direction: a loose rock'n'roll sound rather than the sweeping romanticism of its predecessor. The vast crew of musicians and the services of Gregg Jakobson that had made *Pacific...* such a magnificent achievement were abandoned. *Bamboo* was to be largely a collaboration with Dennis' new writing partner Carli Muñoz.

---

[1] The wealth of Beach Boys material, never mind Dennis Wilson material, still unheard or unknown is probably unprecedented for a band of their stature. In Stephen Desper's words: "I like to tell people who ask me what it was like to record Brian Wilson that I have erased more BW tracks than most people have heard!"

Carli had long-term links with the Beach Boys even before becoming their touring keyboard player in 1973. Born in Puerto Rico and brought up on the sounds of Liverpool and California, he was a member of the group Space in the late 1960s who were managed, coincidentally, by Jack Rieley. Encouraged to travel to LA at Rieley's behest, Carli met up with Beach Boys backing musicians Eddy Carter and Mike Kowalski through mutual acquaintances and was soon performing as a temporary percussionist with the *Sunflower-Surf's Up* Roadshow in 1970–71. A year later Rieley became the Beach Boys' manager and in 1973 the vacancy for a full-time keyboardist arose when Daryl Dragon left to form The Captain and Tennille. Carli, who had already impressed Carl Wilson with his musical virtuosity and was temporarily unemployed following a tour for Wilson Pickett, was the obvious replacement. With additional recommendation from Jack Rieley he was to remain for the next six years.

Along with Bobby Figueroa, Putter Smith, Ricky Fataar and Blondie Chaplin, Carli was part of the new flavour ushered in by Rieley to project the Beach Boys as a hip multi-ethnic force. Blessed with the technical abilities to play jazz as well as the "straight" hits of the '60s his was a significant contribution to their resurrection as a live act. And around the mid-70s they were simply awesome, filling the stage with musicians and still willing to play obtuse material from *Sunflower* and *Surf's Up* in tandem with the Brian Wilson confectionery box of hits. The sweltering summer day in 1975 when the Beach Boys blew Elton John off his own Wembley stage is still talked about by those who attended in hushed reverence. Indeed, the evidence of 1974's *In Concert* album highlighted a band at the height of their performing powers, the extra backing providing those famed Californian vocals with the necessary muscle to compete with the best of their contemporaries.

Yet despite this strong musical current, Carli did not play on *Pacific Ocean Blue* and became a permanent fixture too late to play on any of their great '70s albums. His association with Dennis was as a touring companion and based, initially at least, on competition rather than songs. As seen in my interview [see Appendix] their relationship bloomed through a macho rites of passage on joining the band, a competition for women and then, only finally, through music. Carli had a great many songs written from his days in Space as well as a batch of lissome rockers and by 1977 he was openly auditioning them in front of an appreciative Dennis and Carl. Like the classically-trained Daryl Dragon, he was a far more accomplished musician than Dennis ever would be. However, this combination of the technically complex and the exotic Caribbean was more than intriguing enough for Dennis, rising to the challenge, to start working with him.

According to Carli, the initial sessions for *Bamboo* were upbeat affairs, brimming both with the confidence of *Pacific Ocean Blue*'s critical success and the chance of exploring new genres. Despite an often gruelling tour schedule Dennis remained highly focused, loving this extended opportunity to bathe in artistic freedom outside the pressure cooker of the Beach Boys. With *Harmony* berthed close by at the marina they had a ready-made escape pod to relax in after marathon sessions in the studio. Completing this idyllic scenario Dennis would fill the rumble seat of the vintage Model T he was driving with beer from a Venice Beach deli on the way to another day's work. "He had a passion for sailing plus he loved recording, and good honest music. He also cherished good friendship, so, I could honestly say he was happy and optimistic."

This was a scene reaffirmed by Roy Carr[2] of the *NME* who happened upon sessions at Brother Studios by chance in September 1977 just weeks before the release of *Pacific Ocean Blue*. Arriving with Dean Torrence who was delivering some promotional mugshots, he was soon roped into singing backing vocals. He remained there for two days. "Dennis said, 'You'll know this one' and it was 'Only With You' from *Holland*. The whole backing was done but he said he wanted to do a layered vocal on it. So he did a guide vocal himself in about fifteen minutes, doing two or three takes, and we spent the whole afternoon just layering this song and another one I can't remember the name of." The session was only interrupted halfway through when Dennis donned a pair of rollerskates and promptly disappeared, only to return an hour later wearing a huge beaming grin. Apparently his current lunchtime routine involved intimate relations with a waitress in a nearby diner.

"When he got back we worked on this other song. He said that too many artists wait too long between albums and his idea was that as soon as one record was dropping off the charts the next one should come out. He said that when he was recording *Pacific Ocean Blue* there was enough material for at least two-thirds of the next album and he always wanted to have over half an album done. He also wanted to go back and revisit at least one or two of the old Beach Boys songs. I don't think his ego was so large that he wanted to disassociate himself with the band and there were old songs of theirs he had always wanted to sing. As far as I can remember this new version of 'Only With You' was close to the original except of course his voice was that much more intimate, a lot more heartbreaking. When he was singing this he'd play-act and put his hands up to his chests and say, 'This'll break the little girls hearts'."

Dennis was fully aware of the paradoxes in his media perception. He was the Beach Boys' resident fool and cocksman – forever introduced in concert as a "naughty boy" with reference to "the ladies" or being drunk – but Dennis was in admiration of other drummers who had branched out into other fields of music. "He was saying to me that most people think of a band as a bunch of musicians and a drummer but look how many great jazz drummers have fronted great bands, like Art Blakey or Buddy Rich or Gene Krupa. He had a lot of admiration for Ringo because I think people perceived him as the Beach Boys' own version, you

---

[2] Roy had met the Beach Boys in London in 1965 when a member of The Executives. During the recording of a Radio Luxembourg show he had taught Brian and Carl the correct chords to a number of Beatles songs that they were getting wrong – a number of which turned up on the *Beach Boys Party!* album later that year – and remained a champion of the group when he became a music journalist some years later. Striking up a friendship with Dennis and Carl he met and interviewed them on numerous occasions in the '70s.

know, that sort of happy-go-lucky character."

Dennis' appreciation of jazz had been evident since his *Pet Sounds* days spent watching the superior drumming technique of Hal Blaine. Working with horn players such as Joel Pesking, Glen Ferris and Zal Marquez this influence had spilled significantly into his songwriting and was immediately obvious in the complex structure of songs like "Time" and "Dreamer". Inherent curiosity was the source of an insatiable desire to learn and to master anything thrown before him: musically, physically or romantically. In this sense Carli Muñoz represented a whole new style of music and Dennis quickly latched onto it – as Tom Murphy, Dennis' oft-time producer from this period, verified in the *Endless Harmony* sleeve notes: "[he] had the greatest respect for Carly. He thought Carly was so talented". When they finally worked together in 1978 the results would be markedly different from what came before.

Pacific Ocean Blue had been a deeply sensual album, ultra-marine and dense; and while some of its soulful textures would also find their way onto *Bamboo* at least half of the new songs were low-down and sleazy rock'n'roll. The sweeping seascape of strings and the huge roll call of musicians was replaced dramatically. So much so that the dramatis personae working alongside Dennis and Carli consisted of a defiantly basic set up – usually Tommy and Sterling Smith on guitar and percussion, Dave Hessler on bass and long-time players Pesking and Figueroa. As Dennis' personal life tipped towards its alcohol-sodden descent so the music reflected its wayward course of its creator. His new songs gravitated towards a celebratory good-time boogie or the piano-based ballads which was their downside.

Left over from the 1976/77 sessions, perhaps even earlier, were "School Girl" and "Wild Situation". The former was as crude lyrically as the title suggested[3] but featured a driving off-beat drum rhythm and an isolated high-toned bass line. Complete with female backing vocals it shuddered on the verge of falling apart and sounded like the bastard offspring of Big Star's "You Can't Have Me" and the funky mid-song breakdown of the Stones' "Can You Hear Me Knockin'". "Wild Situation", the song that originally contained alleged references to the Manson girls, had now become a cliché-ridden tale of licentious groupie encounters ("she's an angel on the ground") and concluded in a call and response finale of "She took off her clothes and moved in my direction, she got it hot and now it's a big erection". Subtle, not. The music was great though, a slow meandering blues topped off with three or four-part Beach Boys harmonies and Carl Wilson noticeably high in the mix. Also in the 12-bar bracket were the Wilson/Muñoz compositions "Moonlight" and "New Orleans". Booze-drenched and primeval slabs of trash – "everyone knows my name, no one's gonna guess my age, the young girls go into a rage... under the moonlight" – Dennis was singing out a parody of his excesses: a 33-year-old sex symbol on the slide.

---

[3] In a case of life imitating art Dennis was arrested for contributing to the delinquency of a minor in April 1978, after a gig in Tuscon, Arizona.

Since splitting finally with Karen Lamm the sight of Dennis coked-up or drunk on stage was causing regular tensions within a band solid in surface but cracked beneath[4]. In an attempt to court the *Endless Summer*-loving masses Mike had long replaced his holy robes with a more diplomatic stage persona. The Beach Boys were a corporation – a reflection of their audience – and it was important they were perceived as good, clean American fun. In no particular order the set list ran the gamut from surfing to cars to girls, encompassing the nauseating "Be True To Your School" along the way. There could be no deviation from their image. It was like Murry's authoritarian stance all over again, the petty regulations and the striped shirts, and Dennis would consistently and wilfully undermine it. As the band became straighter he became wilder. His beard and hair were by now lank and unkempt, his clothing beat-up and old, and when the alcohol had really taken hold his playing was for a different band in a different place. On those nights that usually energetic onstage contribution had become merely unpredictable: barking into microphones, losing rhythm on the drums and disrupting songs in mid-flow. While the band innocently sang "C'mon pretty baby and dance with me" Dennis would counter with "C'mon pretty baby and fuck with me". To Mike's displeasure the crowd still cheered for Dennis but he was losing control and spending as much time in the wings as on stage – if he even turned up at all. Like Brian – a fading background presence behind an unplugged keyboard, wheeled out like an antique relative – he was becoming redundant to the whole razzmatazz that was a Beach Boys concert. As the happy-happy show rolled on, his only constant was an obligatory rasped and discordant take on "You Are So Beautiful".

The recreational activities that were spilling over into the workplace had first come to a head during the Beach Boys' record-grossing tour of Australia in 1978. At this point, much to the disgust of Mike and Al, all three Wilson brothers were dabbling in hard drugs. Brian was liable to swallow anything once free of his minders and even Carl was entertaining a flirtation with a variety of powders, in addition to collapsing drunk onstage in Perth. But it was Dennis who was singled out as the most destructive influence since he had been buying for and taking coke with Brian, and thus tarnishing the image of the whole organisation. According to Stan Love, "Dennis had been hanging round and he got Brian to buy maybe fifteen thousand dollar's worth of cocaine. Brian would snort up to five or six grand in a half an hour, and they'd have to put their hands in his mouth to stop him swallowing his tongue". When Brian was found in possession of a $100 bag of heroin in Melbourne the blame fell instantly on Dennis and the ensuing arguments very nearly split the band. In the aftermath he was ostracised even further from what remained of the Beach Boys' creative centre, with Mike clamouring for his dismissal: "Dennis is not a kind of person who you can give another

---

[4] After marrying in May 1976, Dennis and Karen were divorced by September 1977. Continuing an on-off relationship through much of the next year they remarried in July 1978 only for Dennis to file for divorce a mere two weeks later. Their second marriage was not annulled until 1980.

---

chance. He's not the kind of person who's trustworthy. People who like drugs lie, they are not trustworthy." For the time being Dennis remained, but Mike would not have to wait long for his wish.

The demon seeds of wanton self-destruction were evident in several others of the *Bamboo* tracks – most notably "He's A Bum". Cut as a very rough demo in September or October 1977 the song was another classic slice of Dennis Wilson. Lines like "he's a dog – a hot dog – he loves to do it on his hands and knees" or "he's a bum, he's a sailor, some people said he lost his lady... but he's alright" were all lewd bravado and macho posturing. That the song was autobiographical didn't take a genius to conclude. The bar-room rag of the music covered by '80s style synths and a great melodic bass line showed Dennis at his arrogant best. This was true too of "Companion", a Carli Muñoz composition that nailed spiritual lyrics to a rich Latin score. It was a truly bizarre concoction: a searching, soulful vocal about living life with a "constant companion" set against a mighty wall of percussion and the sound of Rio Carnival unleashed. Santana meets the Beach Boys under Sugarloaf Mountain. Of all the songs on *Bamboo*, it was the strong hook lines of "Companion" that sounded like hit potential – certainly compared to "Peggy Sue", the latest instalment of 7" woefulness committed by the band to the airwaves.

Yet if the sheer looseness and boogie of *Bamboo* was a return to the reckless abandon of Dennis' youth there was also much sadness in evidence. The other half of the record, dedicated to art of balladry he had been perfecting since the start of the decade, told a different story. Beneath the chest-beating was the sound of a heart breaking. Hence there was Carli's "It's Not Too Late", written in the late '60s and featuring Carl Wilson's pitch-perfect tones. It was a mid-paced number of gently progressing chord patterns that built politely to Carl's aching repetition of the title. Hinting at the optimism of reconciliation that was absent from the other clutch of slowies "It's Not Too Late" would have graced any Beach Boys LP from the late '70s.

The remaining ballads that should have appeared were not nearly so positive. Constructed around minor-key notes and chords Dennis had a trio of songs that were obsessed with themes of loss, loneliness and despair. The spectre of Karen Lamm still loomed large over everything he did. "Love Surrounds Me", which actually appeared on the Beach Boys' 1979 *L.A. (Light Album)* in a more processed form, was resolutely bleak in outlook. From the opening line "All alone again, left alone..." the song was a realisation of a life doomed to worthless affairs in the wake of true love dying. Though girls were always around to momentarily ease the hurting, ultimately the protagonist was left empty to suffer what could have been – "I gave up our love but it won't disappear... desire, seems as though everywhere I go it's all around me... but there's no, there's no love of my own." The over-produced version that surfaced on *L.A.*, and featured Christine McVie in the fade-out, was too glossy by half but to hear Dennis playing the song back in 1978 accompanied by the dirge of a pipe organ was something else. The hurt so evident in his voice was barely palatable.

Dumb Angel

Dredging the same dark waters was another Carli Muñoz song, again written some years previously, called "All Alone". Following the fatalistic themes of "Love Surrounds Me" (it was ushered in on another tragically emotive opening line: "If I could live my life again, I wouldn't do you wrong") Dennis made the pain all his own. "If I could ever love again"... more tearful pianos, more wrenching saxophone, more impassioned vocals: the emotional meters were flickering constantly between red and a deep, deep blue. Whatever Carli's original intentions had been, in Dennis' voice the song became an expression of personal pain – despite the groupies and adoration, probably because of them, the all-consuming emptiness ensued. Dennis sounded marooned, utterly despondent, any hopes of salvation extinguished by the sheer unreality of LA living. At times like this it sounded like an unwholesome existence inside the most joyless Hank Williams howl – "I'm So Lonesome I Could Cry". In songs like "All Alone" and "Love Surrounds Me" Dennis was playing out the dramas of his mind; the dawning dread that the lifestyle, the city, the touring, the booze – everything that defined his image – were conspiring against the spirit. The overbearing expectations of who he was and what he represented meant Dennis Wilson could never find fulfilment, the lines between rock stud fantasy and stark emotions were becoming blurred beyond recognition. "My love, where's it gone? In the sadness that our love left behind I'm standing all alone."

The final piece to this triumvirate of lost love and tears was perhaps the most beautiful, a towering song co-written with Karen Lamm and Gregg Jakobson entitled "Baby Blue". A close cousin to the fantasy world of "Cuddle Up" or the orchestral undertow of *Pacific Ocean Blue*, "Baby Blue" was a lament to romance soundtracked by the most gorgeous arrangement. Over a delicate guitar-picking Carl ran away with the melody, his angelic tones the perfect Greek Chorus, all misty-eyed at the thought of this perfect girl. "Feel the pull of a lonely day... I wonder where you were today." In the verse, Dennis took the whole affair back to earth, his tender vocal incarcerated by guilt and remorse – "Late at night when the whole world's sleeping, I dream of you." By now love is just a memory and the coming day a distraction from the pleasures of night – dreams are all that's left to hold on to. By the song's conclusion the two voices were multi-tracked to harmonic Wilson heaven. It was a sublime performance. Magical. Enormous.

The music was something else again. A sparse arrangement of bass harmonics, strings, piano, and momentary stabs of brass. The descent into bombast that other hands might have wrought never came. The sound remained forever intimate and empty; staring with tear-stained eyes into the rain-soaked darkness. Recalling the conclusion of "God Only Knows" where Brian had somehow made snare drums sing and stop the heart in such swift arresting bursts, Dennis supplied a gently rolling and intermittent percussion. It sounded like midnight waves lapping against the Santa Monica shore.

Unlike "Love Surrounds Me", the version of "Baby Blue" that appeared on *L.A.* was far superior to a demo version that had omitted Dennis' emotional vocal for whistling. The album itself, mauled on release and suffering an awful reputation thereafter, actually contained some stellar moments. CBS President Walter Yetnikoff had famously commented, "Gentlemen, I think I've just been fucked," in response to its premiere playback and Nick Kent at *NME* described it as "more mediocre pop", but *L.A.* was debatably the finest Beach Boys LP since *Holland*. Jostling with Dennis' two numbers was the sublime "Good Timin'" – written years previously by Brian and Carl and described by Dennis as "another 'Surfer Girl'" – while Carl's "Angel Come Home", though workmanlike, at least contained Dennis' distinctive vocals. Of course it was obligatory for there to be lashings of ridiculous to compliment the sublime, and this was provided in spades by a disco version of 1967's "Here Comes The Night" and a putrid rendition of the campfire "classic" "Shortenin' Bread". The inclusion of the former was another creative low point with Dennis refusing outright to promote it. Needless to say when released as a single it was a minor hit ("Baby Blue" was the B-side), proving there was no accounting for taste as America prepared for the shock of the Reaganite '80s. While punk was slaying rock dinosaurs in the UK, anodyne AOR still reigned supreme on the American charts. By 1979, with the wane of *Saturday Night Fever* and Studio 54, disco officially sucked. Meanwhile a new generation of poodle-haired hopefuls (Foreigner, Rush, Styx, Van Halen, REO Speedwagon) were spawning, all ready to take over the soft rock mantle. With the likes of Supertramp's *Breakfast In America* setting the pace it seemed as if US Pop culture was coming to an end.

For those who cared, the appearance of "Love Surrounds Me" and "Baby Blue" on *L.A.* were the first signs that the momentum to finish *Bamboo* was floundering. Mirroring the situation in 1972 when "Make It Good" and "Cuddle Up" had book-ended *So Tough* instead of adorning a Dennis Wilson solo album, their inclusion propped up an otherwise lightweight record. In this way his talents were being abused in the same way as Brian's: shut out of formulating group direction but expected to make sacrifices to the cause when there was a dearth of quality material. Indeed, this was the first time since 1973 that a Dennis Wilson track had even appeared on a Beach Boys record – the first time since 1972 that he had sung one of his own songs. This was a quite remarkable fact since without question he was the most talented and prolific band-member throughout this entire period. That his work should appear so belatedly was a tragic irony: for it signified the end of his solo aspirations, not any kind of new beginning. By late 1978–79 Dennis' career was seriously floundering through a combination of bad luck, bad decisions and, from some of those around him, complete indifference.

In truth the *Bamboo* sessions had been a continuation of *Pacific Ocean Blue* rather than part of an official project. Self-exiled from the Beach Boys, Dennis had simply carried on recording without constraints. While the rest of the group decamped to Iowa for *M.I.U.* or Westlake for *L.A.* in an attempt to make Beach Boys-sounding records, he always returned to Santa Monica and the familiarity of Brother Studios, of which he was part owner along with Carl. So despite the distractions that came with touring the globe Dennis was always able to walk straight in and pick up the thread – he could work in total freedom to his own timetable without the restrictions or pressures provided by a record company. This situation changed markedly in mid-1978 when Brother Studios changed hands and was sold to jazz musician Tom Scott. Overnight the opportunity to experiment disappeared and his work would start to lose focus. Operations were switched to Tom Murphy's home studio or George Hormel Jnr's Village Recorders and sessions had to be booked weeks in advance. The time away in Australia and Europe now became an issue as sessions became more and more protracted. For Dennis, used to working on a whim at Brian's house or the Brother complex, this was simply an alien concept. Any vision he held for *Bamboo* was fractured in the stop-start reality of the business.

This situation was exacerbated from November 1978 by Dennis' burgeoning relationship with Christine McVie, which was starting to keep him anywhere but the studio. As a member of Fleetwood Mac, Christine was part of a "family" every bit as insane and incestuous as the Beach Boys – only it was they who were now the biggest California-based rock act in the world, easily dwarfing the '70s achievements of the Wilsons. The album *Rumours* alone had reached near iconic status, the possession of seemingly every other adult in the Western World[5] and spawning huge FM hits like "You Can Go Your Own Way" and "Dreams". In 1978 they were busy working as individuals on *Tusk*, the sprawling double-album on which the prayers of the US record industry rested but which was soon baffling critics and fans the world over. When Dennis moved into an out-house on Christine's Coldwater Canyon estate Fleetwood Mac were at their commercial zenith and riding the creative and sales success that for the Beach Boy was a distant memory.

For the next two years Dennis would spend a good proportion of his time around the Fleetwood Mac entourage. Though he did start some joint-sessions with Christine in 1979 and 1980 this was exercised mostly in a non-professional capacity. She described him as "my multi-faceted jewel" and "delightfully eccentric" while generously loaning thousands of dollars for Dennis to launch himself headlong into her own band's hedonism. Fuelled mainly by booze – vodka and orange – but also by increasing amounts of anything available, the Los Angeles lifestyle was accelerating to a blur and Dennis was leaving a trail of carnage in his wake. His aftershow drinking contests with John McVie (Christine's ex-husband) reached epic proportions – so much so that Mick Fleetwood considered Dennis "like a man with twenty thyroid glands, not counting the gargantuan amounts of coke and booze and pills he was always shoving into himself". The whirlwind that Christine had unleashed into her personal life had soon written off her Rolls Royce, wrecked her home in drunken rages, burned down her pool house, taught her to water ski and planted a heart-shaped garden in her backyard – the romantic

---

[5] *Rumours* itself sold over 25 million copies while the October 10th release date of its follow-up was afforded the honour of "Fleetwood Mac Day" by Los Angeles Mayor Tom Bradley.

sentiments of this last gesture dampened somewhat considering Dennis' generous gesture was actually billed back to Christine.

Dennis' wild streak had always been countered by an equally powerful urge to work and create but during his two-year involvement with Christine his energy was literally soaked up. He was by now hopelessly addicted. Christine commented that "Dennis has awakened things in me I'd have been scared to experience and made me feel the extremes of every emotion", but in the process he was losing touch with any semblance of reality, bouncing from one disaster to the next. Beneath the veneer of indestructibility was the fragile wantonness of a child, compulsively driven to teeter on the limits. Lindsay Buckingham, who would later include the tribute "D.W. Suite" on his *Go Insane* album, hit the nail on the head: "...he was a good guy. He was kind of lost, but I thought he had a big heart. I always liked him. He was crazy just like a lot of other people, but he had a really big heart, and he was the closest thing to Brian Wilson there was, too. He was halfway there."

Around 1979 the *Bamboo* project was put on hold. Though scarcely comparable to the loss of *Smile* over a decade earlier, the ramifications of its demise would be equally tragic. *Bamboo* should have been the record that cemented Dennis Wilson's career in the firmament; another critical success in the vein of *Pacific Ocean Blue* would surely have distinguished him from the pitiful efforts of the Beach Boys. But the evidence of his talents is locked up in vaults awaiting a record company brave enough to release them. Like Brian's "Teenage Symphony to God" the songs from *Bamboo* remain some of the most sought-after unreleased material in the Beach Boys canon.

During the two-year party with his Warner Brothers label-mates, Dennis' status as a Beach Boy was disintegrating on a daily basis. The kudos afforded by *Pacific Ocean Blue* did not sustain beyond 1978. By the end of that year Carli Muñoz had escaped the madness to bring up his kids, while Dennis' sessions with Christine were thwarted by arguments, separation and band commitments. Now denied the time and the equipment to record at will there was no longer an outlet for his talents. Following the heroin debacle in Australia and his consistently unpredictable behaviour on stage Dennis was viewed as a liability. Brian's presence, though he had contributed nothing new to *L.A.* and was merely a passenger on tour, was required to provide credibility, but Dennis... he was an embarrassment. Mike and Al were busy promoting the band as good squeaky-clean Republicans (by early 1980 the band were dedicating "Long Tall Texan" to George Bush) and Dennis simply did not fit any longer in any capacity beyond the drum kit. Drunk and disorderly behaviour was simply not sanctioned within the slick, family-orientated Greatest Hits show. There was simply no room for such an untamable force as the band strived away from rock'n'roll towards retirement.

Events would finally come to a head at the Universal Ampitheatre in the early summer of 1979 as Dennis staggered over to a microphone to drawl an incomprehensible sentence about cocaine and Quaaludes. The next moment he was seen brawling on stage with Mike Love and the following day he was officially thrown out of the group. It was a scenario to be replayed several times in the next four years. The gloves were now off: Mike Love's vision of the Beach Boys had finally succeeded. For Dennis, who had provided their name, their identity and their spirit, and who had sacrificed his own solo career less than six months before, it was a devastating blow. The Beach Boys, who were once a by-word for creativity and ingenuity, were now an empty vessel and all three Wilsons were playing peripheral roles in their own creation.

Bamboo never came out, was never realised, was never talked about, was never given a final track-listing – and the Beach Boys continued their tragi-comic descent into show band hell. Dennis would never play on a record again. There were attempts – with Christine McVie, in Hawaii, and finally with Brian in 1981[6] – but they were all aborted due to personal problems. He belonged in a hospital ward not a recording studio. The physical ravages wrought by accidents and self-abuse had been swift and devastating and that once beautiful voice was now nothing but a dry wheeze; as painful to behold as it plainly was to use. Dennis sounded utterly defeated and a lonely echo of his former self. His cartoon depiction on the jacket of *Keepin' The Summer Alive* (1980) was the only evidence of his existence as the decades turned.

The unreleased productions he made with Brian in 1981 were the probably the last. After that date there was no more music.

"The Beach Boys made Dennis and broke him too."
　　　　　—Stephen Desper to the author, 2000

"I'm lonesome. I'm lonesome all the time."
　　　　　—Dennis Wilson on the day of his death, 1983

Those final three years were the living end. Dennis was falling – accelerating – downwards into a bottomless hole, aware of his condition but unable to alter the course of a life spent on the edge. He could never change who he was. I do not concur with the idea that Dennis had a death wish (quite the opposite, he had too much life, too much energy) but to anyone who witnessed a Beach Boys' concert in the 1980s the writing was on the wall. The sight of the band's sex symbol barely able to perform – though still able to exude raptures from the crowd through his mere presence – was akin to watching a sick animal in the throes of death. As the lights dimmed for the encore he would somehow stumble through a few verses of "You Are So Beautiful", though the irony of what passed through his lips was all too obvious. His voice had almost ceased to be. The permanent smile he held as he sang could not mask the pain. Over-riding any show of bravado was the reality of self-abuse that had turned his surfer's body to a corpulent bloat and worn his complexion to the pallid grey of cirrhosis. An Alan Bergman photo from August 1983 – an image that would form the centrepiece of *Rolling*

---

[6] From these Dennis-produced sessions came the compositions "Night Blooming Jasmine" and "Oh Lord".

Stone's obituary within five months – was of a man who had seen too much. Dennis looked like he'd come through a war. The fading light that added years within months to the still-young corpses of Brian Jones and Jim Morrison was chillingly similar.

Purged from the band, Dennis was drinking and coking away the pain in the back streets and dives of Venice. Like anything else, he pursued it with an almost superhuman vigour until it became a way of life – consuming kilos and running up bills of thousands, never considering the consequences. Funding all manner of barflies and hangers-on, the figure he cut was like a punch-drunk version of Brando's Terry Molloy, a defeated man whose dreams were destined to remain unfulfilled. As one of the self-confessed messengers of the Beach Boys, without the music and the band he had nothing. In 1981, compounding the sensation of wings fully clipped, even the *Harmony* was taken away – repossessed to pay bad debts.

James Taylor, remembered seeing his former *Two-Lane Blacktop* co-star back in 1983: "I was out visiting Peter Asher. I had had a traffic accident, and Dennis came over looking absolutely wild, in some altered state... he was green and foaming at the mouth. And a month later he was dead." Since the mid-60s Dennis had been nothing but approachable, even during the periods of gargantuan fame he still acted like just another kid on the Strip. As a superstar he had always been available. Back then he and Brian seemed to own the damn place – between them they had practically invented it – but here they were full-circle, reduced to the status of bums. The heart-throb of yesterday was unrecognisable and the streets that were once his kingdom had become alien and lonely. He now stalked them like a wounded creature, a jug of vodka and orange permanently affixed to his hand, reduced to cadging his drinks and smokes from strangers in bars. The one time resident of one of L.A.'s most opulent mansions was now renting a tiny house on Wavecrest Avenue in Venice Beach. The hangers-on soon followed and Dennis was forced to live in a closet underneath the stairs while tens of people shared his home.

Various attempts were made by the band or by business manager Bob Levine to hospitalise Dennis, but each time he entered a clinic vowing to change he would leave prematurely and relapse. The addictive behaviour of nearly 40 years was proving impossible to unravel. Yet somehow he still performed with the band, sometimes officially but often uninvited, as they played to ever increasing audiences. The highlight of these shows would be their command of nearly 250,00 people on July 4th at the Washington Monument in celebration of America's birthday – along with pumpkin pie and Budweiser they were now officially institutionalised as part of the American Dream. This was a status cemented with the election of Ronald Reagan in 1979. The über-conservatism of the ex-Californian Governor was seen as the necessary antidote to successive years of failure, marked by defeat in Vietnam, prolonged economic depression and the hostage situation in Iran. Wishing to rewrite history and depict a simplistic golden age, with the White House reinstated to a "shining beacon on the hill" the Beach Boys became providers of innocence to the patriotic flag-waving majority. To see the band in 1981 or 1982 was not unlike watching the Stones crank out their back catalogue – given the crowd participation and the familiarity of the material these events were beyond rock'n'roll and tantamount to a rally. The audience came for the music and to reaffirm faith, to eat barbecue and sing along to "Barbara Ann" – it hardly mattered who was up there singing. Yet when Dennis, the people's champion, turned up he was more than capable of upstaging Mike. Despite his bedraggled appearance, his latent charisma still connected with the crowd.

The last 4th of July Show for Dennis was in 1983 at Atlantic City. The concert had followed controversy in the weeks preceding when Secretary of the Interior James Watt infamously banned the Beach Boys from the nation's capital. Ludicrously proclaiming they were a heavy rock band who attracted "undesirable elements", his decision was overturned personally and publicly by Ron and Nancy. Watt received a statuette of a foot complete with gunshot wound for his blunder while the Beach Boys were afforded humble apologies. The triumphant show would be the last attended by all six members. It would also be the second time that year that Presidential intervention would affect Dennis' destiny.

Despite it being one of their proudest moments together, the film footage and photos that followed the event would be some of the saddest and distressing to feature the Beach Boys. It had been over twenty years since their conception and here they were: the whole group stood around the President and the First Lady, upon the manicured lawns of the White House. Yet it was difficult to picture those five clean-cut boys in their checkered shirts for the dysfunctional adults they had become. Now balding, bearded and fat and wearing a curious ill-fitting clash of cowboy hats and jumpsuits they looked even more unlikely pop stars than they had in 1963. Back then of course it was crazy Dennis who provided some semblance of reality to their image, his golden surfer boy looks always the focus of the camera lens. But that day he looked disheveled and unwashed, like a tramp had somehow snuck into the picture. Dennis was utterly wasted.

The press conference where the President declared his lifetime love for the band was even more grotesque. As the flash bulbs illuminated the podium Dennis lurched forward several times with his hand outstretched trying to make contact. He seemed desperately out of control and it was obvious that Mike Love was acting as a barrier to keep him off screen and away from Reagan. Sweating profusely Dennis somehow seemed smaller, like he was shrinking to nothing. That Nancy would ultimately become synonymous with the much maligned "Just Say No" campaign was one of several ironies apparent to anyone watching their TV screens. There she was on her own front lawn smiling and sharing prime-time space with an incurable addict.

Meanwhile, the final twist to the ongoing Wilson-Love power feud became apparent when Dennis' daughter Jennifer introduced him to her 18-year-old friend Shawn. It turned out she was Mike's love child from a short-lived '60s tryst, but Dennis slept with her anyway. It was a relationship of twisted convenience: Dennis provided Shawn with access to a father who denied her existence, Shawn provided Dennis with the ultimate way to piss her father off. Their disastrous union was final hammer blow to a relationship long since soured. Mike despised Dennis for his "immorality" (or at least its potential effect on the Beach Boys' audience) and was jealous of his continued popularity and his success with women. Dennis saw Mike as a hypocrite since he had been married five times himself.

What could have been the ultimate revenge tactic turned sour when Shawn became pregnant and the couple entered into a short, volatile and loveless marriage. A mutual adoration of their newborn son, Gage, was the only element keeping them together. Dennis had filed for divorce within weeks.

His last show would be on September 27th 1983 at the LA County Fairgrounds. A month later he was officially homeless, and while Shawn and Gage were rented a room at the Santa Monica Bay Inn he was dependent upon the kindness of friends for places to stay. Half a million dollars in debt his 39th birthday came and passed, and days before Christmas he would discharge himself from the St John's Hospital where Bob Levine had entered him for a last shot – for Gage's sake – at detoxification. Prescribed 100mg of Librium every two hours to quell the incessant cravings of the bottle it was one shot too far. Disorientated and aching from accidents and batterings his body could not take the strain. In days he would be dead.

The end, when it finally came on December 27th, was straight from the pages of Hollywood. Dennis had hooked up with Bill Oster, skipper of the 52-foot *Emerald*, and spent the day on board the yawl berthed at Marina Del Rey. Nearby was the empty space where his beloved *Harmony* had once been moored. He had been drinking vodka since early morning from a bottle which Oster's family tried in vain to hide while plying him with turkey sandwiches. And though he was plagued by depression with the thought of growing old Dennis also showed signs of jubilation, since Levine had apparently dangled another carrot in front of his nose: if only he could dry out in thirty days in any clinic of his choosing, then plans would be made to finance a buyback of *Harmony*. Thus, even though he was "staggering around pretty good" according to Oster, "Dennis was in a good mood, happy. We were plotting how to buy his boat back."

Fuelled by the booze Dennis suddenly announced he was going swimming, wearing nothing but his cut-offs. The water was cold – about 58 degrees – but his head was full of bravado, the usual half-clown half-daredevil. With protests ringing in his ears Dennis dived thirteen feet down to the marina bed looking for treasure. Intermittently he would surface laughing after retrieving small rivets or pieces of rope: all remnants of the boat he had once so lovingly restored. Miraculously as he came out for a breather he held a silver frame that had once contained the wedding photo of a younger, fitter man with the beautiful Karen Lamm. It was six years since Dennis had tossed it overboard in the midst of another argument. They had been the happiest days of his life and perhaps the only time he had known true contentment.

Back on board and wrapped up in blankets the shivers started, but Dennis remained obsessed with finding more. The sea had taken his memories and he became adamant that in the dark waters there lay a treasure chest within his reach, a box full of gold. Everyone laughed but begged him not to return. "It was probably a toolbox," said Oster, "He was just being Dennis, entertaining everybody, being his lovable self, goofing around." As usual it was impossible to stop him and Dennis dived back.

His lifeless body was retrieved some 50 minutes later. The ocean that had given him life had finally claimed him back.

On January 9th 1984 Dennis Wilson slipped gently into the Pacific. The special dispensation required for a civilian's burial at sea had been duly granted by President Reagan. (A remarkable life might have been over, but to the end Dennis managed to bend the rules.) The official verdict to his death had been "accidental drowning" though the autopsy reports had shown significant traces of cocaine and alcohol in his blood mixed up with the Librium. In truth, he was already a broken man and those last few years had often seemed like a prelude to this moment. Stephen Kalinich considered Dennis a dead man before he even hit the water while his second wife Barbara asserted similar feelings fifteen years later, "I felt he died before his actual body died." The fight within had diminished and you felt that if they had opened him up, Dennis' heart would have been in several pieces.

The *Times* obituary read that Dennis was "the most volatile of the three brothers" but that his "contributions to the group included a series of sombre compositions notable for imaginative musical settings and suited to his slightly hoarse delivery". Of course this was all true, but there was more than that. The real significance of events would only be seen when the shell-shocked faces of his brothers confronted the TV cameras. Carl vowed there and then that the Beach Boys would continue because it was what his brother would have wanted, but everyone in the room knew his loss was inestimable. Brian would later recall watching events on the evening news in a state of disbelief: "Dennis [was] lying on the cement covered by a large body sack. His arm and leg stuck out. I knew the picture was real but I still hoped, expected, Dennis to get up and yell 'Surprise!' He didn't. He couldn't. I thought, My God, that's the last time I'll ever see Dennis." He had been their inspiration, their engine, the bane of their lives: the almighty force that dragged them to the surf in the first place. For the last decade he had also been their prime creative force. With his passing went the true soul of the Beach Boys. Without Dennis Wilson they would be nothing.

When the debris sweeps away, what is left?

For all his reputation Dennis Wilson was a fragile soul. The reckless macho persona – the surfer, the fighter, the lover – is belied by the music he left us with. A fact evident from the day his incredible voice was showcased on "Be Still" back in 1967. Dennis flourished in extremities but his generosity and free-spiritedness – facets of character he always retained when so many of his contemporaries bowed down to cynicism and greed – sat uneasily in such a mean-spirited decade as the 1980s. In the sensationalism that followed his death and decline this was a fact often lost. Certainly it was seldom written about in the papers and obituaries and was brushed over in certain biographies about the band. Personally, I picked up a second-hand copy of *Pacific Ocean Blue* after consuming the repackaged 2-on-1 Beach Boys LPs 1966–1973 and can still remember the revelation when needle hit groove. That rare tingle of discovery, like some tremendous secret, when voice and music resonate together so perfectly was all I really needed to know. How many eyes had passed over that strange bearded cover on their way to inferior choices? At that one moment I felt sorry for the rest of humanity. I wanted to grab every pair of strangers' ears and force this on them. How could music this good, this soulful, this beautiful be lying vanquished and forgotten?

Dennis was no fool, he understood the needs of commerciality – he was a Beach Boy after all – but his guiding artistic principles were, and always remained, truth and honesty. And while these principles could be errant in his personal life, in the music and in his voice there was no hiding. For 39 years he had revelled in the role of pioneer – inspiring his brother to songwriting greatness before seizing the mantle of experimentalism as Brian took to his bed. When it came to the music Dennis proved incapable of playing out his defined rock star role, of sacrificing the need for expression. "There's no escape from being honest. On the inside, we're always honest. On the outside, we can bullshit. Inside, there's no escape..."

The efforts of Mike Love to push the Beach Boys down a populist alley were met with unstinting resistance. Either inside the studio or on the road Dennis merely upped the ante by pushing his lifestyle and his music even further out there, seeming to revel in upsetting his lead vocalist. If Mike preached abstinence and a policy of control then Dennis would get wrecked, ridiculing transcendentalism and lurching ever further out of control. Shifting through the gears he accelerated into an inevitable fate. But to judge the man without hearing "Cuddle Up" or "Thoughts Of You" or "Baby Blue" or "Be Still" was ridiculous. On tracks like those and many others Dennis bared his soul and bared it with a raw purity few others would have dared explore. Maybe he belonged to a more innocent time, but those ideals have been outlawed now.

His reward? During those 39 years, limited. *Pacific Ocean Blue* was a minor success and through the '70s he provided B-sides for six Beach Boys' singles, but only the tip of what he actually wrote made their finished products. Where now are the demos from which the highpoints of *Sunflower* were drawn, the solo album he made with Daryl Dragon, the sixteen songs he worked on with Stanley Shapiro, his mid-70s experiments coinciding with Brian's comeback, the ambitious symphonies he planned with Stephen Kalinich, the *Bamboo* sessions and the collaborations with Christine McVie? Undoubtedly some of these, reworked and remodeled, surfaced on Beach Boys' albums, but the majority are still buried unheard. For the majority of fans brought up on the "image" of the Beach Boys and the Californian myth Dennis Wilson's attractions were not musical. He was the sex symbol, the surfer, the playboy, the drummer. The freewheeling image of sunshine and happiness that defined the band would be his for life.

As the century closed the Beach Boys would split into three separate and acrimonious factions, all proclaiming their own take on the band. In a climate of revisionism and lawsuits a ghost-written autobiography was issued in Brian's name and Mike Love, despite the paucity of musical evidence, would claim his own hand on their greatest musical achievements. After the death of Carl Wilson in 1998 this situation was exacerbated further in a climate of misinformation and outright lies. One could probably guess where Dennis, always Brian's muse and champion, would have stood on this. But there was no longer anyone to answer for him and his songs were never played. Only Brian would even acknowledge the importance of Dennis Wilson. When the rejuvenated former genius broke into an emotional rendition of "Lay Down Burden" from his eponymous 1988 solo album the image of his brother Dennis was solemnly projected onto a screen.

Yet Dennis Wilson's songs, straddling two decades, caught an inherent vitality and timelessness retained by few other performers. Those who slavishly followed fads will be forever locked in their era as period pieces – in the recent words of Van Dyke Parks, "Music in the '60s was like a cloud of flamingoes – one agitated creature took to the sky and pretty soon you saw an entire pink cloud rise up". Dennis created a music that was truly unique and it is here that he lives and breathes, not in the faded photographs of his youth. Decades pass but pure emotion is impossible to date-stamp; the sheer intensity he delivered time and again would never successfully be bought and sold as a commodity.

The Beach Boys of course would continue down the road they had travelled since 1978. The apple pie road of Country Fairs and Republican rallies that would inevitably lead to Nashville – now home of unabashed sentimentalism – "Kokomo" and appearances on *Baywatch*. Little more than a travelling sideshow they melded perfectly into the gentrified era of *Top Gun*, Huey Lewis and MTV as creativity was sacrificed before a love of the Greenback. Their concerts remained celebratory affairs but stuck in an ever-increasing timewarp. Mike Love cast a revisionist eye over the glory years claiming now to have masterminded their greatest triumphs, and even influencing the Beatles when he met them at Rishikesh[7]. Without the genius of Dennis or Brian the path they chose was the lucrative one.

And this perhaps was the ultimate paradox. Dennis Wilson had dreamt the Beach Boys into existence. His lifestyle had been the inspiration behind his brother's greatest songs. Thirty years later that same lifestyle had become an identity for California itself – synonymous with the plasticity and vacuity of a whole region. For the rest of the world

---

[7] Strangely enough, his own solo records hardly bore out these claims. Without exception they were truly witless and nauseating. Albums like *Looking Back With Love* were such exercises in bland mediocrity that who knows what even more ignominious fate they would have met had their maker had not been a Beach Boy.

---

the Beach Boys, and Dennis in particular, exemplified the whole freedom myth of surfing, cars and two girls for every boy.

The reality of course was quite opposite. Dennis had long since broken free of these constrictions and for the majority of his short life lived way beyond them.

He was not a star in any current sense of the PR-driven wannabies that fill the pages of *Hello!*. In rock'n'roll he remains something of a rarity. He created from the need to create, not merely for the success and the trappings. Like few others his music remained a direct reflection of his lifestyle – a lifestyle where anything was permitted, a lifestyle that was dedicated to joy but remained unbearably lonely. When making music everybody had to get involved.

Dennis stood for a different, nobler America. The frontier wilderness where the perimeters were unmarked and unexplored. An America filled with extraordinary natural beauty that the likes of Kerouac, Steinback and Whitman had documented. These, not the illusionary trappings of wealth, were the foundations of the real American Dream. The canyons, mountains, rivers and oceans: The Promised Land as opposed to Disneyland.

And he was flawed too. Like Brian that is an essential part of the legend and was at the heart of his fans' devotion. He could be as crass and pathetic and egotistical as any rock star. And yet that strange juxtaposition between brute force and extreme sensitivity was at the heart of his attraction, for Dennis never shirked from his failings or attempted to hide his emotions. Good or bad he never gave less than his everything and for those reasons his musical legacy remains so strong. (For Dennis there was no censorship or pretence, and even when falling apart personally his music and his soul could still touch perfection). While his non-surfing bandmates stuck with a formula that brought worldwide success his own notions of freedom reached out far beyond the beach until they became all-encompassing. This same universal freedom that led Brian to make *Pet Sounds* in 1966 was what Dennis dedicated his whole existence to. Accelerating forward, always instinctive, there were no boundaries: Dennis wished to be a free spirit and live without consequences. It was an almost Faustian desire for kicks that would send him from the depths to the skies. The same force that saw him serenading dolphins from the deck of his beloved *Harmony* or striving to create magic in his music would also destroy his marriages and his life. Ultimately, Dennis Wilson was as untameable as the ocean he loved so deeply.

And now all we have left is the music. Beyond the drug abuse, beyond the alcohol, the infidelities, Charlie Manson, everything Dennis was ever blamed for... this is all that remains. Unknown symphonies conducted from the soul, sung in a ragged voice that experienced too much. Reputations disintegrate to a meaningless nothing before such sublime beauty. After we are long gone the ocean will remain. (Had he lived who knows what might have been? After all, look at Brian who seemed on the point of irreversible decline for much of the 1970s but has now returned with some style). Dennis truly was a dumb angel, one of the most profoundly gifted songwriters and performers of his era and destined to throw it all away.

Is it possible to have too much freedom? To exist outside the boundaries, or at a constant 160mph on the dragstrip? For Dennis the question was irrelevant. He did it. He lived it. He sang it.

His soul is out there in a Pacific Ocean Blue.

AN INTERVIEW WITH
STEPHEN KALINICH

In 1967, with Brian Wilson about to enter a state of hibernation, Dennis, like the rest of his fellow Beach Boys, began the pursuit for a new direction. The first fruits of this search became apparent on the 1968 LP *Friends* and his two collaborations with Californian poet Stephen Kalinich: "Little Bird" and "Be Still". Simple and beautiful, they were the first evidence that Dennis possessed a huge talent for songwriting, and could scale the same heights of emotion as his older brother. The pair later hooked up in the mid-1970s and Stephen wrote the lyrics to "Rainbows", which appeared on side two of *Pacific Ocean Blue*. A number of other compositions were also attempted at this time but never finished, as was an ambitious project embracing poetry and classical music, entitled *Life Symphony*.

I spoke to Stephen Kalinich on 4th September 1999. Before the interview Stephen read me an excerpt of a poem he wrote on the news of Dennis' death in 1983[1].

So you wrote that when you heard of Dennis' death?

Yeah I wrote that right after he died – I showed it to Karen Lamm, to Carl Wilson and Marilyn Wilson. But not many people have seen it. It's a biographical thing like when I and Dennis would go to the Santa Monica

---

[1]   The full poem reads as follows: "You pass through time like a rider from another dimension. / You were never tied to things – you knew that material things could not be possessed, / That they were only ours on loan. / That we could never own anything – only have the illusion of owning it. / Though we were surrounded by the attractions of wealth at times, and the media paints a picture of you that sells magazines and papers you would laugh now. / You knew that fame and all of its attractions could not endure. / You knew that the real reality was giving and love. / You used to tell me when you did something you thought was wrong, "Why did I do it? I didn't even want to". / You gave to me as I tried to give to you. Not out of our mutual needs but out of an abundance, an overflowing. / You have been released from time. / You seem more real to me now. / Thank you for helping me to know that we are after all not here to accumulate wealth, but we are here to help each other. / It even seems absurd to me that anyone could do anything just for money. / Money is fine to use to feed a family with, to buy necessities with. / But it is not a god, a deity. / It is not worthy enough for us to set our lives around. / It seems sometimes that it is the God of this world. / It seems to be what draws people and motivates them more than anything. / But there are areas of life it cannot touch. / It can free us to explore new possibilities, but it only strangles most of us. / Makes us slaves, it computes our real desires with other thoughts: profits and benefits. / It could liberate us, it could be used for good not just excess and indulgence. / It is not the reason we are here. / You made me see it clearly."

---

open air theatre and I would do a poem and he would direct me and it was so inspiring.

He was compassionate and cared about people. The media usually says all the negative and terrible things about him and chasing women. And some of them might have elements of truth, but the point is none of them capture his soul. He had soul in music and he was a master. And yet a primitive master in the sense that he may not have heard all of Beethoven or Bach but he had a feeling of combining the pain and the joy together. And we had many songs that we wrote together that no one will ever hear.

I always thought that the songs that you and Dennis wrote together had a real positivity about them. Particularly "Rainbows" off of *Pacific Ocean Blue*. I think that song really stands out on that album in between melancholic numbers like "Farewell My Friend" and "End Of The Show".

Yeah, I tried to bring that element to it. "Be Still, as I told you", I got the idea when I read, "Be still know that I am God", in The Bible. That in stillness and in listening we can find many answers instead of thinking we know everything. To be quiet and have humility.

And Dennis was humble before creativity. He was in awe of it, in reverence of it. I never once heard him say "I want this to sell". But (rather) this is my heart, this is my expression. This is what I oughta communicate. That is what I thought was beautiful about Dennis.

So you first met Dennis in 1967?

No it was 1966. 1965 or 1966. We hit it off straight away. Then I became a contract writer for Brother Records and I had a group with Mark Buckingham and we wrote a song called "Leaves Of Grass" that couldn't get played because it was thought to be about marijuana. Even though it wasn't – it was based on my reverence to Walt Whitman as a poet.

Did you think when you met him – I'm going to be writing sings with this guy sometime soon? Was there some sort of immediate connection?

Well I was already signed with The Beach Boys because of Brian so I knew we were going to write, but I didn't know it would happen that quickly. He heard me recite poetry and he went wild. He was really moved by it. But instead of being selfish he said, "You and Brian have got to write together." He was very generous in spirit – I loved the guy. His body was electric, he was vibrant. He was like, "Stephen we're gonna take this around the world."

Were you surprised by Dennis' talent given his reputation in the band as the playboy and the drummer?

I never had that sense. I mean he was always a power. I always thought he had a great talent and a great generosity of spirit. I never saw him as just the drummer – he was a creative genius in his own right. Creatively he understood as well as Brian, but he never used it for commercialisation. He wasn't as studied and it just came from his heart.

Was he self-indulgent sometimes? Sure. Were we all? Sure. When it came to creativity you could see the spiritual in him and his belief in doing good, in love, in God. And though humanly he fell short like all of us, his music came from a beautiful source. He wasn't just some wild crazy guy who partied a lot. His heart maybe never accomplished all it wanted to but had the intention to do good. To bring joy and happiness to people.

Do you think he was always searching for something?

Yep. I think that's how we connected. Also I never did drugs and he did. He said one day on acid he could become one with a drop of water and I would do that anyway.

But do you think he was a pioneer in the way that he worked? I mean, in the way he approached things. He always seemed to be the first in the band to try anything.

I think he got hold of an idea that worked. I think he was even friends with Marlon Brando, he wanted to share it with the whole world. He would get so excited and enthusiastic.

He would let the music rise up out of him and he would let it take him and not impose his will on the music. He had such a reverence and humility it was almost like "white gospel".

That crack in his voice that sometimes people didn't like too much, I loved. He had soul. He was a white soul singer. He had a purity in his creative approach that wasn't in his regular life maybe, 'cos I know he had a lot of girlfriends and stuff. He was like a virgin mind of creativity. He knew it was something that came through him and went beyond him so there was a transcendence of ego and a total of humility.

We wrote a song together, which had a line, "A child's joyous tear". We never finished it but Carl really liked it and Brian, Dennis and myself were going to work on it. It was in a song called "Grateful Are We For Little Children": "A Child's joyous tear was innocent, he has no fear. Now I know what love is".

It was just searching through words and melodies and just as a song can be an opportunity to celebrate life or to celebrate surfing this was to celebrate feelings. Urgings of the heart. What is the real purpose of life or the soul? What is the purpose of creation?

Dennis was close to an untrained Bach. Dennis was Johann Sebastian Bach without the training in the sense that Bach did everything for the glory of God. (I'm speaking creatively here). And yet his life had strains of Beethoven. Torn soul in a lot of ways – always searching and that inability to grasp was probably the reason why he always wanted to get high. It was hard for him to realise that. I thought that Dennis drowned before he ever hit the water. I think that his spirit just wasn't breaking through some boundaries there and mentally he had already gone under and submerged and drowned.

How would you work? Would you just recite poems and Dennis would pick up on something and go with it?

I told you about "Little Bird" where I left the poem on his piano. He called me the next day and he had the music. He changed a few lines, this and that. He didn't like the word "strife" which I had in the original poem. He was funny about words even though he had that purity.

Did you find much difference working with Dennis in the '70s? Did you go into the studio with him then?

I think that by that time he was more tortured and that innocence remained but it was more from pain. So I don't think the compositions were as clear even though the songs were good. I think "Be Still" and "Little Bird" were the purest forms. Maybe you don't agree but that's the way that I see it. The purity and the nakedness. What is the man when you strip the bones away?

There were so many layers on "Be Still" that didn't make it to the finished record. Dennis and I talked about putting the Mormon Tabernacle choir on there. That's where we were heading with *Life Symphony*. It was going to be life flowing, love flowing. OUT ON THE STREETS. THE HOMELESS. THE DESTITUTE. YOUTH SYMPHONY. THE CORRUPTION AND THE BEAUTY OF YOUTH. GIVE LOVE. BEING LOVE. BEAUTY. TIME. BOUNDARIES. WAR. PEACE. HARMONY 1 AND 2. COMMUNICATION. INTENTIONS. MOTIVES. DESIRES. PRAYERS. PROGRESS. PERSPECTIVES. DRUGS. PUT DOWN YOUR NEEDLES. WHOLENESS. BEING. CONSCIOUS-NESS. DIVINE DECREE. DEATH. WAR NO MORE. SYMPHONY. POETRY. CHILDREN. PEOPLE.

Life Symphony would be every note of life. The sad, the beautiful. Every colour. We wanted to take this symphony to the whole world with his music and add symphonies around it and choral singers. We wanted to get the top orchestras in the world. That's what we wanted to do but we fell short on a lot of it. Nobody knows that. And I'm still going to do it and I'm going to dedicate it to Dennis

There was another song "Tale Of Man" that Dennis did start putting music to. It went: [sings] "Man In his greatest age, through every prophet and every sage, The wars the hate, the cheating and the lies."

It was something like that but he never finished it...

What was the feeling like when you had written a poem with its own distinct rhythm and then it came back with music on it?

It was so exciting because I only recited it to him once and then he sang it back to me. I mean Brian is a genius and he would do exactly the same thing as Dennis.

Do you think that playing in the touring band of the mid-70s satisfied Dennis's notions of commerciality and allowed him the freedom to experiment?

He loved being part of the band. If Brian was the heart and soul of the Beach Boys then Dennis' enthusiasm and excitement and sincere humility was also part of the Beach Boys. When he sang "You Are So Beautiful", the Joe Cocker song, he was able to touch people. He was a really exciting guy.

The music was more god-like but the life and the women and the other stuff was more like the temptation, the lust of the flesh and the spirit, which don't have to conflict with each other, because if you can merge the feeling of the physical and the esoteric and the erotic with the spiritual and not just follow the animal laws, there is a chance for purification and redemption.

I think that part of love is not just that mad feeling from our sexual organs but also the element of choice in love. It's also a decision and a consciousness. He had that feeling of love and that sincerity of love but he also recognised that he could choose. My assessment was that he tried to cooperate that love that he got in his music, and bring it into the rest of his life. I don't think that he quite got that tie-in.

Dennis had the music in the pure form and to take that energy and love that came out of his music and to apply it to his personal problems, to his life, to take drugs, to not be in control of your passions and your desires... he did not know or realise how to translate that into his own life.

I think that if he could have used that power in the music and the creativity he wouldn't have had to fall so far when he fell from grace. Because grace was good to him but I think that what happens is, like with Brian, when you fall into that dark hole, that vortex, that outer space, that quasar, you lose the perception of reality and you walk just looking for the high and the elation. When Dennis was on the road it was just such a high and when he came back just to everyday life you get to crave that love and that affection. I think it was hard for him to love just one on one.

I guess that's just a classic thing in bands...

And if I get more girls is that going to make me happier? And you realise that it really won't after a while. If I do more of this because I've done every drug. Maybe it was hard for him to orchestrate the symphony of his life. Like his everyday life. Like maybe it was easy for him to be the baby but not be the father – although he loved kids. So to take that feeling from his music and transfer it to the rest of his life was difficult.

What about the Helen Keller song?

We never finished it. The song went along these lines: "She touched me in stillness. No sky could she see, no sound could she hear. Though she

---

smiled when she walked, As if something within gave her eyes, gave her ears, gave her hope. And I who could see the morning sunshine, And hear the ripples in the gentle stream, Did not see in life as much as she. Could not hear the many silent voices. She touched me in stillness".

I think that whole thing was that in some ways Dennis was more blind than Helen Keller – and more deaf, and more dumb. And I don't mean that unkindly but in the sense that the stillness in the music could have pulled his heart up. I'm thinking that now (i.e. that it wasn't written with Dennis in mind). Dennis could see divine love in his music but could not transcend it in his life like Helen Keller could with all those obstacles before her.

You've got to combine intelligence and discernment with these things and sometimes Dennis did not have the ability to say no, to consider what was overall best for his being. He had a lot of impulsive and impetuous qualities.

I think that the crack in his voice was the crack in his life between beauty and pain. Between pain and liberation. At the same time as he had the pain he had the joy. Not knowing that the same thing that caused the joy could be applied to where the pain was. So it's blurred for him rather than integrated.

Do you think the pain was something he was born with?

That disposition towards the melancholy? Probably he never outgrew that whole thing with his father. He thought that he never deserved wholeness. He was a fragmented, beautiful soul.

So did you ever think at a point he's not going to live through this?

I thought that the conflict in him was going to have to be resolved one way or another. If somebody could only have broken through with enough love. He never knew how loved he was and I don't think he believed in himself enough.

AN INTERVIEW WITH
JOHN HANLON

After stints as a technician at the Record Plant, Cherokee and A&M Studios and as a roadie for Rick Springfield and Little Feat, John Hanlon became a technician and engineer at Brother Studios in 1976. His first project was the *15 Big Ones* LP. Initially working a 9–5 shift with the band he became more involved with the ongoing work for Dennis Wilson's *Pacific Ocean Blue*. By 1977 he was working round the clock with Dennis and engineers Stephen Moffitt and Earle Mankey to complete the project. Interviewed on October 17th 2000, he gives a personal insight into the making of that record and the musical genius of Dennis Wilson.

When you started working with the band was Dennis already working towards the release of a solo record outside of the Beach Boys?

He was working simultaneously with the Beach Boys who were finishing up *15 Big Ones*. At the time the focus was all on Brian. He had been lying in bed asleep – he'd pulled the cover over his head and disconnected from the Universe for the time after *Holland*. They hadn't brought in Dr Landy yet, but that whole "Brian's Back" junk was going on and they were trying to get him back interested in the studio again.

So what at that point did you make of Dennis' material, especially in the retrogressive light of what the band as a whole were doing?

He was a genius. Dennis was a genius. He had more of Brian in him than anyone else. Carl was a great, great guy – Mike was a little different – but Dennis was a genius and you heard it instantly in his music.

I had got into music because of The Beatles and *Sergeant Pepper*. And I also I heard "Sloop John B" and all of those *Pet Sounds* songs. Even before that, songs like "Shut Down" and "409" – all those songs co-written with Gary Usher were amazing. Brian was always a genius to me and those songs on *Pet Sounds* just blew me away. They changed my life. Between that and The Beatles my life changed.

I'd look at the back of "Little Deuce Coupe" and see palm trees, sand, and girls in bikinis and hot rods and the ocean and I'd say, "What land is that!?" And they'd say, "That's California!" So I made plans from that moment on to move to California from New Hampshire where I grew up.

Then later I'd hear stuff like *Surf's Up* and it was just so far ahead of its time. I'm amazed that no-one noticed on that last Madonna LP, that she did with William Orbit, *Ray Of Light* ...that on the second song titled "Swim" the intro guitar and keyboard seem influenced by the melody of "Feel Flows" from *Surf's Up*. Listen to *Surf's Up* and those incredible melodies written with Jack Rieley and Van Dyke Parks. You'd have to be

---

deaf not to hear it. I mean Brian's just had such a tremendous influence.

With Dennis, he was writing melodies and writing really strange time signatures with the drums and really cool things that I'd only heard in jazz. I just thought he was really avant-garde – he was an amazing artist. He wasn't afraid to experiment, he wasn't afraid to fall into space. He used to sit there with a bass harmonica and sit on the floor and play it because that was the only way he could get enough air to hold it properly. And he'd say Charlie Manson used to show him stuff. He was very out there. He wasn't afraid of being different – even though that whole subject was real taboo because of what went down in '69.

He was extremely creative. He would play the drums, he played the bass, he played a lot with synthesizers like the Mini Moog, the ARP, all the analog synths. They had harmoniums, Chamberlains, they had a clear plexi-glass electric harpsichord, they had a lot of really cool instruments there in the back of the studio.

Dennis was always wanting to work when he felt the emotion. And that meant he would work at night. He was just incredible in terms of his writing. There are songs that have never been heard or released that I still remember the melody to. There was one called "Holy Man" which might have gone through some title re-changes that was just total genius. The track had been recorded before I started working with him and I was totally mesmerised by it. It was a spiritual song. I've never heard a melody and a rhythm embodied in a song like that and I haven't heard it since. If I ever I could accomplish one thing it would be to go into the vaults and find that song. Just to hear it one more time, I wouldn't care if it never even came out.

There's stuff like that I remember that was just magical. It was every bit as talented as what Brian had done. I thought some of Brian's greatest work was on *Surf's Up* and *Holland* – that little 45 ["Mount Vermont & Fairway"] is just amazing.

A lot of people have talked about this so-called *Bamboo* or *Bamboo II* or whatever. But nobody's been in the vaults yet... ever. There's a lot of stuff there that I hope no-one screws around with. I was there when they did those 16 Tracks and 24 Tracks and there's been so much garbage [on bootlegs] that I've heard. They're nearly all just rough mixes on cassettes or quarter-inch tape and a lot of those house mixes that came out are just bogus. They don't include any of the songs that Dennis had in the can. What I would do is go in and re-trigger the drums with more modern samples, but the performances are there and the keyboards are there and the vocals are there. I would love to do an album for him – that's still a dream.

He was just an amazing guy. He went out of his way to give people a break. I mean, I was a nobody who didn't know anything and he gave me a break and he just delighted in helping other people. He had a lot of love in him for other people but he didn't know how to accept love. So he had a rough way to go.

Could you give me some idea of how Dennis worked?

He really didn't overdo anything. That really impressed me and I was amazed with his production work. He would always layer things on and then strip them back. He was a very self-critical guy in terms of editing himself and always seemed to see the bigger picture.

One time we were working late on the song "Dreamer" and he decided he wanted a guitar solo, but nobody was reachable at 10 or 11 at such short notice. So I stuck my head over and said, "Dennis, I've got my guitar here." I'd never even played on tape before but he told me to plug in and play a solo and be great or whatever. He had two girls with him in the studio at the time and I was so nervous I told him to take them to the French Restaurant – The Bellevue – at the corner of Ocean and Santa Monica Boulevard. Just leave me alone for one hour.

He told me that there were 16 bars for the solo but that the Fender Rhodes keyboard, which he played, was to take over for the last 8 bars. I was a big fan of Lindsay Buckingham's solos so I kind of had that in mind when I started. Only I didn't realise that the tape plays back all your mistakes so I rolled back and tried to punch myself back in which was rather difficult to do while playing guitar at the same time. Finally I managed to pull it off and really got into playing this solo – only I forgot about the Fender Rhodes and erased the hell out of it.

Dennis came back after an hour by which time I was all panicked. We played back the tape and he kept stopping it short on the eighth bar. He just said "It's good, but you really get great in the second half." Finally he played the whole thing but he didn't even care that I'd erased the Rhodes. I wasn't even that good a guitar player but he gave me a break. I mean, I'm on Dennis Wilson's solo record. I had no business being on that. He gave me a shot and kept the solo, and kept it on the record. With things like that he was a really generous man.

Would that have been a similar situation for a lot of the other players on there? The list on the jacket is huge, so was he just always drawing people in?

Yeah. I think that Earle Mankey played a lot on there. Earle was a great guy – extremely patient and hardworking. He was on the staff and had a lot of training and experience. Stephen Moffitt was the studio manager who did all the mixdowns – so basically it was me, Earle and Stephen who worked on *Pacific Ocean Blue*.

How about Gregg Jakobson?

Gregg was a sounding board for Dennis in that they had a lot of ideas. They were buddies... they were bro's. He was level-headed when Dennis was acting crazy. He could reel him in. When Dennis was too conservative on something Gregg would egg him on. It was a really good working relationship – I thought Gregg was a fine guy.

So what would be a typical day in the studio with Dennis Wilson – how would he compose?

He would get in at around 10 in the morning and either start putting a tape up or start playing the piano. He wrote a lot on the piano but he also wrote on the drums. He'd have melodies in his head that he would work out with rhythm and time and then he'd build a song around that. He'd then transfer those ideas to different instruments like the Moog and the Oberheim. He was a big fan of working with different bass lines. He also encouraged letting go. With respect to horn arrangements, he hired great cats and let them blow. Improvisation was his vision here, to see how far you could go. You know – hitting the envelope and still be able to get back.

He would encourage improvisation and that was what was so amazing. He was like a jazz guy. He used to scoff at himself that everybody thought he was just a surf drummer and he was almost ashamed of that. He acted guilty about making all his money from being a Beach Boy – like, "what do I know? I play the surf beat..."

And then he'd go into this other stuff and it was like trying to prove he could be as creative as Brian – though he would never, ever, say that out loud. But you could tell there was that sort of angst inside of him. It was like he had these strong creative impulses kicking against the public image of the sex symbol, the surfer and the drummer.

That must have been a weird couple of roles to play. Playing along with the Mike Love axis on one hand that wanted Brian back in the studio churning out the surf hits and then pushing his own music to places that the Beach Boys were just never going to go...

Yeah, I mean that was the Beach Boys and then Dennis would stretch out on his own stuff that was completely in another place. He brought the Double Rock Baptist Choir in to do this gospel singing ["River Song"] and it was amazing. I just felt really fortunate to be working with him.

Aside from those little bits that made it to the record you just couldn't possibly describe to somebody what went on in the studio. We'd work in the morning like that from 10 to 1 and then he'd go out to dinner with Karen to some fancy Beverly Hills restaurant or go out on his boat and invariably he'd come back later. Sometimes he'd leave at 6 or 7 for the night and other times after a fight with Karen he'd stay late. He was at his best after his emotional outbursts. That's when he was a wreck and he was just emotionally fragile. And he was incredibly creative then. I hate to say it but it was like Lowell George, his best work was done when he was emotionally strained. He was not afraid to emote and to put down on tape exactly how he was feeling.

There were a lot of great sessions that would go on from about 7 until midnight where he would be a wreck, but if you channel that energy it would be amazing.

Were there any particular sessions that stand out personally?

"End Of The Show". That was a great song – I can recall April 15th 1977 [from my studio notes] we got Bruce Johnston to come in and do a bunch of harmony vocals like parts that Brian would have sang. He had Ed Carter on bass and Billy Hinsche on guitar, and Dennis on the drums. But he just did these background vocal arrangements that rivalled what Brian had done in four or five-part harmony. That [version] didn't make it on the album and it became one of these *Bamboo* things. *Bamboo* was just a working title of what he was going to start next, but because other of circumstances that never came to fruition.

There was a lot of 16 and 24 track masters of "End Of The Show" and "Holy Man" and some other songs they had worked on with Gregg Jakobson. To this day I can't wait to hear that melody again and I've never heard it yet on any bootlegs. I hear cassettes and rough mixes of stuff we were doing in the studio while working on *Pacific Ocean Blue* and it's just ridiculous.

"Cocktails" was the working title of another song that he was working on in June 1st of 1977. Then there was another thing which he called "The Album Tag Song" which was a working title for March 23rd 1977. That was done in a really weird time signature, like a 9/4 time signature that was really mesmerising.

What about the song "Thoughts Of You"?

Oh, that was just amazing. It was totally about Karen. He was very, very in love with her. They fought hard and loved hard. They both lived in this house on Broadbeach in Malibu where he had this upstairs bedroom where the wind just blew in and that made you understand where he was coming from with that song.

There would be nights where we would both be commiserating. Me over some surfer girlfriend and him with his broken heart over Karen – a boys' night out, that kind of thing. We would have candlelight going and get food in and then he'd sit down at the piano and play these songs. And with "Thoughts Of You" he just totally captured the vibe of heartbreak and being alone in his huge house on the beach and wind coming through the curtains. The lyrics and the starkness of the performance captured the view from that house.

And he would probably do that vocal at 10 or 11 in the morning. He had the ability to sing like that. You would think that sort of vocal that would be recorded at midnight but he could shut out the world and plug right in creatively to the message that he wanted to get across.

Stuff like "River Song" and "Pacific Ocean Blues" were really uptempo by comparison. He was really into the power of the ocean. He would sometimes take me out on the *Harmony* and sail up the coast or over to Catalina. There was one time when he decided he wanted to do some recording in Hawaii and he'd call up and say get over here and I'd check out the studios for him in Honolulu on Waikiki Beach. He was just amazing and it's just so sad that it burned out.

What were Dennis' influences musically?

To be honest I don't know. I never heard him listen to anything else but his own music. He was very much like Neil Young in that regard. Neil only listens to what he's working on and if he's listening to anything else he keeps it to himself.

Was he hanging out with other musicians at the time?

No, he was hanging out with women. Dennis was into his star status and using it and making it work for him. He played it to the hilt because he could. He was funny.

So why do you think Dennis has been portrayed as such a one-dimensional character in so many of the books and articles about the band?

Dennis just suffered. He felt other people's pain and was very emotional. He always loved the underdog and he loved to be the underdog. He loved to give people chances. He was one of the most generous people I've ever met in my life. He was always encouraging and he would always tell me "Don't ever settle for anything but the best. Don't ever accept second best". He gave me my break in the business – I can't say enough good things about him.

He wanted to be the common man and sometimes he took it too far. Dennis had a lot of demons in his life. He had a rough time – when you give, give, and give and you don't know how to accept love you pay a price for that. Dennis loved his wives tremendously, he loved Gage his son, and he meant well. But he fell in with the wrong people, and though the responsibility was ultimately his, he just got bit by the disease.

He was always trying to prove himself and I think that's what also drove him to greatness.

Dennis was just down to earth. Like with the Transcendental Meditation stuff he would just say, "Screw this – let's just be people and be warm". He had an incredible sense of humour and wasn't afraid of laughing at himself. He never took himself too seriously and that was joy to be around and it was so unlike the Beach Boys. Everybody was trying to maintain this image – like being told to record 9–5, what a joke. What a farce.

So was it a very fractious situation to be working in?

In my opinion he had a very well-defined boundary with his work vis-à-vis the Beach Boys. When it was a Beach Boys session he would try to be a team player and try to do what was best for the group. He was definitely trying to push Brian into being more experimental. He just wanted a reality on the tape – he didn't want to see the Beach Boys become some sort of Bubblegum Greatest Hits Vegas attraction. He abhorred that – he saw it as a big sell-out and bullshit. He wanted to push new ground and create whatever fertile environment he could to watch Brian unfold and come back to earth and start writing music again.

He was encouraging of *15 Big Ones* because it was letting Brian get into signature songs like "Blueberry Hill" and the Ronettes and getting him used to working again. What I saw him get short-tempered with was settling for this Maharishi crap that would go down. Like the M.I.U. album and "Roller Skating Cuties" and some of those songs were like drivel and he couldn't stand to work on them.

He was extremely deferential to Brian and did not want to see him get influenced by anyone outside of the group. He was always trying to encourage him.

Do you think there was ever the chance Dennis would leave the Beach Boys and go solo?

I never got that feeling. He loved his brothers, he got into it a lot with Mike Love – but there was a love/hate relationship there. God only knows what went on... in fairness to Mike I don't know what he had to put up with in regards to Dennis. Dennis could be a royal pain in the ass too. He loved flushing phonies out and what he thought to be shallow or false behaviour. But he loved the Beach Boys and was very supportive of them and it put food on his table for a lot of years.

What about *Bamboo*? Do you have any idea where that title came from?

I think it was more of a working title. It's what he was going to call a studio in Hawaii if he got one built there. He loved going to Honolulu and he really wanted to record there. I think they sold Brother in 1978 and Dennis was quite lost without it. It was proving difficult to keep financially – Elton John recorded some background vocals [on "Blue Moves"] there and some New Wave bands like The Quick. They had to run it like a commercial business and then Dennis couldn't get in when he wanted because it would be booked up. At some point I think it became impossible and that really tore him up.

What was Dennis' reaction when *Pacific Ocean Blue* came out? Even though it sold 200,000 copies and received good reviews it seemed to disappear pretty quickly.

If it bothered him he never said anything about it. He didn't put anyone down, he just moved on to the next record, the next thing. He was really upbeat. He went out and partied when we finished and then he was in the studio the next day. It was just priceless working with someone you knew was a genius. He was just down-to-earth – I don't know how to put it really – he had a huge ego but he was just so easy to deal with. You know, he gave me his 3-litre racing Porsche as an album bonus. He had like $20,000 in the engine alone – it came with a German mechanic. It was ridiculous. I went from a 30-horsepower Volkswagen to a 300-horsepower racing Porsche and promptly drove it off the road. I'd never been in a car with that much power. It was insane. I was a little long-haired hippy with a Volkswagen Bug living in a beach house in Malibu, and then I had a racing car.

AN INTERVIEW WITH
CARLI MUÑOZ

Carli Muñoz, Beach Boys' percussionist and keyboard player, was the last person to collaborate with Dennis on a project of any significance. After the critical success of *Pacific Ocean Blue* the two worked together on songs that would have formed the basis of a second solo LP, *Bamboo*. Several of these – "All Alone", "Companion" and "It's Not Too Late" – were written by Carli and interpreted by Dennis. In a move away from the dark atmospherics of its predecessor, *Bamboo* was to incorporate Latin grooves, jazz and full-tilted rock'n'roll. Aside from "All Alone", which appeared posthumously on the *Endless Harmony* compilation of 1998, the remaining Muñoz-Wilson compositions were never released, while the project was shelved. We spoke on February 24th, 2000.

How did you come to work with Dennis individually outside the Beach Boys?

Since the very beginning when I started working with them, Dennis was always a very confrontational type of person and also he also had a large ego and/or a sense of competition. He had a sense of competition with everything, particularly women and power. So the first time he saw me he challenged me to arm wrestle, which was something he was always doing – like challenging the bouncers to wrestle and things like that – and I beat him. I was probably the only person I saw beat him. So I think that was where he got a lot of respect for me.

So, some sort of macho thing then...

Yeah, in his own macho way. In his sporting, challenging kind of way.

But there was more to it than that. We were both kinda horny guys, always after the prettiest girls. So another thing that was bonding was that one time we were on a tour in Ohio and it was one of those long drawn-out tours and we were all going a little crazy and we both saw this girl in the dining room of the hotel we were staying at. We both really liked her, she was a total knockout. So, before the concert Dennis came up to me and was like that he'd asked this girl out and they were meeting up this evening and I said, "That's funny, I asked her out too and she said she was going to go out with me." So then he proceeded to get real hard and there was some exchange of power, he was kind of insinuating who are you?", and I told him we'll have to fight about it. So we went out to fist-fight, and we actually started fighting like two animals over a piece of meat.

We few a few punches and then stopped and looked a each other kind of thought what are we doing here acting so crazy? So, I had an idea and said, "Why don't we ask her if she'll go out with both of us?"

---

and we both agreed on that. So we approached the girl and told her what had happened and that we'd been fighting over her and would she go out with both of us. And so we both ended up dating her at the same time. The details of which I don't want to get into...

So it was always a challenge thing – that was the nature of going on tour: there was always a lot of boredom, a lot of sexual energy and a lot of pretty girls around, eager and willing.

From then on Dennis and I became a team and we would get all the girls. They could not believe that two guys could be unanimously doing this and not competing against each other. Nobody else stood a chance. And so that was our kind of bonding there.

The other thing is we would have very deep conversations. He was a very spiritual guy. Not about any dogma in particular but in general we talked about the spirit world and a lot of very spiritual things.

And then of course the music. It was Dennis and Carl who got to hear my original musical ideas. Carl always supported me and backed me up very much. In fact he wanted the title song of an album to be one of mine – a song called "Companion". It was an example of what I've been talking about, the song talks about a   constant companion", which was a spiritual companion.

I think that song is quite interesting for a Beach Boy to be involved with, because it's a sort of Latino number isn't it?

Well he had a very wide range of emotions and a very wide conception of who he was. All the way from the very competitive, physical type of guy to the highly spiritual, searching soul. To me that made him a very whole person. I think he might have liked somewhere in between but that's just the way he lived his life and how things turned out.

Had you heard much of Dennis' solo material like *Pacific Ocean Blue*, before you started working with him individually?

I really liked it. I was familiar with that material because he had played it very often for me on the piano. I didn't participate in those sessions though, since I was having kids. That's also one of the reasons that we did not complete *Bamboo*.

So those sessions for *Bamboo* were in 1978. Can you remember any of the other songs you were working on?

"Under The Moonlight", he liked that a lot. It's a song that goes, "I want to be a rock'n'roll star, under the moonlight," and is kind of like a fantasy sort of thing – almost a parody.

There was also "All Alone", which just came out on that *Endless Harmony* album.

You wrote that in the late '60s didn't you?

That was actually a mistake [on the sleevenotes] and I confused it with another song called "It's Not Too Late". That was the one I wrote in the '60s and "All Alone" was written in the early '70s, probably 1971. That's also a very spiritual song for the love of someone. There was also a song called "Shootabout" that was never really completed but he liked that song a lot. I'd still like to finish that one. Beyond that there were many more experimental things but as they were not finished they were untitled. So it was "Companion", "All Alone", "Under The Moonlight", "It's Not Too Late" and possibly "Shootabout".

Which studios were you using to record these?

Mostly Brother Studio in Santa Monica. We also did a few things, but very informally and we did not get very far with it, at Tom Murphy's home studio. Before he had his commercial studio in Venice. We didn't do too much there but I can remember re-recording "All Alone".

What was Dennis like to work with on a composing level?

I would give a Dennis a song, like "Companion", and then he would sit on the piano for hours and work on it. Also I'm a jazz musician and he heard me do some more complex things – I had one song called "La Plena de Amor" that had a very complex rhythm – but he loved it and he spent the whole day working on it from noon until dark. It was a very difficult song with a lot of counterpoints. When he was with Christine McVie he would call me up at 4'o clock in the morning and ask me for the words to "All Alone". Basically he worked very hard at it.

The songs I've heard like "Companion" probably weren't completed, but what kind of direction were you hoping to move with them?

It was never completed but it was more of a spiritual direction. We became very close at the time and he would share with me things that I don't know if he told anyone else. In the same way I reciprocated and we had a very, very special bonding.
    When there was big turmoil within the band the Loves and the Jardines and the Wilsons had bouncers to protect them. One time a fight was going to break out between Dennis and Mike on their private plane and Carl's manager at the time Jerry Schilling came and asked me to come over as I was the only one who could get through to Dennis. So I went up and held Dennis back in the aisle because he was going to punch Mike Love. I whispered to him that he'd better cut this shit out, and he just whispered back, "Shhhh, I'm only faking it". And that was so typical of him. He wanted to create such tensions and he knew no end how to piss Mike Love off.
    He would drive everybody crazy by creating dangerous situations. We would be on a limousine ride with an escort in front of us of several cars taking all the group, and he would tell the driver to pass the escort. The driver would refuse so Dennis jumped over while the car was still

running, moved him over and then floored it until we passed the other cars. He liked to keep people on edge. Another time we were flying to New York and we were going past the Twin Towers in our Falcon jet and he asked the pilot to go between the towers. Fortunately this time he didn't take the wheel. We were so scared we just put our heads between our legs.

Nobody could get near him. If one of the bouncers tried to control him then he would want to fight them. There was a very long time when he wouldn't trust anyone and that's when we bonded. At some time though I started to move away from him because he was starting to do too much and getting too crazy. He was doing a lot of drugs and that's when he started going out with Mike's fourteen-year old daughter. It got to the point where he was getting incoherent and it just hurt me to see him like that and I decided I just didn't want to be around him. I didn't know what to do at that point to save him from himself.

I think he saw me as a strong person who could help him out. I had done drugs but back in the '60s, and I had been through that and I wasn't going to again. It was just devastating to see him and I decided to keep my distance.

When you see the concert footage from the '80s it's incredible how much he aged in about five years.

Yeah, he deteriorated very quickly.

He always had a deep-seated grudge with Mike. I don't know whether it was because of competition but they were very different persons. Totally incompatible people – like night and day. I asked Dennis one time what the root of it was and he claimed that one time Michael gave him acid put him on a motorcycle and then took him for a ride. A really scary ride, that freaked him out.

How did you get on with Mike?

We were never really buddies. He was like the other side. It was the opposite of Dennis and Carl.

So were the lines drawn that distinctly in the late '70s with Dennis and Carl on the left, Mike and Al on the right and Brian sort of incapacitated in the middle?

Right. The line as far as I know was always drawn.

Did you ever think that Dennis was going to leave the Beach Boys and start up a solo career?

I think if he'd had tremendous success he might have ventured out but he also loved being a Beach Boy. He was really supportive of the group in his own way was and really proud of it too. He loved his brothers and he was very frustrated that Brian was so distanced. He was always very close to

Carl, particularly when their father died.

When you were writing with Dennis in the late '70s were any other Beach Boys collaborating with you?

I sat often with Carl and played him my music but we never wrote. Brian and I sat one time, and, it was kind of like a brief encounter, but it was meaningful because he wasn't talking to anyone at all. He asked me how I could play his music to the intention of what it was meant to be, and I told him that when I took my first acid trip in Puerto Rico I heard *Pet Sounds*. LSD opens up a lot of channels in the psyche and I told him that I had perceived his soul and I got it" and knew what the core of it was about. I understand he had been doing LSD himself at the sessions. But anyway, he kind of looked at me weird and then he hid. He was completely isolated.

Was there ever a finished track listing for "Bamboo"? Was it ever likely to come out?

It was not just an exercise, there was a lot of effort put into it and there was money put into it.

But there were problems of domain. The group were supposed to be produced by Caribou Records and all our sessions were unauthorised. We just did it because it was Dennis and he wanted to record these songs. But it wasn't an assignment from a record company. We had the studio, we had the creativity, we had the songs, we had the urge, we had the talent. We had the tools to do it. So we did it.

But somewhere along the way... I don't know what happened. I truthfully don't. I was having kids and then Dennis started going off the deep end and then he met Christine McVie and he started doing a lot of drugs and then that was it. That was the end of it: I was going in the direction of home and the family and he was going to the deep end of drugs and craziness.

I was pleased when "All Alone" made it onto the *Endless Harmony* album but I would like to know where those masters are now. If they found them I don't think there would be any objections to releasing them. There were some important songs on there. "It's Not Too Late" with Dennis and Carl singing together was a beautiful song. And with them both passing away "Companion" seems really relevant since it was being with someone from the spiritual world.

When was the last time that you saw Dennis?

I left the band in 1981 because the inner group relationships were deteriorating. I saw Dennis when he was going out with his niece, Mike Love's daughter, and he was going to marry her. It was in a house in Malibu and I went for a last attempt to see where he was at and if there was any hope of straightening up his life. He looked really bad and he was upset and said he was having dreams that were frightening him. I think he had done a promotion or something but he had a room full of sneakers and he offered some to me. I forget whose house it was – it was up on the hills in Malibu.

He was very disappointing and I thought I would have very little contact with him because he was so frustrating for me. I was one of the last people to give up on him – everybody else had, but I was still working with him. I thought maybe it was a ray of hope and he would notice what he was doing to himself and to other people around him. But at that point I saw that the transformation wasn't going to happen.

At that point I had new people in life with my kids and I decided I should take care of them and not get drowned in this situation. So that was the last time I saw him. Then the next thing I heard was that he'd passed away when I got a call from the office. But I wasn't surprised... I *was* surprised, but I wasn't.

I could see exactly what he did when he passed away. He did that sort of thing all the time: jump off the boat, show off, clown around. One time we went on a trip together along with Christine McVie and my ex-wife and some other people on the *Wild Goose*, which was John Wayne's boat, and he was a clown through the whole thing, a daredevil clown. This was a big yacht, a converted minesweeper, and he would jump from the deck with skis into the cold water. He did not know fear and had no respect. He didn't care how cold the water was.